Protean Poetic

Sylvia Plath. Photo reproduction by Jim Kalett, reprinted by permission of Harper & Row, Inc., and Olwyn Hughes.

9/24/81

Protean Poetic

The Poetry of Sylvia Plath

Mary Lynn Broe

University of Missouri Press

Columbia & London, 1980

Copyright © 1980 by The Curators of the University of Missouri
University of Missouri Press, Columbia, Missouri 65211
Library of Congress Catalog Number 79–3334
Printed and bound in the United States of America
All rights reserved

Library of Congress Cataloging in Publication Data

Broe, Mary Lynn.
  Protean poetic.

  Bibliography: p. 208
  Includes index.
  1. Plath, Sylvia—Criticism and interpretation.
I. Title.
PS3566.L27Z585   811'.5'4   79–3334
ISBN 0–8262–0291–8

For Wilhelmina, Patrick, and
in memory of Rolla Edward

Preface

In the mid-1950s, at the time when Sylvia Plath was writing her first serious poems at Smith College and then in Cambridge, England, two major poetic movements were gaining prominence. Robert Conquest's anthologies, *New Lines I* and *New Lines II*,[1] introduced the genteel rationality of the Movement poets to England, while slightly later in America, Robert Lowell's *Life Studies*[2] offered stark insights into the literature of psychological stress and suffering. At different points in Plath's career, each group provided a milieu for, as well as some formative influence on, her poetry. Each offers a touchstone for distinguishing Plath's individual voice and poetic.

Perhaps Conquest's provincialists were more accurately defined by a few "don'ts" for which they became famous than by a positive party philosophy. These poets of the quiet, "plain line"—Philip Larkin, Elizabeth Jennings, John Wain, and Charles Tomlinson among them—broke from the Pound and Eliot allegiance to paradox, symbol, and myth to speak a new sober kind of statement closer to prose than poetry. They called it "neither empty rant nor . . . bloodless chinoiserie," "neither howl nor cypher, but the language of men."[3] Politely empirical, they refused to abandon the old orthodoxies and rational structures for the "unbridled Id," the barbaric yawp, the forties cry of the "ring-tailed roarer," or for the seamier side of human nature—the "sort of upper-middle-brow equivalent of the horror-comic"—uncovered by the new psychology.[4]

The Conquest anthology betrayed everywhere its bias toward the traditional forms and metrical exercises. A number of the contributing poets were university faculty or librarians who exercised the caution of logical positivists in running their academic paces. They never surrendered to subjective mood. Their language permitted only what could be verified by logic. Their unflinching belief, according to Alfred Alvarez, was that "life is always more or less orderly, people always more or less polite, their emotions and habits more or less decent and more or less controllable, that God, in short, is more or less good."[5]

Firmly wedded to English roots, these Movement poets

contrasted with the confessional camp—Sylvia Plath, John Berryman, Theodore Roethke, and Anne Sexton. The new confessional poets, as Sylvia Plath puts it, made an "intense breakthrough into very serious, very personal emotional experience" by bringing private pains and intimacies to the center of the poem.[6] The naked ego wriggling on a couch won a dramatic authority over that healthy and whole gentility of the New Liners.

Psychic realities replaced social understatement as the focal point in this new poetry. Personality itself, according to James Dickey, with its weight of experience and memory, became the writing instrument:[7] "I myself am hell / nobody's here—" Robert Lowell reminded us.[8] By his clear-eyed scrutiny of the reciprocity between history and his own family stress, nervous breakdowns, and frequent hospitalizations, Lowell created in *Life Studies* the living tissue of a man in the process of becoming himself. By exposing a vulnerable psyche, the new poets formulated a high-risk, percussive "poetry of departures" that countered the perfection of the Movement.

Among the pioneer theorists of that contemporary consciousness we now call "confessional" or "extremist" are M. L. Rosenthal and Alfred Alvarez. According to Rosenthal, brutality and "universal angst" were heaped on the post-1945 sensibility, forcing it to become the scapegoat for world violence—two wars, genocide, concentration camps, and mass technological alienation. In contrast to the heroic subjective mode of the Romantics, the confessional self was placed at the poem's center so that the speaker's psychological vulnerability and self-recriminations meshed with the wider forces of disintegration in the civilization. The betrayed quality of life was absorbed back into the self in an exchange of the privately and culturally symbolic.[9]

The challenge common to the new poets of psychological stress, Rosenthal held, was an artistic or imaginative one: "Self, the subjective side of what used to be called 'civilization as we know it,' has been fragmented by everything that has 'laid all the world waste.' Perhaps it can be reconstructed in the aesthetic process."[10] In this cult of vulnerability, however, the self became a hero-victim attempting to dictate the curve of the aesthetic process by the discoveries made—and the energy of the insights arrived at—in the act of experiencing. The more painful the experience of exploration, the better. But as the self picked up the baggage of modern psychology and sociology, the original importance of the transforming energy and sensuous excitement within the confessional mode gradually succumbed to clinical notation of trivial neuroses. The artistic form and measure of energy yielded to a fashionable "t-group" sort of self-exposure. Pathology was equated with poetic power, self-indulgence with self-revelation.[11]

Alvarez isolated another basic element of this new beyond-the-gentility principle poetry with his definition of "extremist art" as a kind of psychic Darwinism, the survival of the creatively fittest. The modern artist pushes his intimate insights to the edge of breakdown and then beyond, straining urgently until paranoia, manias, and depressions of his "inner space" assume the importance of the old Romantic commonplaces, Beauty, Truth, Nature, and Soul. According to the extremist canon, there is a certain dispassionate toughness required of the artist, a wariness of being trapped in any easy emotion: "he shares this cool with his audience; so the more ruthless he is with himself, the more unshockable the audience becomes."[12]

The wide critical currency of the terms "confessional" or "extremist" in recent years makes it more limiting than helpful to define this new poetic reaction to Eliot's cult of impersonality: "the progress of the artist is a continual self-sacrifice, a continual extinction of personality."[13] An overwhelming responsibility is placed on the artist of the confessional mode, according to Alvarez, for the poem's success or failure is contingent upon the balance or subtlety of the poet's personality. The real measure of success is the "convincing imaginative reality" of the poetry, not confession or the intensity of pain. The artist must have cultivated a certain critical assurance that he can move away from narcissistic self-absorption to artistic and emotional enlargement within the poem. The dramatic authority of suicide or the psychiatric ward cannot substitute for creativity and artistic control.

In a BBC interview shortly before her death, Plath emphasized that the more horrid the psychological experiences the poet encounters, the more mandatory informed and intelligent control becomes.[14] Yet in the late fifties and early sixties the "man who suffers" was revered above the "mind that creates." Lowell spoke of his sterile marriage, his institutionalizations; Sexton of incest, masturbation, and abortions; Berryman's "Henry Pussycat" of his lusts for women and for walking into the water in his pajamas one dawn. Each created a new value for self-exposure. By virtue of simple shock effect, candor and spontaneity became confused with sincerity and authenticity. In short, Alvarez's important reminder—that "the more subjectively exposed the theme, the more delicate the artistic control needed to handle it"—was ignored as confessional poems dwindled to mere verbal snapshots, discrete instances with little reverberation.[15] Careful verbal notation of an object or an event could be no substitute for the imaginative transformation of the private life through the process of art.

Unfortunately, the brief history of Plath criticism has been, to borrow the words of John Berryman, largely a matter of "hitting our heads on the nail" in the name of confessional art. The poet died by suicide early in 1963, an event that set in stony relief images of terror, death, insanity, and melodrama in the poetry. Soon she received top billing as the Pyrrhic goddess of suicide who defied the last societal taboo. Her art appreciated only as the poems were devalued into slide tissues for the biographical drama. Because she managed to elude the literary world with the record that prefaced her suicide, Plath and her poems were assigned an artificially compelling value. Qualities of intensity and urgency made her work seem all the more costly and authentic. To the suicide buffs of the late sixties, Plath meant what she said.

Since 1963 a remarkable range of poems have been autopsied, reduced to snippets of coroner's reports, and then reassembled every few years in some new literary exhuming. (We can only recall Plath's self-irony—"I am your opus, / I am your valuable"—and her warning to those probing psychovoyeurs: "There is a charge / For the eyeing of my scars . . . a very large charge.")[16] Critics have split between the speculative and the biographical; the craft followers and the cult devotees; the mythmakers and the demythologists; those Gradgrindians who praise the cast-iron discipline of her prosody and the necrophiliacs who probe the poems for sufficient pain and suffering to require a deadly consummation; the crowd that hears her literary ventriloquism and the one that watches her stage-direct her own Gothic romance. Even feminist critics have just begun to give proper credit to Plath's more muted domestic poems. In citing her passive victimization and railing against her "jailor," the "stink of fat and baby crap," or the "viciousness in the kitchen," they have generally overlooked the self-irony and expansive emotional range that rescues her art from her costly rite of femininity, suicide.

Recent psychological criticism has denuded the poetry by citing the poet's basic Oedipal nature, her demanding schizoid art, her Laingian false-self system, or her Jungian imbalance. Followers of this approach relish the discovery of Plath's regressed libidinal ego or the false logic of her private phenomenology that saw death as rebirth.[17] Often with movingly passionate rhetoric, these critics argue ways to justify the poems as death prescriptions: "Life, the poet has repeated over and over, is a greater violence than death."[18]

In the years since her death, Plath's works have been ransacked for every sort of clinical symptom or verbal notation that might explain her suicide at the peak of her career. What ought to be read forward as the creative skill of poemmaking informed by artistic control has been read backward as the footnoted suffering of a broken psyche. Plath's poems are viewed as cryptograms, scrawled in an idiolect decipherable only by reverent feminists and mythmakers of the Plath legend.

An elitist cult grew up not so much around Plath the poet as around her colossal risk and sacrifice. Club members were other artists, critics, poetasters, even psychologists. They crowded the suicide bandwagon, as the legend goes, envying Sylvia Plath who "constructed" her own death. In the words of Anne Sexton:

Suicides have a special language.
Like carpenters, they want to
Know which tools.

They never ask 'why build.'[19]

Plath, of course, was assigned a charter membership in this suicide club. She earned her merit badge by her first attempt at nineteen and "completed her art" by a successful suicide at thirty. Alvarez's attempt to defuse the suicide in *The Savage God*, by a personal account of his own failure in contrast to Sylvia Plath's completed act, has worked inversely to refocus attention on the artist as prime representative of this death-track sensibility.[20] The better the artist, the more vulnerable she is.

At the present time, an illogical publication chronology, spotty biographical information, and an incomplete corpus of her works have not served Plath's art well. A number of things have contributed to making the reconstruction of the poet's life

and the critical estimation of her work an extremely difficult
task. Among these are the publicity that accompanied Plath's
death in 1963, the highly selected detailing and documenting of
her life in recent years, the posthumous appearance of three out
of four major volumes of poems, small collections, and a battery
of single poems.

The state of the poems themselves—many published
seriatim in limited editions, others housed recently in the Lilly
Library at Indiana University, and some forgotten in the Sophia
Smith Women's History Archive—is, in the words of Marjorie
Perloff, "surely one of the [greatest] scandals of recent publishing history."[21] The fact that the entire Cambridge Manuscript of
over forty poems remained undiscovered for twelve years
suggests the possibility that still other poems may be extant but
unpublished. In his introduction to *Johnny Panic and the Bible of
Dreams*, Ted Hughes tells us that a long fragment of a novel was
"lost somewhere around 1970."[22] Of seventy extant stories,
only twenty have been collected; of Plath's notebooks kept over
ten years, we have only four brief fragments in *Johnny Panic*.
Hughes's two articles on the chronological order of the poems
describe the specific occasions of composition for several
poems, but fail to sketch the outlines of the entire oeuvre,
which, he claims, builds to a single, elusive mythical center.[23]
The task undertaken by recent bibliographers seems to be the
most appropriate answer to this confusion in the Plath canon.[24]

In the chapters that follow, my aim has been somewhat
remedial: to demythologize Sivvy, to describe her "theatrical
comeback in broad day" to the art of poemmaking—the changing nature of her imaginative vision, her developing poetic, the
growth of her creative sensibility, the singular daring achievement of her voice and tone. Plath's work incorporates a wider
and more exciting range of emotions and responses as well as a
greater degree of artistic control than recent critical history
suggests. From the early Smith and Cambridge poems, Plath
has assigned a lively new value to ambivalence—making a
strong case for passivity and inertia on the one hand and the
authority of pure motion on the other. And in her earliest
writing, Plath recognized her complexity, that she had "one too
many dimensions to enter":

    . . . Time
    Unwinds from the great umbilicus of the sun

Its endless glitter.

I must swallow it all.[25]

"Give me back my shape," "tell me my name," Plath
urged. Keeping in mind the poet's own imperatives, I have tried
with quiet habits of reading and, according to classical stan-
dards, to do just that.

"There is no great love," Plath has said, "only tenderness."
Great tenderness is owed to people whose mark is, in some
indelible way, on this work: the late Miriam Leranbaum, savvy
and generous critic; Myron Hack, whose abrasiveness was more
cherished than any milksop praise; John Hagopian who turned
my vague metaphors into "blunt indefatigable fact"; Joan Joffe
Hall, advisor, mentor, and muse; Paul Ramsey and Robert
Wooster Stallman who saw the ragged beginnings, though
from different perspectives; Robert Hoover who "made
notes"—endlessly; and Joseph N. Bell for whom perfection is
not terrible but a habit of life.

Like Plath, I have always had "one too many dimensions to
enter"—most particularly during the past year. Special thanks
go to Derek and Elizabeth Colville, Mario and Lee DiCaesare,
Gayle Whittier, Gerald Kadish, Jacqueline Van Baelen, and
Katherine Bidney who have, by their loving nurturance, eliminated at least one dimension each.

Additional thanks are owed to Sheldon Grebstein, Eugene
Flood, Al Carpenter, Gloria Gaumer, Ella Kalinich, Jean Ives,
and Beth Spiro for help in various ways. Finally, I wish to
express my gratitude to the SUNY Foundation for a Faculty
Research Fellowship enabling me to work on the book during
the summers of 1976 and 1977; also to the staff and personnel of
the Sophia Smith Collection, Women's History Archive, for
their kind research assistance.

Contents

I.

Early Fiction and Poetry
"the fact of doubt, the faith of dream"

A Brief Overview

"If only I can weld the now—where I'm living so hard I have no energy to produce—into art and writing later on."[1] Even as a teenage diarist, Sylvia Plath recognized the particular challenge of the human condition in art as well as in life. She suggested that her task would be one of translation: finding the proper imaginative and rhythmic forms for the breakneck experience of hard living; discovering where her own voice and developing poetic impulse were abused by running the academic paces within a fixed poetic tradition; reconciling the zestful readiness of her imaginative life with the practical concerns demanded by a world of physics grades, Yale flings, and competition for the big publishing slicks. For, like the colossal statue in "Letter to a Purist," Plath spent her adolescent years virtually astride two worlds:

> . . . with one foot
> Caught (as it were) in the muck-trap
> Of skin and bone [she]
>
> Dithers with the other way out
> In preposterous provinces of the mad cap
> Cloud cuckoo
> Agawp at the impeccable moon.[2]

"Just to find a balance is the first problem," claimed the young poet in 1950. And the search for this balance, the fitful improvisation with argument and technique, is the one problem we find Plath best describing in her early writing.

With its vacillating energies and charming disproportions, her story is one familiar to adolescence. Plath's letters home during her Smith College years (1950–1955) show the development of her paradoxical attitude toward existence. She thought of herself as a philosophical pioneer in that eternal system of weights and measures. Numerous versions of the fact-imagination polarity were deeply rooted within her sensibility.

1

Each swing in that cosmic "cycle of joy and sorrow" absorbed the poet totally, depleted her emotional and physical energies, yet offered slim prescription for finding the balance between the poetic impulse and mundane existence.

With the first discovery of her social and creative powers, Plath was heady and intemperate: "I want, I think, to be omniscient . . . I think I would like to call myself 'The girl who wanted to be God' " (*LH*, 40). To the perpetual romantic, there were no impossibles:

> Oh, I love *now*, with all my fears and forebodings, for *now* I still am not completely molded. My life is still just beginning. I am strong. I long for a cause to devote my energies to. . . . (*LH*, 40)

But Plath, the work-study "Smithie," was also likely to remind herself that only by humble gratuity did she gather crumbs from the tables of the richly literate: "I have to keep on like the White Queen to stay in the same place . . . If only I'm good enough to deserve all this," she wrote to her mother late in 1950. At times she could be giddy about the present moment, posing as that perfect romantic, snatching time at its gilded crest. At other times, vying with brainy coeds for dates and acceptance, or slanting her stories for the big-money magazines, she cultivated practical skills with the gritty determination of one rehearsing rote lessons:

> All that I write or paint is, to me, valueless if not evolved from a concrete basis of reasoning, however uncomplex . . . Poetry and art may be the manifestations I'm best suited for, but there's no reason why I can't learn a few physical laws to hold me down to something nearer truth (*LH*, 66).

As if in proof of her claim, many later poems that "seem often to be constructed of arbitrary surreal symbols are really impassioned reorganizations of relevant fact,"[3] according to Ted Hughes. Plath's best work, he insists, is rooted in the bits and pieces of her notebooks, what she called those "things of the world with no glazing" (*JP*, 3). Later, when she wrote an autobiographical essay for *Punch* about her early school years, the "rabid teenage pragmatist" declared her motto to be unquestionably Machiavellian: "Usage is Truth, Truth Usage."

In her lengthy introduction to *Letters Home*, Plath's mother, Aurelia Schober Plath, describes a childhood legacy riddled with the same crossfire that is evident in her daughter's earliest writing.[4] Claiming "psychic osmosis" with her daughter, Mrs.

Plath gives us a glimpse of her own Austrian background. Despite the fact that her father decided early that she should become a "practical business woman," Aurelia Schober cherished romantic novels and ideals about self-education. Louisa May Alcott, Horatio Alger, and Gene Stratton Porter taught her the rags-to-riches theme. She completely identified with the poor and virtuous, believing that they always triumphed. That her daughter Sylvia inherited these idealistic notions is evident from the way she carved her own heterogeneous achievements. Yet Hughes has emphasized her high-powered professional bent, her need to be a "big earner," to "master a difficult trade," to "hammer her talents into acceptable shape" (*JP*, 2–3). As she wrote in her journal: "Wakeful last night. Tossed and turned. *New Yorker* fear, as if I could by main force and study weld my sensibility into some kind of articulateness which would be publishable" (*JP*, 4).

Another legacy introduced Sylvia to the conflict between the poetic impulse and the world of compromise, if not diminished reality. Mrs. Plath maintained what she called an "upstairs-downstairs" household during Sylvia's childhood. Upstairs, Sylvia and her brother made up rhymes and lyrics in a fantasy playworld populated by Matthew Arnold's Forsaken Merman and Mixie Blackshort, the heroic bear. Downstairs, in an alien world severed from the warmth of family affection, Otto Plath died a slow, agonizing, and self-imposed death of diabetes mellitus, refusing lifesaving surgery and choosing complete solitude. These two contradictory dimensions of existence were inextricably bound up in Sylvia Plath's youth. They required her comprehension, perhaps even encouraged the new, positive value she gave to ambivalence, which she clearly cultivated throughout the early poems.

What distinguishes Sylvia Plath's display of youthful contradictions suggested by *Letters Home* is not the variety of analogues that rehearse the same childhood theme, but the volubility with which Plath states and restates this dilemma. Throughout the early poems and fiction, an oracular voice echoes the central argument, one that seems worthy of summary.

More for convenience of description than chronology, we can cite three groups of early poems that describe the conflict riddling Plath's childhood. Ten poems were published in the *Smith Review* between 1952 and 1955.[5] Another unpublished manuscript of eleven Smith College poems, each an English Department prize poem in 1954–1955 under the pseudonym of Robin Hunter, remains in the Sophia Smith Women's History Archive.[6] The third and most substantial collection is the Cambridge Manuscript, named for the forty-three poems Plath submitted to her "twelve black-gowned examiners" in 1957 to fulfill partial requirement for the English Tripos at Newnham College. Left behind in the faculty library at Newnham, the manuscript was discovered there twelve years later by two college librarians.[7]

The choice running through these poems is frequently either that of intellect versus imagination or of fact versus the poetic impulse. Allegorical figures in one of the early poems state the conflict in a slightly different way: "lantern-jawed Reason," "squat Common Sense," or "King Egg-Head" toppled by "the barbarous Prince Ow." From metaphysical sobriety to fanciful public bravado, the poems cover an expansive range of emotion. The poems baldly restate Plath's concern to find a balance in the elements of choice in critical opposition. In fact, knowing that the "choice . . . is always to be made" becomes a touchstone for the young poet against which she will measure her failures and improvised solutions:

> The choice between the mica mystery
> of moonlight or the pockmarked face we see
> through the scrupulous telescope
> is always to be made; innocence
> is a fairy-tale; intelligence
> hangs itself on its own rope.
> (*RH*, "Metamorphosis of the Moon")

Foreshadowing Esther Greenwood in *The Bell Jar*, Plath recognizes the odds involved in the difficult task of orchestrating dualities: "I'll be flying back and forth between one mutually exclusive thing and another for the rest of my days."[8] We see the speaker of various poems repeatedly choosing *not* to select one dimension of existence over another. Her preference, instead, is to grasp intellectually the need to make a choice: "suspense / on the quicksands of ambivalence / is our life's whole nemesis" (*RH*). With what will become a characteristic blend of whimsy and deadpan humor, Plath understands that true sensitivity to the human condition does not invite glib partisanship. What she suggests is the development of a comprehensive sensibility that can grasp ambivalence:

> Either way we choose, the angry witch
> will punish us for saying which is which;
> in fatal equilibrium
> we poise on perilous poles that freeze us in
> a cross of contradiction, racked between
> the fact of doubt, the faith of dream.
> (*RH*, "Metamorphosis of the Moon")

In her attempt to balance the major contradictions rooted deep in her sensibility, Plath engages in a dialectic in which oppositions are as clear-cut as they are effectively miscalculated. The question raised in the early work is whether a comprehensive view of life and art—one that joins proportionate "actualities of intellect" with illusions of the imagination—is possible.

Both the poetry and prose written in the decade before 1960 attempt to answer such a question.[9] While much remains unknown about the range and composition of the poet's writing before *The Colossus*,[10] the known work thematically chronicles disillusionment with life and art. Disenchantment results from exclusive allegiance to romantic love mythology and sole reliance upon the independent existence of the imagination:

> Stars shoot their petals, and suns run to seed,
> However you may sweat to hold such darling wrecks
> Hived like honey in your head.
> (*CM*, "Epitaph for Fire and Flower")

What is at first a very general disenchantment with ideals in the *Smith Review* poems becomes more specific, more personal, and more ominous in the mid-fifties poems of the Cambridge Manuscript. The imagination is found to be a poor risk, a tool left behind in the idyllic state of childhood and now recovered at only too great a cost. Practical facts invade the privileged domain of the imagination; "this cracked world's incessant gabble and hiss" demands attention:

> However I wrench obstinate bark and trunk
> To my sweet will, no luminous shape
> Steps out radiant in limb, eye, lip
> To hoodwink the honest earth which pointblank
> Spurns such fiction
> As nymphs; cold vision
> Will have no counterfeit
> Palmed off on it.[11]

In sum, the youthful Plath is unable to find a balance

between "muck and dream." Nor can she poetically resolve the dilemma of a life careening from imaginative to practical concerns; from, as Ted Hughes says, "what was expected of her and what was finally exacted" (*JP*, 9). Stalled in a notebook catalog of physical objects, Plath jeopardized her power to rearrange: "the sheer objective presence of things and happenings immobilized her fantasy and invention" (*JP*, 7). "No spark of sap leaps up to light the fire" in these "transfixed" verses, no "countermagic can undo the snare" that holds them in their static rhetoric (*RH*, "Prologue to Spring"). Her poetic forms remain elaborately structured and staidly traditional with only slight variations. Her themes are mannered and falsely overstated. Plath raises arguments "like sitting ducks" in these earnest poems that are like philosophical tracts, but she always meets with the same implacable response:

> Nothing changes, for all the blazing of
> our drastic jargon, but clock hands that move
> implacably from twelve to one.
> (*RH*, "Love is a Parallax")

There is some redeeming value to these poems that jangle the cosmos and, at the same time, challenge the sobriety of unobtrusive verse form. Unable to suggest an aesthetic resolution to contradictions or disillusionment, Plath makes a temporary, at best ameliorative, adjustment. She either chants an ethic of cautious warning against imaginative flings (a potentially less skillful recourse) or sounds a note of self-mockery in ironic recognition that the "facts will out." Despite a vigorous life of the mind, a powerful disillusionment is inevitable, the poems claim. Only by witty celebration of incongruities or mocking recognition of her puny stance in the universal scheme can she gain any protection against inevitable disappointment.

Bolstered by views too impersonal, "ready-made big themes," her wit does not derive from her sensibility and is not yet apparent in its own imaginative form. Rather, the fledgling poet is still weighing balances, striking compromises, and juggling complicated verse forms. The forms she chooses—terza rima in particular—are archtraditional, relying heavily on repetition and closure for their effect. The risks they invite—the only ones she takes—are lexical. Plath makes these turgid early poems playfields of prosody, slanting verse forms to mock her grandly overblown illusions. The best poems strain toward the truth of her diary claim: "Always I want to be an observer. I want to be affected by life deeply, but never so blinded that I cannot see my share of existence in a wry, humorous light and mock myself as I mock others" (*LH*, 40). The worst dwindle to a battery of precious effects, studied and artificed, a cavalier mixture of metaphors that suggests an undergraduate's diligence and perception:

> Grasshopper goblins with green pointed ears
>   caper on leafstalk legs across my doorsill,
> and mock the jangling rain of splintered stars.
> (*RH*, "Epitaph in Three Parts")

What follows is a frank survey of both weaknesses and strengths in Plath's early, uneven, and sporadically published writing. A careful scrutiny of the early poetry should help us better judge the "typical" mature poem by providing a basis ignored by recent biography sleuths and psychological speculators. Thematic concerns in the early fiction and prose often prove germane, so I have included them as well. A clear-cut analysis of either thematic concerns or prosody is difficult to achieve given what remains unknown about the range and composition of the early work. For this reason I have occasionally integrated the two approaches where I feel it is most helpful in describing Plath's early talent and creative direction.

From Illusion to Self-Criticism: Love, that "ultimate orbit"

Plath begins predictably. Her early writing celebrates a world lost to us, stuffed into the back of some cedar chest with all those embarrassing love pangs and crushes, dance programs and capezio slippers, nosegays and fraternity lavaliers. As a tartan-clad coed in a 1953 issue of *Mademoiselle*, Plath raved about the "astronomical versatility of sweaters / and men, men, men." She predicted a favorable "ultimate orbit" for herself and nineteen other guest editors. Likewise, a few early poems ("Apotheosis" and "Wreath for a Bridal") sound this positive note by praising physical love, though in a plodding, rather dull manner that seems more epitaph than celebration. Ceremonial elegance suggests the sacred love union of two people who are "paragons of constance":

> . . . let sun surpliced in brightness
> Stand stock still to laud these mated ones

Whose stark act all coming double luck joins.
(*CM*, "Wreath for a Bridal")

But it is not the paeans to creative natural love nor the "bright future" of "favorable forecast" for the guest editors that moves Plath to write. Rather, posturings, sighs, sober laments, and harsh warnings about the inevitable romantic disappointments create the fabric of both the early fiction and poetry. Plath constructs a fiction and a poetry from only a fleeting awareness of that gap between reality's blunt indifference and one's private imaginative world. She magnifies the moment when self-delusions break down in the face of rude facts to a gesture worthy of Isadora Duncan.

Alfred Alvarez has suggested that even when she employed the most jejune imagery—fickle love seen as a spring frost, a love-jilting felt as "cold blind rain" of winter—Plath never lost a "certain critical edge of dissatisfaction" with her poetic achievement. Her sharp self-awareness, particularly in the early fiction, has been observed by Lois Ames who noticed that, although the poet's subjects are drawn from the usual cache of teen romance and tears, the endings of the early poems and stories run counter to the admittedly banal subject matter. The final insight is often a lowkeyed and ironic divergence from the apparent subject. Such insight suggests the poet's sharp, chiding recognition of how little her subjects represent her actual intent and inner vision.[12]

Her earliest piece of fiction, "And Summer Will Not Come Again,"[13] is a good example of this peculiar perspective and its limitations. An ingenue falls in love, carefully following all the steps in a prescribed ritual of adolescence. Her final disillusionment ("Just how do you go about forgetting a guy, anyway . . . A freckle-faced guy named Bruce, tall with knife-blue eyes . . . ?") pales in comparison to the elaborate—if usual—imaginary world that the young woman has constructed for herself. Plath's particular skill with the portrait is the counterpoint of the sentimental refrain of a stammering, blushing young woman ("Never, never again . . .") and her budding sense of irony: "The whole day had been hateful . . . The silence was like an expectant vacuum. It's like when you're waiting for the phone to ring, Celia thought. There's an empty unfilled place in the atmosphere just waiting to receive the sound. But when it does come, it's not for you" (*Seventeen*, 275).

Like most of Plath's early fiction, this story ends with a note of self-awareness: "She has turned him away and that was what hurt." It makes the point that the excesses of the imagination and the romantic myth are one and the same. Both are ill-starred. But self-awareness is bathos; it is maudlin, if not canny, in this case. There is no development after the young woman's discovery, no moral coming of age, nothing beyond mere recognition of the bitter twist of fate. In a precocious literary moment, she quotes a poem by Sara Teasdale:

> On the long wind I hear the winter coming,
> The window panes are cold and blind with rain;
> With my own will I turned the summer from me
> And summer will not come again.
> (*Seventeen*, 276)

A much later fragment from a novel, "Stone Boy with Dolphin" (1957–1958), describes a young Cambridge coed's antisocial behavior at a party. She glories in her own maladjustment and scorn for others. In a fit of drunken intensity one night she bites a notorious womanizer on the cheek. Throughout the story the girl has identified with a delicate sculpture of a boy holding a waterless dolphin, his "wings of stone balancing like feathered fans on the wind." The statues's precarious poise and lidless, anonymous face remind her of her own yearning—particularly in her early short stories—to "leave her mark." Yet the mark she leaves, the infelicitous bite, is as self-conscious and comical as that youthful disproportion between physical detail and imaginative vision in the story's narrative:

> This Friday night, waiting for Hamish, Dody wore a black jersey and a black-and-white-checked wool skirt, clipped to her waist by a wide red belt. I will bear pain, she testified to the air, painting her fingernails Applecart Red. A paper on the imagery in *Phèdre*, half done, stuck up its seventh white sheet in her typewriter. Through suffering, wisdom. In her third-floor attic room she listened . . . to witches on the rack, to Joan of Arc crackling at the stake, to anonymous ladies flaring like torches in the rending metal of Riviera roadsters, to Zelda enlightened, burning behind the bars of her madness. What visions were to be had came under thumbscrews, not in the mortal comfort of a hot-water-bottle-cozy cot. Unwincing, in her mind's eye, she bared her flesh. Here. Strike home.
> (*JP*, 175)

"Stone Boy" ends on a brief note of awareness, less wry than the previous story. The tone is soberly beyond vaudevillian postures, and perhaps more resonant with despair:

> The cold took her body like a death. No fist through glass, no torn hair, strewn ash and bloody fingers. Only the lone, lame gesture for the unbreakable stone boy in the garden, ironic, with Leonard's look, poised on that sculpted foot, holding fast to his dolphin, stone-lidded eyes fixed on a world beyond the clipped privet hedge, beyond the box borders and the raked gravel of the cramped and formal garden paths. A world of no waste, but of savings and cherishings: a world love-kindled, love-championed. (JP, 195)

Overstatement in the poetry has been a matter of lexical and syntactic strategies that demonstrate a melodramatic prowess, not a personal dramatic vitality. According to Hughes, "she could no more make up an objective ingenious narrative than she could connect up all the letters in her handwriting, where nearly every symbol seems to sit perched over a gulf" (JP, 5). Exaggeration in the fiction results from her catalog of too many "moments of awareness," each savored for its flash of bitter irony. The theatrics of such moments suffice for verbal action, resolution, or imaginative growth. It is as if the energy of discovery substitutes for the application of wisdom, producing an exaggeration in character, conflict, and action. As Alvarez has said: "in these earliest poems . . . there is often a tense and excessive thickness of texture: the diction is rich but self-conscious, the movement dandified, the landscape ornate; the action, in short, is nearly all on the surface."[14]

Things happen grandly, never simply, in the early poems. Subjectivity is lost in a drum-banging melodrama, the clatter of heavy sound effects. One finds the entire metaphysic of Plath's poetic world collapsing in cataclysmic images: "God topples from the sky, hell's fires fade / Exit Seraphim and Satan's men." "Blood runs in a glissando from the hand" (RH, "Epitaph in Three Parts"). Personae have whips, blazing swords whirling about their heads, or roses in their teeth. In the villanelle, "Doomsday" (SR), the hyperbolic action seems appropriate to a Hollywood stage set for The Day of the Locust: painted stages fall apart while things crack, crumble, topple, are blasted or fractured. Time goes awry as the "idiot bird leaps out and drunken leans / Atop the broken universal clock." Even the actors here "halt in mortal shock." Lost love is likened to a bankrupt circus or to a spring day strangled by an unexpected late frost. Clock time and heart time war incessantly; a red rose and nightingales side with uneducated and "intolerant beauty" against those revolving wheels of time; cavorting lovers seize their brief moment in the face of the grave, asking "where to go when clock strikes tomorrow / and the bitter gauge / marks time at zero."

In brief, a tour through Plath's early imagery is not unlike picking one's way backstage among old dusty stock props of a vaudeville act or a parlor drama. The nexus of images—what Plath herself speaks of as ready subject matter for all those who lack inner experience—includes sundials, circus acts, crowing cocks, striking clocks, silver veils, crystal caskets, lapis lazuli seas, and honey fountains. Using these props, the poet chooses sides in "cosmic pro and con": the frailty of the human heart versus mechanistic society; reality versus illusion; fact versus imagination; the vanity of human wishes versus the ravages of time.

Verse form becomes a kind of textural overstatement that is too dense, too turgid, too able. In addition to the regularly clumsy use of the metaphoric mode, Plath relies heavily on assonance, consonance, internal rhyme, and even compound adjectives—all an undergraduate's homework in prosody from a handbook on literary forms. Patterns of interlocked rhymes carefully develop an overly disciplined logic while the poet's hallmark is the masterful, slightly off-rhymed ending.

Many of the early poems draw from a common lot of technical characteristics and stock themes. They include highly fanciful dream narratives told oh-so soberly, long-winded dialogues, exaggerated use of color and the senses, a gathering of sensational public personae, usually women—queens, fortune-tellers, acrobats, even liontamers. The women are invariably mocked for their camp and spectacle, and finally humbled by a practical lesson. Their toppling occurs either in the narrative event of the poem or in the poet's manipulation of form, occasionally in both. But rarely does the medium of the poet's own voice betray itself in this action or strike a personal identification with the put-down of these flamboyant women: any risks she takes are syntactic and lexical, never personal.

Familiarity with all of this raw awkwardness reminds us of Theodore Roethke's belief that conscious imitation is probably the one great method of learning. The most original can come from the most imitative, according to Roethke, but the final triumph is "what the language does, not what the poet can do or display."[15] Although much of her language is the fare of debaters and the trade of philosophers, Plath does develop an idiolect with general and archaic terminology. Perhaps the key to her idiolect is betrayed by the "gorgon" reference—"gorgon prospects," "gorgon-faced"—and the aura of accompanying images of things deadlocked, transfixed, frozen, dissevered, hardened, and metallized. The contradictory nature of the alluring yet deadly gorgon is the single paradox that runs throughout these early poems: the lure of beauty yet the threat of petrifaction; the intrigue of the imaginative and aesthetic realms, yet the inevitable debunking by the physical world.

In addition to peculiarities of language, her apprenticelike verse calls attention to itself because of one particularly glaring fault: the "periodic" metaphor. She simply exhausts this rudimentary poetic mode in a kind of technical and thematic overkill that bears some brief illustration.

Metaphor is an elementary tool, familiar to readers through the workings of its complementary motions: the outreaching or extending meaning (epiphor), and the creation of new meaning by combining or juxtaposing (diaphor). Plath adopts the epiphoric mode. Many of her poems emerge, however, as a sort of poetic groping because she fails to maintain energy tension in the comparison. Similarities are often hackneyed and obvious: love likened to a bankrupt circus or spring described as jeweled wealth. While facets of her chosen vehicle express similarity to the more elusive tenor (usually the love relationship), little semantic motion is transferred beyond that first, literal comparison. No energy moves us through newly sparked awarenesses, and this is perhaps the key: her exercises become diligent but dispassionate displays empowered by less and less transforming energy.

In "Winter Words," one of the Smith College prize poems of 1955, the tenor—the more elusive part of the metaphor—is the time between night and the first dawn. Time is described by the vehicle, a landscape approaching winter. In turn, this vehicle is a book whose content is authored, quilled, entered, scribbled, and inscribed by various creatures of nature. The result is little more than a greeting-card allegory dragged out by an accumulative style. The force of comparison dwindles into the tritely precious and static:

With fur and feather,
    buck and cock
softy author
    icebound book.

No chinese painter's
    brown and buff
could quill a quainter
    caligraph.

Chipmunks enter
    stripes of black
in the winter
    almanac.

A scribbling squirrel
    makes a blot
and hides a rural
    rorschach nut.

Inscribing cryptic
    anagrams
on their skeptic
    search for crumbs.

A posthumously published broadside, "Million Dollar Month,"[16] presents a trite and overextended vehicle that is actually an epiphor enclosed within another epiphor. Love is cheapened to a jeweled, affluent spring:

. . . princely uncles flower on plants;
    amethyst aunts
pamper all our lavish wants;

Forsythia waves telegrams
    of topaz whims
willing us liberal diadems.

. . . till fortune of diamonds adorns my dear,
    all debonair
in the affluent emerald atmosphere.

There is certainly no intuitive vibrancy in the poet's use of precious stones to describe the colorful bounty of spring. Nor is fresh meaning gained in the poem's imaginative transformation.

What occasionally rescues the work from its overwrought or lumbering use of metaphor is Plath's skill in varying traditional form and technique. Unlike other moderns—Robert

Creeley, Charles Olson, Theodore Roethke—Plath never goes
so far as to formulate an organic theory of poetry where the act
of expression creates the precise idea of the poem. But Plath the
academic is a sinewy athlete-in-training, showing a looseness
with, and subtly abrasive critique of, many conventional forms
that she employs.

Like her "Aerialist," one of the campy performers in the
Cambridge Manuscript, Plath is adroit and "cat clever" on her
"perilous wire" of craft. At times the "outrageous nimble
queen" controls and mocks the banality of her subject matter by
slightly manipulating conventional forms. Like the crowd-
pleasing acrobat in the poem, the poet performs well in tryouts,
running the tightwire of sonnet, terza rima, and villanelle. She
is "gilded" by critics for a "tough stint" well done:

> . . . the girl
> Parries the lunge and menace
> Of every pendulum;
> By deft duck and twirl
> She draws applause . . .

Then, again miming her prize performer, the poet turns the
original public challenge about to a realistic end, one subtly
self-mocking, earned only by "sighting the stratagem." Her
clever successes—when she does succeed in these early
poems—are in knowing how to leap through the hoop of traditional structures: technically she overcomes thematic clichés of
love and disillusionment, and the absence of a clear, declarative
personal voice in the poems. Her skill demonstrates that prosodic form and technique are not always to be dismissed simply
as self-conscious and imitative artistry. And as her work matures, her self-critical, self-measuring optic becomes more
sharply focused, more cleverly designed.

But Plath is still a neophyte in her command of verse forms.
In "Admonition" (*SR*), for example, traditional form reverses
the propositional sense as the final tenor of the metaphor reverses a carefully structured series of vehicles. The result is a
bitter comment on human love, but one whose subtle message
is lost amidst the appositions. Four stanzas, parallel in syntactic
structure and natural image, present a series of warnings: life
that is dissected dispassionately, or intellectually scrutinized,
risks losing its very animating principle:

> If you dissect a bird
>   To diagram the tongue
> You'll cut the chord
>   Articulating song.

Iambic trimeter suddenly drops to dimeter in the third line of each stanza, hammering the dire consequence of the warnings. In the final stanza, the natural metaphors are undone, ironically reversing the vital function of the previous forms of life that are now used to comment on *human* love. The point is that human exchange ("syncopation") has not the vitality or the smooth-running naturalness of the bird-beast-fish metaphors:

> If you pluck out the heart
>   To find what makes it move,
> You'll halt the clock
>   That syncopates our love.

"Life is so difficult and tedious I could cry. But I won't; I'll just keep writing villanelles," she wrote home in 1950. Plath's aim was to find a balance between the familiar practical world and an insistent imaginative life. Perhaps it is significant that the sonnet, the terza rima, and the villanelle—each a complex but formulaic pattern of balance and structure—were Sylvia's favorite forms. They appear frequently in this early work and provide conventional expectations for the "artful dodges" of her strategic balance and self-mockery.

One of her early apparent strengths was her shrewd use of the French villanelle. Paradoxically, this form creates the impression of simple spontaneity through complex artificial schemes. The nineteen lines of the villanelle communicate at once an illusion of stasis and movement: the first and third lines are alternately repeated through five tercets, only to be juxtaposed at the end of the sixth, and final, four-line stanza. The illusion is one of stalled repetition, of sameness, of neatly enveloped thought. Nevertheless, an argument develops insidiously through the nineteen lines.

In a 1953 villanelle, "To Eva Descending the Stair" (*SR*), Plath precariously balances worn themes, clock time versus heart time. The suspension of these themes stands against the weight of the logical argument that dashes any hope of permanence in human beauty and passion. The first and third lines of the initial tercet set up the dialectic between the force of human emotion and the ravages of time:

> Clocks claim stillness is a lie, my dear;
> The wheels revolve, the universe keeps running.
> (Proud you halt upon the spiral stair.)

The argument, in five tercets, presents a series of astronomical images that suggest that the universe is engaged in a massive conspiracy against the feeble assertions of enduring human love, desire, or beauty. Asteroids "turn traitor," planets "plot with old elliptic cunning," stars are "cryptic" in their movement, and suns involve themselves in solar "schemes." A responding group of images (the third and fifth tercets, the rose and the nightingale) counteract the insidious calculation of the universe with open guilelessness of physical beauty and desire. As representative of this beauty, Eva is uncompromising in her attempt to stop time's course: "proud" is wrenched out of syntactic structure. But what she fails to realize is that her defense of immortality by means of passion is subtly enfeebled: hypotheticals hint of the fickleness of emotions—"if the heart be burning," and "if the flesh be yearning." The point is that, logically, the argument weakens as the villanelle progresses. But the form allows the poet to hold both sides of the argument—the running down of time against the stubborn insistence of the flesh—in the last quatrain. A balance never won in life is here achieved in form.

In her favorite villanelle, "Mad Girl's Love Song" (*SR*), Plath juggles imaginative schemes with the romantic myths by means of tone and structure, managing yet another self-critical comment. The form itself shows the young girl's self-centered struggle with thwarted romantic illusions:

> I shut my eyes and all the world drops dead:
> I lift my lids and all is born again,
> (I think I made you up inside my head.)

In place of subtle, mature control of tone and imagery, this poem appears to jangle with all the catch-phrases of dashed romantic hope: stars go "waltzing out in blue and red"; a false lover bolts while the speaker claims "I dreamed that you bewitched me into bed / And sung me moonstruck, kissed me quite insane."

Of the villanelle's two repeated lines, the first line is a prosaic, even boastfully puerile statement that the poet can, with emphatic bravado, admit or refuse to recognize the outer world. In as simple a gesture as opening or closing her eyes she can murder or create reality. But the third line of the tercet sounds a colloquially portentous note. Hesitancy, by virtue of its repetition in the villanelle, gains significance. In the reluctance of "I think"—versus "I shut" or "I lift"—the poet is not certain where her imagination has shaped factual matter. Thus the form poses an important question and ends with a hint of self-criticism: is it possible that the romantic jargon itself might have shaped the real person before her?

> I should have loved a thunder-bird instead;
> At least when spring comes they roar back again.
> I shut my eyes and all the world drops dead.
> (I think I made you up inside my head.)

"Second Winter" (*RH*), a sonnet from 1956, is perhaps her most intricate example of a tensive balance between subject matter and chosen form that offers an oblique self-measuring perspective. The whole sonnet deserves close scrutiny as representative of early achievement:

> And so it goes: just as the greening bud
> is about to leap from the cage of winter branch,
> just as the coiling plant within the seed
> prepares to strike through stubborn shell and launch
> bright fireworks of flowers in the air
> till radiant petals dart their scarlet tongues
> and kindle all the eager atmosphere
> to flame in a phoenix ecstasy of wings,
>
> suddenly the traitor climate turns
> and strangles the sweet fluid in the stem
> while sun is frozen in a crown of thorns
> and honey stiffens in the honeycomb;
> and the tender season falls with falling snows,
> and so my love has gone, and so it goes.

As in so much of the early poetry, the subject matter is quite ordinary and obvious. The fickleness of a love relationship is compared to a sudden spring frost. Less obvious, however, is a sophisticated emotional tension captured in the way that Petrarchan and Shakespearean sonnet forms are played off against one another to express finally the unpredictability of love and the mockery of human expectation. The poet has coupled the Shakespearean sonnet form (twelve lines followed by two brief lines) with the more symmetrical Petrarchan octave and sestet. The tight, logical unity of the Petrarchan rhyme scheme (*a b b a /*

a b b a for the octave; *c d c d c d* for the sestet) is abandoned for
the interlocking scheme of rhyme in the Shakespearean form
(*a b b a / c d c d / e f e f / g g*), which is more attuned to a principle
of development. That visible Petrarchan "turn" of line nine is
challenged by the final couplet, the only precisely rhyming lines
in the poem. It is worth noting the traditional expectations of
both forms and their interaction in this particular poem, for their
merging forms create Plath's self-measured view of love.

The octave and sestet of the Petrarchan form portray the
two-sided emotion of pressure and release, a movement rem-
iniscent of inhaling and exhaling, or muscular contraction and
release. This tumescence-detumescence dynamic—certainly a
wry comment on the subject matter—occurs neatly within the
verbal frame: "And so it goes . . . suddenly . . . and so it goes."
A tense, kinetic aspect of early spring, "coiled" and "about to
leap forth," is dramatized in the octave; the sestet portrays a
sudden shift to the unexpectedly stifled, stiffened, and stopped.
Implicit, too, in the Petrarchan turn is a shift in rhetoric that
invites a broader, more leisurely view of the subject matter. In
contrast, the traditional Shakespearean resolution must be
managed in two brief, summarizing lines.[17] Thus the invitation
for wit, barb, and paradox.

The point is that the Petrarchan turn here is not the final
release or resolution; rather, it is a false or deceptive center in the
same way that the cycle of the seasons—at once the echo of
man's own decline, yet a bitter contrast to his noncyclical
mortality—demonstrates an uncharacteristic lack of predictabil-
ity. A sudden frost halts spring in its usual seasonal progression. The brief Shakespearean couplet at the end of the sonnet
thwarts the longer, more reasoned denouement of the Petrarchan form in echo of the action of the seasons and the abrupt
passing of love. This false center of the sonnet (traditionally the
Petrarchan line nine), the shift in texture of imagery and in
meter from anapest/iambic to the dactylic, support this sense of
a traitorous turning. This philosophy of form strongly suggests
that the same quality of unpredictability in the seasonal, the
interpersonal, and the aesthetic realms is found here. Despite
the worn subject matter, Plath achieves a particularly subtle
union in "Second Winter."

The poet advances the argument in the second quatrain,
solving a perpetual problem inherent in the Petrarchan form
and foreshadowing the poem's concluding wisdom. For all the

physically charged violence of the verbs in the first quatrain—leaping, coiling, striking, and launching—the distinctly coital energy seems to disappear in the imaginary airiness of the second. Nature in bloom disappears in a mighty poof with "bright fireworks of flowers" kindling the air. Other ephemeral images connote the same imaginative insubstantiality, at once real yet mocked by the sudden turn in line nine.

Instead of merely embellishing this image with the second quatrain, the poet builds toward a quiet irony in the final two lines. Against that sense of solid, intractable resistance of branch, seed, and earth, she offers the fire-and-air insistence of a universe all abloom, a "phoenix ecstasy of wings." In its own way, such a universe is as fragile and contingent as the poet's own love. The implied difference, however, is that nature has within itself the capacity for regenerating from its very ashes, as man has not. Thus we see perhaps the most bitter facet of the love relationship.

Action in this first octave prefigures the leaden dismissal in the few lines devoted to the resolution of the metaphor: "the tender season falls with falling snows / and so my love has gone . . ." Even this usual opportunity for barb and wit is ignored for the casual sense of "And so it goes." The seriousness of the concluding disillusionment may be felt in the onomatopoeic sound of falling (*f* and *l*) and the hollow weight of the *o* in the couplet.

Any post-Shakespearean reader assumes that the seasons are reliable, human love is not. The poet, in so subtly meshing the two sonnet types, achieves a formal mockery of the vanity of all human expectations, but particularly of her own gullible faith in the endurance of love. The enthusiasm of the octave, stalled in the first four lines of the sestet, yields to the imbalance of the final couplet's despairing resolution. Romantic illusions yield their energy to the insubstantial nature of love: Plath subtly manipulates two sonnet forms to make this comment. In such a way she anticipates the tone of weary exhaustion in later poems from the Cambridge Manuscript.

A fairly large segment of the early work, however, is not so seriously admonitory about the course of love. Poems range instead from the gently mocking to the bitterly sarcastic. They create their effect by shrewd coupling of craft with surface action.

In another attempt at balance, "Circus in Three Rings"

(*SR*), Plath simultaneously portrays the painful, ephemeral nature of love, and the persistently stubborn defense of its illusions. Metaphors of a circus and a hurricane comment on a love that is ominous, frivolous, perhaps even campy in its excesses:

> In the circus tent of a hurricane
> designed by a drunken god
> my extravagant heart blows up again
> in a rampage of champagne-colored rain
> and the fragments whir like a weather vane
> while the angels all applaud.

As liontamer and trapeze artist, the poet and her lover feign cheap postures of bravery for the crowd's approval. Likewise, the poet-craftsman juggles poetic tools to discover how far she can defy fixed, traditional form. While the poet turns those "gnawings of love" into power and public bravado in the narrative, she nevertheless chides herself for the dashing theatrics of her act by exaggerating the formal elements of alliteration, consonance, and end rhyme:

> Daring as death and debonair
> I invade my lion's den;
> a rose of jeopardy flames in my hair
> yet I flourish my whip with a fatal flair,
> defending my perilous wounds with a chair
> while the gnawings of love begin.

What underscores the poet's public hijinx here is the heavy and unvaried alliteration that emphasizes the tone of self-mockery. These qualities work to save the poem from too much sober confession. The image of a brave liontamer defending against wounds is a ridiculous posture to describe the pain of love. The trimeter, the enclosing rhymes in lines two and six of each stanza, mockingly heightens the foolish posturing of the poet expressed in the tetrameter lines in each stanza.

In this way—the visible mechanics of prosody and not the certainty of a single, developed poetic voice—the poet seems to mock her own gullibility in love as well as her immature use of metaphor. What she seems to be saying is that the poetically contrived world of make-believe is not so different from the circus world of flourishing whips, which in turn is not a far cry from that deceptive, showy love. Each one can "vanish with devilish ease," ultimately mocking any previous belief as they fail to obliterate personal pain and disillusionment:

Mocking as Mephistopheles,
eclipsed by magician's disguise,
my demon of doom tilts on a trapeze,
winged by rabbits revolving about his knees,
only to vanish with devilish ease
in a smoke that sears my eyes.

If the chief fault of the early poetry is metaphoric over-statement, then the particular success of the earliest poems is Plath's distanced, but formally clever, debunking of ideals. The craft of prosody is more than a training ground for her to mimic Dylan Thomas, Emily Dickinson, Theodore Roethke, or William Butler Yeats. It is often her private tool for exposing foolhardy illusions about love and the imagination. While the moment of ironic divergence focused in the fiction seemed awkward, perhaps even static, several poems improve upon this theme of traditional love gone "amuck." Humor is more evident as she finds forms more colloquial and more appropriate to express that gap between the practical and the imaginative life.

Plath favors a peculiar repertoire of comic female personae whose greedy reach exceeds their grasp in "Ella Mason and her Eleven Cats," "Ballade Banale," "Complaint of the Crazed Queen," and "Snowman on the Moor." While they do dem-onstrate some superficial differences—they range from crone-like fortune-tellers to intractable young wives—these women are all subjected to the same fate. Each is rudely disciplined by the failure of extraordinary wants and loves. Moreover, the form communicates the recognition that the bitter lesson each learns about herself and about love is usually a mocking and self-berating one.

We glimpse Ella Mason, "the sphinx queen of cats," in a playful six-line stanza similar to the sprightly bob-and-tail of Robert Burns's Standard Habbie:

a fashionable beauty
Slaying the dandies with her emerald eyes:
Now run to fat she's a spinster whose door shuts
On all but cats. (CM)

The reality of this warped beauty finds its kindred form in the anapestic and iambic lilt, the great metrical leaps from pentame-ter to dimeter, and in the self-conscious diction ("Rum and red-faced as a watermelon, her voice / Long gone to wheeze and seed . . ."). This prankish and unpredictable form suggests the fate prescribed for the "minx-thin and haughty" spinster:

> But now turned kinder with time, we mark Miss Mason
> Blinking green-eyes and solitary
> At girls who marry
> Demure ones, lithe ones, needing no lesson
> That vain jades sulk single down bridal nights,
> Accurst as wild-cats.

Although the poet seems to mock the frail or the stubborn who do not risk loving—figures such as Ella the spinster or the one virgin sister of Persephone—at the same time she recognizes the inevitable pain and disillusionment that follow from the customary participation in a love relationship. Old Gerd the fortune-teller has mastered the art of orchestrating others' futures. But she tries to "govern more sight than is given to a woman / By wits alone" with respect to her own life. As a result, she finds only "gorgon-prospects":

> . . . each bud
> Shrivelling to cinders at its source,
> Each love blazing blind to its gutted end—
> And, fixed in the crystal center, grinning fierce:
> Earth's ever-green death's head.

Occasionally a giant or godlike lover hastens the ironic reversal of all illusions about love. With mock-epic grandeur he adds to the speaker's wry self-depreciation. Once again, Plath seems to dwell on the impact of the momentary revelation—that distinctly biblical rule that to win you must lose. In "Ballade Banale," a poem from the *Crystal Gazer*[18] edition of Plath's early work, the main character turns her myths of love and idealism against herself by an ill-timed discovery. "Consciousness does not pay," seems to be her lesson. Alone she poises on the bitter turn of the discovery. The maid is a real man-killer who speaks of her own naiveté in the same breath that she leaves a wake of broken hearts:

> Bored by the boys I was one spring,
>   Each like the other, soft and pale,
> Willing to dance like dolls on a string
>   Just for a kiss and a wedding bell.
>
> So I churned the butter and baked the bread,
>   Laughed at will you and scoffed at please;
> Nights I sailed in my small white bed
>   In search of someday to change to is.

A juggler, a man of the moment, invades the maid's private life and presents her with a fanciful scene. Swords of flame whirl about her head. His ballads preach to her that age-old practical lesson of scheming in love, for the chase is more spirited than the conquest:

> 'Love me, darling, in your own way,
>   Indulge in every kind of folly,
> But if forever you'd have me stay
>   Never say you love me wholly.'

On the day that she candidly admits she loves him wholly she is left with a snowdrift, an empty bed, and a universe that jeers with the juggler's refrain.

The moment of insight is often double-edged, paralleled in Plath's form. A hulking giant runs amok in the chessboard kingdom of the "Crazed Queen":

> With hands like derricks
> Looks fierce and black as rooks;
> . . . .
> Her dainty acres he ramped through
> And used her gentle doves with manners rude; (CM)

By the feminine ploy of crying, the queen stops the giant's pillage. But the price of this miracle is her seduction, desertion, and future dissatisfaction with mere lovers of the "greenhorn lot." The tone and structure of this poem skillfully present the queen's ambivalent situation: her self-deluded imaginative flights coupled with her realistic assessment of other "doughty" men. A five-line stanza swells and then shrinks to dimeter lines at the center of each stanza; the narrator's storytelling voice maximizes drama for the sake of a good tale but minimizes the actual terror by controlled, chatty intrusion ("I tell you" and "Why, all the . . ."); the rhyme pattern interlocks with lines of matching meter, leaving at the center the unrhymed dimeter line. In this way, the structure of the poem contributes to the sudden bitter awareness of the queen that, having experienced the extraordinary, she is no longer fit for the paler, mundane world: "How sore, alas, it is / To see my people shrunk so small, so small."

The best mock-epic tradition embellishes the moment of insight in "Snowman on the Moor" (L). The tradition forewarns of the outcome. We glimpse the metamorphosis of a young woman from a Joan of Arc to a patient Griselda as she bids for dominance and self-sufficiency in love:

> Stalemated their armies stood, with tottering banners:
> She flung from a room
> Still ringing with bruit of insults and dishonors . . .
> He did not come
> But sat on, guarding his grim battlement.

In grand martial tradition, the young wife musters her forces—admittedly not the most self-reliant thing to do—by summoning a "fire-blurting, fork-tailed demon" to help her subdue her unruly husband. What she finds in her "stone-hatcheted, grisly-thewed helper" is a far worse woman hater than the man she wants to trounce:

> . . . o she felt
> No love in his eye,
>
> Worse—saw dangling from that spike-studded belt
> Ladies' sheaved skulls:
> Mournfully the dry tongues clacked their guilt:
>
> "Our wits made fools
> Of kings, unmanned kings' sons: our masteries
> Amused court halls:
>
> For that brag, we barnacle these iron thighs.

Although the pursuing giant finally crumbles to smoke, the woman trots home dutifully, humbled and gentled. The form is just right for embodying such an experience. Interlocked rhymed stanzas of terza rima draw us formally onward, while the wildly disparate line length and the heavily modified and alliterative texture of the verse are themselves comic archaisms. As carriers of the wife's fantasies about supernatural aid, these elements of the verse set us up for the final submission. Here, as in so many early poems, what might be taken for self-conscious imitative form is employed, particularly in the dramatic narratives, to mock the poet's sentimental illusions about romantic love. As she says elsewhere, she is caught in a "cross of contradiction, racked between / the fact of doubt, the faith of dream." The only remedy is to celebrate a comic endurance of the plight.

What is absent from Plath's early forays into the craft of poetry is a mature, confident feeling of balance between a virtuosic agility with form and a distinct personal voice. The letters and arguments of the poems show how desperately she wants this balance. She recognizes the poet's chief contradiction: that fine and tenuous line between restraint offered by form and the challenge to break initial poetic impulses against fixity. Plath arrives with a grave lexicon of philosophically weighty or cliché ideas: her "casuist arguments run riot" in these early poems. She contrives elaborate metaphors whose tensive insight is lost in length or banality of comparison. Most blatant is the gap between her particularly subtle forms (terze rima, sonnet, or villanelle) and the hackneyed imagery and themes. One theme only—inevitable love disillusionment and its effects on the imagination—remains mining ground for the mature poet.

Plath's adolescent tinkering with the elements of prosody is her first step toward an individual theory of poetry. By disrupting fixed, standard form in ghost rhymes, or by varying stanzaic and rhythmic patterns, she fumbles to make the act of expression not a prosaic restatement but her means of discovery or clarification. Imagery remains trite, unfelt, and provides little opportunity for fresh discovery within the poetic process. As her growing technical sophistication in altering traditional form greatly surpasses her choice of impersonal leaden language, the poet herself asks "what countermagic can undo the snare?" (RH, "Prologue to Spring").

Imagination: Irony and the Practical Fact

Plath's overstatement of disillusionment in love becomes accumulative and, at the same time, more specific. Just as she mocks the naiveté of romantic illusions recognizing their hazard, she debunks a singular life of the imagination. Both invariably fail her. She is unable to maintain that duet between the illusions of the imagination (the "mica mystery of moonlight") and the cold realities of facts countenanced by the intellect (that "pock-marked face" scrutinized through the telescope). Plath finds that she cannot join the best of both worlds; she is poised on "perilous poles that freeze us in / a cross of contradiction." Still, any reliance upon the imagination alone is doomed, for it fails to notice a burgeoning world of practical facts. Though she would in these early poems "corral the conundrum of space / at its cryptic celestial origin," she is usually reduced to watching the barometer sink in the face of "a gargantuan, galactic wink" (SR, "Dialogue en Route"). The poetic discovery of this last truth, coupled with Plath's attempt to offer

temporary solutions to this dilemma—either tolerant ambivalence or stark resignation—marks another major achievement of
her early poetry. And the tonal power of this accomplishment
surpasses both the rehearsal of love wounds and the strategic
juggling act with academic verse.

First of all, a number of the early fictional pieces ("Den of
Lions" and "Initiation") cherish the privacy of the imaginative
world at the expense of social belonging. In these stories, soror-
ity debs recognize the pointless rigors of social acceptance. They
do so only after their social composure is publicly shattered. As
one young woman in "Den of Lions" suggests, the awareness
gained, like the situation itself, is too puerile, too self-
congratulatory. Its tone smacks of disciplined rehearsal:

> . . . she would never pay the price. For the cost of admission into
> that brilliant tinsel world was high. You had to sacrifice part of
> your identity; you had to compromise things that were intangible,
> yet terribly important.
>
> Still, it was hard to choose. It was like putting away a Christmas
> ornament. You held the lovely, laquered globe a bit before laying it
> aside. It was patterned with red and blue and trimmed with
> spangles, so you held it tenderly a little while, knowing that inside
> there was nothing, only loneliness, enclosed in a fragile gilt
> shell. [19]

In Plath's earliest short story, the imaginative life of
Elizabeth Minton is a childish and imprecise fusion of things.
Compared to her brother Henry's time-checked world of clocks,
maps, and charts, it is a vital blur: "her mind, a dark, warm
room with colored lights swinging and wavering, like so many
lanterns reflecting on the water, and pictures coming and going
on the misty walls, soft and blurred like impressionist paintings." [20] Tyrannized by Henry's persistent reduction of everything to exact scale, she devilishly merges blue-eyed Henry with
the waters of his Atlantic map. Engulfed by a giant wave, he is
carried to a proper fate. Undignified, he drops through layers of
clouded water "like a porpoise." Even his compass rusts so that
"North is everywhere he turns." Despite the increasingly violent force that propels Elizabeth's imagination, she is led obe-
diently home by Henry. In the end, her stories become ironic
comments on the practical value of a fantasy life, recalling the
situation of the independent young wife in "Snowman on the
Moor" who is humbled by her demon.

When they treat imaginative and not romantic concerns,

the early poems sound a more sober warning about the dangers of a solipsistic life of imagination. Several poems do form a single, polemical statement with "The Wishing Box" and other fiction. Still, the imaginative realm is often disparaged and polarized further from the world of fact because it is characterized as blatant make-believe, dream fantasy, or a child's contrivance, as in "Sweetie Pie and the Gutter Men."

In this story, a young woman visits a prosy class chum who is now married to the new obstetrician in town. She enters a perfectly bland suburban world, boring in its waxen listlessness. Curiously, the only abrasive salvation comes from daughter Alison's imaginary life of violence enacted by her doll, Sweetie Pie: " 'and she goes upstairs in the attic,' Alison was saying. 'She gets splinters in her feet.' Myra checked a sudden impulse to slap the child. Then the words caught her interest. 'She pokes people's eyes on the sidewalk. She pulls off their dresses. She gets diarrhea in the *night* . . .' " (*JP*, 139). The small gestures of this "word-conscious" child, lived through her doll, express all the unspoken exasperation of the main character, Myra. Myra is as doomed as her chum to the adult world of blunt fact, an awareness that the story's chief metaphor indicates but does not develop at the end:

"What do you do to Sweetie Pie when she is *very* bad?"

Alison scuffed. . . . "I hit her."

"Fine . . . what else?"

"I throw her up in the sky," Alison said, her voice taking on a faster rhythm. "I knock her down. I spank her and spank her. I bang her eyes in."

Myra straightened. . . . "Good," she repeated, with little heart. "You keep on doing that."

Myra left Alison standing in the grass . . . she turned only once, and saw the child, small as a doll in the distance, still watching her. But her own hands hung listless and empty at her sides, like hands of wax, and she did not wave. (*JP*, 142)

The threat to an exclusive imaginative life becomes more ominous, particularly when it is prompted by love. Several allegorical dream narratives dramatically isolate such a moment of awareness—Plath's hallmark of romantic disillusionment—yet offer no further solution than did the stories.

In "Dream with Clam-Diggers" (*CM*), a young girl dreams

that she returns to her seaside hometown. Nothing has changed there since her childhood. As she confronts an idyllic world of child's play and is lovingly "plucked back thus sudden to that far innocence," her "fabulous heyday" of make-believe is sobered by the following occurrence:

> Clam-diggers rose up out of dark slime at her offense.
> Grim as gargoyles from years spent squatting at sea's border
> In wait amid snarled weed and wrack of wave
> To trap this wayward girl at her first move of love,
> Now with stake and pitchfork they advance, flint eyes
>   fixed on murder.

In "Pursuit" (*CM*), another deliberately contrived allegory, a meat-craving panther stalks women as prey:

> His kisses parch, each paw's a briar,
> . . . .
> Kindled like torches for his joy,
> Charred and ravened women lie,
> Become his starving body's bait.

When he demands complete sacrifice, mind as well as body, the young woman retreats to her harried imaginative world, the "tower of her fears." The poem ends melodramatically with the panther advancing up the stairs.

Unlike the blatant warnings of the dream allegories, the poem "Battle Scene from the Comic Operatic Fantasy, 'The Seafarer' "[22] raises a more sophisticated but double-edged question: "What price the loss of the imagination? What gain, realism?" A child's play setting—a fanciful world that is a "little Odyssey / in pink and lavender"—spurs the narrator to chide the adult pragmatists whose wisdom quashes such an approach to life. Child's illusion is dismissed, but fact is mocked:

> So fables go.
> And so all children sing
> Their bathtub battles deep,
> Hazardous and long.
> But oh, sage grownups know
> Sea dragon for sofa, fang
> For pasteboard, and siren-song
> For fever in a sleep,
> Laughing, laughing
> Of greybeards wakes us up.

There is a skyrocketing price tag for ignoring the demands

of the flesh and the practical world in favor of those shaping imaginative powers. In "The Wishing Box,"[23] Agnes Higgins kills herself in an attempt to prove her distinctively empty imaginative life worthy of her husband's glittering, tyrannical dream world. Step by step, she tries to recover those fertile, Technicolor dreams of childhood—magic grass, wishing boxes, and turquoise-blue sulfa gum:

> Seized by a kind of ravenous hysteria, she raced through novels, women's magazines, newspapers, and even the anecdotes in her *Joy of Cooking*; she read travel brochures, home appliance circulars, the Sears Roebuck catalog, the instructions on soap-flake boxes, the blurbs on the back of record jackets—anything to keep from facing the gaping void in her own head of which Harold had made her so painfully conscious. (*JP*, 208)

Although she tries novels, sherry, even television, the "utterly self-sufficient, unchanging reality of the *things* surrounding her" triumphs. Things smother her, as Agnes Higgins finds that she cannot tamper with bulky, pragmatic existence.

Finally, when she can no longer sleep, she finds her imagination "condemned to perfect vacancy, without a single image of its own to ward off the crushing assault of smug, autonomous tables and chairs." Only by sacrificing her physical life to art, becoming an icon in Harold's fairy world, does Agnes sustain those fleeting powers of imagination. The ending is wry, bitter:

> When Harold returned from work (he had shut his eyes all during the hour's train trip home, counterfeiting sleep but in reality voyaging on a cerise-sailed dhow up a luminous river where white elephants bulked and rambled across the crystal surface of the water in the shadow of Moorish turrets fabricated completely of multicolored glass), he found Agnes lying on the sofa in the living room, dressed in her favorite princess-style emerald taffeta evening gown, pale and lovely as a blown lily, eyes shut, an empty pillbox and an overturned water tumbler on the rug at her side. Her tranquil features were set in a slight, secret smile of triumph, as if, in some far country unattainable to mortal men, she were, at last, waltzing with the dark, red-caped prince of her early dreams. (*JP*, 210)

Unwitting characters who try to purify themselves of the sensual world are meanly tricked by the stubborn resilience of the physical. In one poem, "On the Plethora of Dryads," the speaker tries to capture the "quintessential beauty" of a warty, knobbly, old apple tree. She has just heard a holy man talk about metaphysics. The tree is pocked and stained, but the speaker is convinced that its real essence is "visible only to the paragon heart." So she chooses the Siddharthan route, starving the senses to fatten the mind, only to find in the end that the confused world of the senses triumphs:

> Battle however I would
> To break through that patchwork
> Of leaves' bicker and whisk in babel tongues,
> Streak and mottle of tawn bark,
> No visionary lightnings
> Pierced my dense lid. (CM)

Instead, sensual, cavorting wood nymphs replace those "visionary lightnings." In spite of her denial, the speaker learns that the miraculous fact of the flesh ("slutty dryads") triumphs at last.

The young woman of another poem wants to "compose a crisis" that will rock the entire universe. But she wants to do it by her fantasy alone. Like the previous young woman, she fails to anticipate realistically the practical limits of the "vaunting mind," or the stubborn intractability of the physical:

> But no hocus-pocus of green angels
> Damasks with dazzle the threadbare eye;
> "My trouble, doctor, is: I see a tree,
> And that damn scrupulous tree won't practise wiles
> To beguile sight:
> E.g., by cant of light
> Concoct a Daphne;
> My tree stays tree.

Again, the last laugh belongs to the indifferent and rebellious physical world:

> . . . this beggared brain
> Hatches no fortune,
> But from leaf, from grass
> Thieves what it has.

The choice between the factual world and the imaginative impulse is unavoidable, but "saying which is which" is nevertheless a reckless enterprise and less than satisfactory, according to the lesson of several poems. The eleven poems collected in the Sophia Smith Archives most consistently present Plath's poetic sensibility "racked between / the fact of doubt, the faith of dream." The Smith poems clearly state her ideological options in the face of her failure to find the balance in that "fatal equilibrium": recognition of the world of stern fact or—knowing the relativity of all absolutes—ironic tolerance of the inscrutable physical world. Both options merit more careful examination.

One tendency of the poet in the Smith poems is to recognize everywhere that dark fate "augured in bleak lines" as a protective device against disillusionment. Earlier poems, such as "Danse Macabre" and "Epitaph for Fire and Flower," have shown a casual, cynical awareness of indifference at the core of her world. No efforts of love can prevail against the grim metaphysical rule with its "stony camera eye":

> You might as well string up
> This wave's green peak on wire
> To prevent fall, or anchor the fluent air
> In quartz, as crack your skull to keep
> These two most perishable lovers from the touch
> That will kindle angels' envy, scorch and drop
> Their fond hearts charred as any match.
> (CM)

Couples "court by milk of moon / sheer silver colors their phantom act." Despite the attempt to disguise it, that "blind lid of land" comes down on all, and the lure of mythmaking proves to be nothing but chicanery. Although the imagination has tried to embellish what is really a mere phantom act, it fails, finally, to delude:

> Lured by brigands in the blood,
> Shanks of bone now resurrect,
> Inveigled to forsake the sod
>
> With kiss of cinders, ghosts descend
> compelled to deadlock underground.
> (CM)

What is so distinctive about the Smith poems is that the note of universal malaise grows increasingly sober and philosophical. The imagery is impersonal, coldly distant, at times metal or ice. It is involved with the seasons, with transitional states and suspended moments, but always accompanied by formal grief. Wintry hardness of stone or ice, things "deadlocked" or "transfixed," the unwelcome clarity of the "scorching sun," or "mangling" of the microscope point toward a final awareness: fables and fiction yield to a rival group of hard facts.

"Prologue to Spring" (*RH*) suggests the New England landscape hanging in balance, "snared in chrysalis formation."
Harsh truth is here felt as a late spring freeze, a world frozen in a
"stone tableau" or something "caught in a brown study":

> In a vault of ice is
>   the sweet world hung,
> transfixed by staring gorgon faces.

The whole natural order is "under seige and the heart of the
earth grows harder, harder." In another poem, dawn "man-
gles" the moon's "fabled horizon of caprice" by its microscopic
scrutiny. The poet issues a stern, perhaps polemical, warning
on behalf of inevitable disillusionment:

> facts have blasted
>   the angel's frame
> and stern truth twisted
>   the radiant limb.
>
> Reflect in terror
>   the scorching sun:
> dive at your mirror
>   and drown within. (*RH*, "Moonsong at Morning")

If Plath presents starkly impersonal warnings about the
limits of the imagination, she also suggests in the same group of
poems that all absolutes are relative in the face of imaginative
failure:

> Perspective betrays with its dichotomy:
> train tracks always meet, not here, but only
> in the impossible mind's eye:
> . . . .
> . . . suspense
> on the quicksands of ambivalence
> is our life's whole nemesis.

Plath insists upon a philosophy equal to the sense of relativity she recognizes. We are reminded again of "Letter to a
Purist": the poet, "dithering" with imaginative pursuits, has
"one foot / Caught (as it were) in the muck trap / Of skin and
bone." Such awareness also recalls the aerialist who has improvised a stratagem for performance, or the lovelorn young lady in
"Street Song" (*CM*) who can "strut it clever," dissembling with
elaborate camouflage to keep the common rout from knowing
the extent of her private pain. But she alone, more "daft than

any goose, / [can hear] This cracked world's incessant gabble and hiss."

One explanation of the poet's ambivalent attitude toward life's paradoxes—imaginative versus factual concerns—is that she greedily tries to grasp a contradictory totality. Appearance and reality are wildly askew for Plath, yet her subjects show no intimately personal recognition of this disparity nor any resulting psychic tension. By offering tolerant irony toward those ambivalences expressed in "Letter," the poet suggests an immediate solution for her failure to make the practical world conform to her unflagging imaginative schemes. Wry irony becomes her protective coloration against the death of the imagination:

> What prince has ever seized the shining grail
> but that it turned into a milking pail?
> . . . .
> For most exquisite truths are artifice
> framed in discplines of fire and ice
> which conceal incongruous
> elements like dirty socks and scraps
> of day-old bread and egg-stained plates; perhaps
> such sophistry can placate us.

No wonder it was with "half humorous, half-stoical acceptance" that Plath, like so many other coeds of the fifties, knew that her carefully cultivated labors of the mind were doomed to failure. A Smith song popular during her undergraduate years captures the edge of irony quite accurately:

> We're ready to wow Life, Time, Fortune, and Luce.
> We've energy, brains, and when we turn on the juice,
> Our style is so subtle it drives men to tears.
> But we're doing the copy for ads of brassieres.[24]

A fighter pilot in another Smith collection poem discovers a kind of cosmic irony as a means of dealing with limitations. In "Metamorphoses of the Moon," the pilot brazenly hurls his plane at the heavens to taunt and "raid the zone where fate begins." In flinging his "silver gauntlet" at space, however—a space that he considers the source of truth and absolute certainty—he is met only by total silence:

> . . . no duel takes place:
> the mute air merely thins and thins.

> Sky won't be drawn closer: absolute,
> it holds aloof, a shrouded parachute
> always the same distance from
> the falling man who never will abstain
> from asking, but inventive, hopes; in vain
> challenges the silent dome.

The odds are always against someone like the pilot who continues that vain challenge to the mute, intractable universe. The design of things appears to bear "truant intent / to double cross the firmament."

> No ancient blueprint builds an ark
> to navigate the final dark . . .
> all absolutes that angels give
> flounder in the relative.

If all absolutes are relative and the universe is unmarked by human logic or action, the only defense against total despair is "scintillant irony." And as Plath reiterates her case for relativity, the propositional sense of her narratives comes to dominate any poetic skill. She finds in these impersonally fictional situations—pilots in silver planes, princes in search of grails—her philosophy of irony.

The Smith poems suggest two temporary resolutions: resignation to the factual world or tolerant irony. Although she develops the stance of irony more thoroughly in later poems, such as "Disquieting Muses" and "Face Lift," Plath describes resignation most convincingly in the early uncollected work. As she rehearses the need to scale down one's fictions to a few well-honed facts, the cumulative tone of her recognition—quite apart from the total texture of the poem—marks her particular skill. In fact, the "same note of dead-end emphasis" actually obscures the texture of the verse.[25] As early as 1948, Plath tried to explain the sources of her creativity by describing the resilience of this voice:

> I write only because
> there is a voice within me
> That will not be still. (LH)

But most often the voice is prosaic, weary, and colored by "multiple shades of gray." Its sheer weight and ironclad emphasis, joined to the expressed idea of physical limits, form the single most convincing quality of the verse.

Frequently, even in the midst of a catalog of cosmic abstractions, Plath's case for the simple monochromatic life leaks through in damaged tones. Previously disillusionment was expressed through technical acrobatics, overextended metaphors, surface action, and a variety of grave but stock concepts: the cosmic upset of ruined love; the war of the great metaphysical polarities, love and the imagination; the moon's illusion versus the sun's candor; the vanity of wishes in the face of love and death; diurnal versus seasonal time. Heroic action happened in books and circuses, love relationships didn't pan out, and imaginative worlds were only ruses. In "Apotheosis" (CM), for example, the tone describing the lovelorn speaker shifts to new, prosaic exhaustion:

> now there is nowhere I can go
> to hide from him;
> moon and sun reflect his flame.
>
> In the morning all shall be
> the same again . . .

Internalized despair overrides the precious metaphor of "Winter Words," the sharp directive of "Moonsong at Morning," even the carpe diem theme that runs through these poems:

> . . . today we start
> to pay the piper with each breath, yet love
> knows not of death nor calculus above
> the simple sum of heart plus heart. (RH)

The same mood of simple, diminished action is communicated by one of Plath's earliest published poems, "Bitter Strawberries."[26] The poem is a glimpse of the workaday world of a group of berrypickers whose hawkish clichés about war (and even some genuine fears about loved ones' welfare) mix with their work in the fields. The poem is a marvel of starkly colloquial understatement and ellipsis. A young girl, Nelda, begs her co-workers to refrain from their "bomb-them-off-the-map" statements, and the response indicates the irony of their status. The quietness of the final image—that simple, practiced gesture of fondling and then snapping the berries—captures all the duplicity and easy habitual violence of predatory human nature:

> "Oh, stop worrying, Nelda," snapped the woman sharply.
>
> She stood up, a thin, commanding figure
> In faded dungarees.

Businesslike, she asked us, "How many quarts?"
She recorded the total in her notebook,
And we all turned back to picking.

Kneeling over the rows,
We reached among the leaves
With quick, practiced hands
Cupping the berry protectively before
Snapping off the stem
Between the thumb and forefinger.

Plath offers another example of this weary tone of resignation in "Superman and Paula Brown's New Snowsuit,"[27] a
story that heralds the death of the imagination. Confronted with
frustration and disenchantment, a young girl makes her first
bitter connection between lying companions, a mistrusting uncle, and the universal pain of World War II prison tortures and
air raids. Paula is "filled with a love of the sheer poetry of flight":
Logan County airport is her Mecca or Jerusalem. Her hero,
Superman, is identified with her blue-suited Uncle Frank. At a
birthday party one day, she sees her first newsreel about
Japanese prison tortures (the main feature, of course, was *Snow
White*). Later that night, her disillusionment grows: "No crusad-
ing blue figure came roaring down in heavenly anger to smash
the yellow men that invaded my dreams."

In another incident, reality proves grimly unavoidable. The
narrator is playing tag with her friends when the bossy kid on
the block is pushed into an oil slick. She has on her new Swiss
snowsuit: "We all froze as she went down. . . . The dull, green
light of late afternoon came closing down on us, cold and final as
a window blind." Paula is blamed for the folly, and her simple,
truthful version of the mishap is ignored: "I told you what
happened, and I can't make it any different. Not even for you, I
can't make it any different."

The story seems to build toward Paula's final, terribly mature, and exhausted sense of destruction. Trust is betrayed
along with her belief in the "poetry of flying," and both are set
off against the background horrors of war:

I lay there alone in bed, feeling the black shadow creeping up the
underside of the world like a flood tide. Nothing held, nothing
was left. The silver airplanes and the blue capes all dissolved and
vanished, wiped away like the crude drawings of a child in colored
chalk from the colossal blackboard of the dark. That was the year
the war began, and the real world, and the difference. (p. 21)

" 'The weed of crime bears *bitter* fruit. Crime does *not* pay,' " urged the Shadow in a 1959 story of the same title.[28] Plath's young heroine, Sadie Shafer, encounters not only the phenomenon of evil in the world but also the sure remedy of triumphant justice. In comic books and radio programs—and never for more than twenty-five minutes at a stretch—crime never *did* pay: "We had no cause to wonder: *Will* the good people win? Only: *How*?" (*JP*, 148).

One day while roughhousing, Sadie bites the leg of a neighbor. The incident gets exaggerated out of proportion in the tense atmosphere of war. Neighbors ostracize her family, whisper that her father is a German spy, and are instrumental in his being sent away "to a place out West." Young Sadie "thought, in rapid succession, of the police, the FBI, the President, the United States Armed Forces. I thought of God. 'God won't let it happen,' I cried, inspired" (*JP*, 151).

> Mother gave me a measured look. . . . "Your father's going away *is* a mistake, it *is* unfair. You must never forget that. . . . At the same time, there is nothing that we can do about it. . . ."
>
> "But you said God . . ." I protested feebly.
>
> Mother overrode me. "God will let it happen."
>
> I understood, then, that she was trying to give me the piece to the puzzle I had not possessed. The shadow in my mind lengthened with the night blotting out our half of the world, and beyond it; the whole globe seemed sunk in darkness. For the first time the facts were not slanted Mother's way, and she was letting me see it.
>
> "I don't think there is any God, then," I said dully, with no feeling of blasphemy. "Not if such things can happen."
>
> "Some people think that," my mother said quietly. (*JP*, 151)

Plath ends "The Shadow" with the mother's understated retort and the young heroine's dashed metaphysic. The soberly ruled philosophy-in-earnest here and in the previous story are typical of the tone throughout *Letters Home*. Plath's deadpan utterances of resolutions and schemes for the future, better work habits, and more realistic schedules are similar to the sentiment of these early poems where the poet vows to have "no glory descend," or that "though the mind like an oyster labors on and on, / a grain of sand is all we have," or when she promises that

today
today I will not

disenchant my twelve black-gowned examiners
or bunch my fist
in the wind's sneer. (*CM*, "Resolve")

Everywhere the letters are filled with rehearsals of that "resonant emptiness." They insist upon a practical optimism that aims to convince by protesting too vigorously that Plath can make the best of whatever comes her way. As she boasts in one letter, "I am growing strong by practice." A 1953 letter shows the same grim heartiness:

> I am determined to be as cheerful and constructive about my mental difficulties as I am going to be about this physical one. Naturally I will be a bit depressed and blue at times, and tired and uncomfortable, but there is that human principle which always finds that no matter how much is taken away, something is left to build again with. (*LH*, 102)

When her father died, an embittered and abandoned nine-year-old Sivvy informed her mother: "I will never speak to God anymore." Her mother was required to sign a contractual agreement drawn up by Sylvia in which she agreed never to marry again. In another letter she insisted with false bravado that "In the cycle of joy and sorrow, there will always be an outlet for me. I can never lose everything—all at once" (*LH*, 59). At other times she indulged in a grim nostalgia of recollection that is held carefully in check: "I can only remember how it was and go on living where I am" (*LH*, 38).

These chanted statements circumscribe the "plain-line" life and are a form of whistling for confidence in the dark. For Plath, they simplify complex things, never emphasizing forward imaginative movement or exploration. For this very reason they portray a condition important to the early work. Vigorous recitals of the surviving, diminished quality of existence are crucial to a description of the emotional dynamics of Plath's sensibility and indicate the shape of her future poetic direction. In the *Colossus* poems, even terror wears a disguise of subtraction as imagination—unreliable as forewarned—is further pared away.

Although the loss of illusion has been costly, and failure of the imagination begs beguilement in the early poems and stories, the "laughing of greybeards" sobers the poet and reminds her that deception is impossible. The practical facts of existence are starkly final in their demand: "Cold vision / will have no counterfeit palmed off on it." With a steady but hollow tone the poems urge clear limits to the imagination. These poems that chart resignation are some of Plath's finest achievements in her early writing. They depart from surface action, trite imagery, and the self-consciously strained voice to employ the best qualities of good imagistic verse: verbal economy and precision; careful rhythm; introspective emotion; no irrelevant, discursive commentary. Absent is the cavalier defiance, the heroic stage action, and the high rhetoric that forms the carpe diem motif of, for example, the following verse:

> Now kiss again: till our strict father leans
> to call for curtain on our thousand scenes;
> brazen actors mock at him,
> multiply pink harlequins and sing
> in gay ventriloquy from wing to wing
> while footlights flare and houselights dim.

Instead, a poem such as "Resolve" (*CM*) treats the theme of exhaustion of the imagination with precise domestic images. A life scaled down to weary, mundane detail is assimilated by the speaking voice:

> day of mist: day of tarnish
>
> with hands
> unserviceable, I wait
> for the milk van.
>
> the one-eared cat
> laps its grey paw
>
> and the coal fire burns.
>
> outside, the little hedge leaves are
> become quite yellow.
> a milk-film blurs
> the empty bottles on the windowsill.
>
> no glory descends.
>
> two water drops poise
> on the arched green
> stem of my neighbor's rose bush.
>
> o bent bow of thorns.
> the cat unsheathes its claws.
> the world turns . . .

The poem does not bother with dramatic performances or spectacles. Here there is no talk of curtains, footlights, toppling tents, "withered worlds," or "puny hells." No voice insists that "in the vein advances / a glacial age." A new introspection, subtly evoked imagery, and words as understated yet precise as "unserviceable" describe disillusionment with a life of the mind. Compare the brag and propositional flare of the following poem with the tone of "Resolve."

> So we shall walk barefoot on walnut shells
> of withered worlds and stamp out puny hells
> and heavens till the spirits squeak
> surrender: to build our bed as high as jack's
> bold beanstalk; lie and love till sharp scythe hacks
> away our rationed days and weeks.
>
> Then let the blue tent topple, stars rain down,
> and god or void appall us till we drown
> in our own tears. (*RH*, "Love is a Parallax")

The images of "Resolve," in contrast, form a hard, clear, unblurred statement that, in the canon of imagism, binds intellectual and emotional complexity in an instant of time. If the "world turns," its measuring stick is "no calculus above / the simple sum of heart plus heart." The images—clumsy hands, a battered family cat, the hearth fire, milk film on a bottle, yellowed hedge leaves, and dewdrops on a rose stem—offer precise emotional description that is an inseparable part of a sensibility. They bring the speaker's daily life before the reader at the moment it presents itself to the poet's mind for resolution. There are no blurring irrelevancies. The world here is her world, a collection of those domestic moments unaffected by any claim for glory or power: "its business is with a mood, with defining accurately and with the minimum of fuss and ornament the kind of slow autumnal melancholy in which inner depression fuses inextricably with the blurred, silent weather outside. . . . Maybe the key is the depression and apparent casualness."[29] Images of steady determination communicate with casual control the mood of diminished weariness. Undecorated by bombast and theatrical action, they lead up to the poet's last resolve: not to "bunch my fist / in the wind's sneer."

The title poem of the Cambridge Manuscript, "Two Lovers and a Beachcomber by the Real Sea," describes the exhausted failure of both love and the imagination. This poem best demonstrates Plath's thematic concerns and technical achievements in the early fifties. Elements of this poem contrast with the obtrusive verse texture and stock metaphors of the previous work. Language is controlled, sparse. It is as charged and yet as familiar as the cold and final reminder about the hazards of illusion and the imagination:

> Cold and final, the imagination
> shuts down its fabled summer house:
> blue views are boarded up: our sweet vacation
> dwindles in the hourglass.
>
> Thoughts that found a maze of mermaid hair
> tangling in the tide's green fall
> now fold their wings like bats and disappear
> into the attic of the skull.
>
> We are not what we might be: what we are
> outlaws all extrapolation
> beyond the interval of now and here:
> white whales are gone with the white ocean.
>
> A lone beachcomber squats among the wrack
> of kaleidoscopic shells
> probing fractured Venus with a stick
> under a tent of taunting gulls.
>
> No sea change decks the sunken shank of bone
> that chuckles in back track of the wave;
> though the mind like an oyster labors on and on,
> a grain of sand is all we have.
>
> Water will run by rule; the actual sun
> will scrupulously rise and set;
> no little man lives in the exacting moon
> and that is that, is that, is that.

The elaborate metaphor of the first two stanzas—the imagination boarding up its summer place after the season—integrates Plath's favorite themes of time's passage, love's inevitable disillusionment, and the failure of the imagination. The once useful exclusiveness of the imagination is under the same mandate of time as that briefly visited vacation spa: both must now be closed down, boarded up, for their season has passed. Everything in its time, the poet says.

The central force of the poem derives from the dramatic shift in stanza three. Metaphoric language is abandoned for single, punched monosyllables: "we are not what we might be. . . ." Precise and exacting reality must be accepted straightforwardly, ungilded by decorative metaphors, underscored by mere simple words. The "maze of mermaid hair" folds away like bat wings. The prosaic terseness of this stanza suggests the sheer effort of the poet to level her vision to the simplicity of the "now and here." There is no forward movement, only a condition of weighty despair whose feeling permeates the language. Curiously, the final childish incantation is at once a solid affirmation of the poet's belief in limitation and, by its very insistence, a light mockery of that belief. Such ambiguity suggests the emotional condition behind so many of Plath's philosophical-poetic chants in these early pieces. The fact is that, given the attraction of the imaginative life and Plath's predisposition to it, she may never be able to adopt the resolve expressed: "and that is that, is that, is that" becomes only another attempt to gain certainty and focus direction through repetitious emphasis.

As a summarizing comment on the poet's development throughout the early fiction and poetry, "Two Lovers and a Beachcomber by the Real Sea" has real significance in its leaden, defeated sense of language and vision. The conflict between illusion and fact, imagination and the physical, always seems to nag at the poet's firm resolve to find some balance. Like the lone beachcomber who pokes among the strewings of seashells, the speaker has not quite accurately assessed the inevitable end of mythmaking. Like the youthful poet, she has deluded herself by her diligent craft and explosive imagery—"probing fractured Venus"—only to be taunted and mocked by the gulls overhead. Unable to check her own imaginative powers or to balance them with factual reality, Sylvia Plath continues to contrive myths of mermaid hair, men in the moon, and white whales in those final images. Distinguished by only a tone of lament and resolution, she has found no final poetic solution to her dilemma.

II.

The Colossus
"in sign language of a lost other world"

Introduction

Before the advent of the posthumous volume *Ariel* in 1965, *The Colossus* poems were heralded as promising examples of well-crafted work. Critics described the poems as hardy in language and sensibility, marked by unsentimental vitality, "mint-new" rhymes and decisive rhythms: "concrete experience arranged in clean, easy verse, ornate where necessary."[1] In addition to her fine handling of language, Plath was praised for humor, cleverness, and exuberance: "Sylvia Plath writes clever, vivacious poetry which will be enjoyed most by intelligent people capable of having fun with poetry and not just being holy about it."[2] Even the most grotesque of *The Colossus* poems prompted another critic to say that "she writes a plump and stumping line that jolts with imagination and clarity . . . she likes life—oh, rare response!"[3] Finally, in a 1962 review of *The Colossus*, E. Lucas Myers almost prophetically suggested that "the poems should be criticized as they are, not as the critics think they might have been. . . . I cannot help but wonder what will happen if, in Miss Plath's second volume of poems, the emotional distance is shortened."[4]

The poet died by suicide on 12 February 1963, leaving a substantial body of uncollected, unpublished poetry, fiction, and prose writing. After the second volume, *Ariel*, critics shifted their focus to the macabre and grisly elements of *The Colossus*: "Always she is aware of the doubleness of things, the shark beneath the surface, the tumult beneath the calm, the glitter beneath the veil."[5] Now described as a "breviary of estrangement," *The Colossus* became a casebook for those seeking evidence of suicidal despair. Richard Howard spoke of the teasing, riddling quality, the allusive technique of the poems, as "disaster within the surface of life": the poet brooded over a "broken landscape."[6] In retrospective comment, M. L. Rosenthal rebuked himself for previously overlooking those "irresistible motives" pushing toward the surface of the poems: "The way in which many of the poems are haunted by images of cold terror, and the empathy involved in her poems about dead animals, are more striking now, and the theme of suicide is seen to be more pervasive than was at first evident."[7]

When Alfred Alvarez suggested that the disciplined art of *The Colossus* functioned as a fence to keep psychological disturbance at bay,[8] critics and reviewers jumped on the "suicide bandwagon" in their eagerness to mythologize Plath. Pathology was equated with poetic power. Any diminished quality of pain or estrangement in the poems hinted that the poet had not yet come to grips with her subject as an artist. With such revisionist views, the critical history of *The Colossus* split between life and art, between the pre- and the post-*Ariel* perspective, a pattern that has determined Plath scholarship of subsequent years.

It is worth introducing another view of these poems, one that explores the broader imaginative vision that shapes both the riddling atmosphere and the particulars of poetic construction (syllabics, slant-rhyme, "ghost" terza rima). For the subject matter of *The Colossus* suggests the quiet elegance of an old painting: "the prospect is dull as an old etching," we are told. "At this wharf there are no grand landings to speak of," merely the "incense of death" mingled with "hours of blankness," stony landspits with a "bier of quahog chips"; classical tragedy (Medea, the Oresteia) with a dull monochrome newsreel; or nostalgic glances backward to the mythical Lorelei, Lucine, or the ruined Colossus of Rhodes set next to the contemporary ironies of Brueghel and Baskin. "What starts as description," we are assured, "finishes as a way of defining her [Plath's] own state of mind"[9] in these distanced and impersonal poems, balanced and framed like artwork. A peculiar emblematic vision of simultaneity—one that Plath describes as a dialogue between "wingy myths" and "blunt, indefatigable facts"—saturates the *Colossus* poems.

In the poems written sporadically between 1950 and 1957, Plath made a general philosophical commitment to the whole gamut of opposite choices confronting her. She dutifully recited the rhetorical polarities. She debated her own position between the "fact of doubt, the faith of dream," often borrowing stale clichés, outmoded metrical forms, and static metaphors. Even the occasional clever variation of traditional form could not redeem the sophomoric subject matter of a circus love "more athletic than a verb":

Treading circus tightropes
  Of each syllable,
The brazen jacknapes
  Would fracture if he fell.

Acrobat of space
  The daring adjective
Plunges for a phrase
  Describing arcs of love. [10]

But as she attempted a "duet of light and shade" between the forces of love and the powers of the imagination, Plath discovered that the imagination collapsed in the face of the blunt physical world. In sobering polemics she urged herself to accept the fact of limitation, of the less-than-ideal, in a world where "no glory descends" and "all extrapolation beyond the now and here" was doomed.

The early poems convinced Plath that her intellectual and theoretical mandates were to no avail: "so much / is vision good for: like a persistent stitch / In the side, it nags, is tedious." The chief difference in *The Colossus* poems is that Plath becomes her own idiosyncratic "literalist of the imagination," nagged by an idyllic union of contradictory qualities, both practical and visionary. And within her poems—those balanced and cropped pictorial compositions—she repeatedly describes a synchronistic state that suspends the rooted and fluid qualities of things in elemental poise: the lovingly tended "greased machines" of "Night Shift" combine the thud of hammers with the silent, "stalled" motion of the machine; "white Niagaras / Build up from a rock root, as fountains build / Against the weighty image of their fall" in "Moonrise"; a gull frozen in motion suggests an extradimensional view of life in "A Winter Ship," for it holds the "whole of the flat harbor anchored in / The round of his yellow eye-button."

Throughout the volume, various poetic devices betray the same habit of vision, the same inclusive pictorial design. With a careful balance of ingredients, Plath dwells in several poems on midpoints or transitional states (day to night, conscious to unconscious). The deliberate two-part structure of other poems ("Aftermath," "Two Views of a Cadaver Room") suggests, by physical analogue, her characteristic imaginative realm. In the latter poem, Plath juxtaposes the cadaver room with a well-known Brueghel painting, joining the clinical "rubble of skull plates and old leather" to satin, music, and romantic love.

Likewise, memory and indifference are meshed in "Point Shirley," while the social and personal responses to tragedy are united in "Aftermath."

Finally, the very shape of the volume itself—the only book of poems to be completely structured and emotionally ordered by Plath—is another version of the simultaneity that obsesses the poet. *The Colossus* gives the impression that an amorphous, mythical world of "a certain meaning green" coexists with crumbling wrecks and tragic aftermaths. The partially formed world grows ominous while the broken world simply decays, but both coexist in sparring commentary that determines the shape of the volume.

By joining mutually exclusive elements, Plath attempts her own "balance and reconciliation of opposites." Given rather startling historical precedents,[11] she cultivates unresolved ambivalence in her habit of vision and tries to formulate the stated contradictions into a working theory of poetic imagination. In doing this, Plath suggests a need for complexity without isolating or separating contradictory aspects of her awareness. Like those dark old crones in the poem "Net Menders," Plath is engaged in the specific labors of her craft, but she never ignores the broader, idyllic vision of things:

> While their fingers work with the coarse mesh and the fine,
> Their eyes revolve the whole town like a blue-and-green ball.
> Nobody dies or is born without their knowing it.
> They talk of bride-lace, or lovers spunky as gamecocks.[12]

Life is cruelly intricate, starkly simple, bitterly ironic, ecstatically joyous. Why choose to recognize merely one facet, the poet seems to ask.

The imaginative order that Plath so insistently describes in *The Colossus* remains psychologically distanced from her poetic sensibility. Like those sharp edges and settled lines of graphic art, "desolation stalled in paint,"

> The scene stands stubborn . . .
> However the grandiloquent mind may scorn
> Such poverty. . . . Here's honest rot
> To unpick the elaborate heart, pare bone
> Free of the fictive vein.[13]

More with Coleridge's mechanical power of fancy than with the creatively unifying imagination, Plath constructs this ideal realm on a variety of poetic levels. She catalogs her examples as industriously as an omniscient nineteenth-century narrator not yet familiar with Joseph Conrad's Marlowe, or F. Scott Fitzgerald's Nick Carraway:

> At the essential landscape stare, stare
> Till your eyes foist a vision dazzling on the wind:
> Whatever lost ghosts flare
> Damned, howling in their shrouds across the moor
> Rave on the leash of the starving mind
> Which peoples the bare room, the blank, untenanted air.
> ("November Graveyard")

While her forms prove that she has done her homework on the great masters (Emily Dickinson, W. B. Yeats, Wallace Stevens, W. H. Auden, Theodore Roethke, Dylan Thomas, and others), and that she has dutifully consulted her thesaurus for precision with synonyms, the subjects of her poetic world remain bloodless, generalized, stalled in their aesthetic perfection. She cannot pyschologically integrate the examples that she so elaborately describes for the development of her own poetic perception. Visual descriptions remain flat; they lack the energetic playfulness and teasing ambiguity of her later poems.

That she fails to incorporate imaginatively this perfectly synchronized world becomes the central focus of *The Colossus* poems. Decay and menace, casual processes of the natural world, threaten the development of her poetic vision. Even the cultivation of distance and memory offers no safeguard against the insidious threat everywhere part of the "essential landscape" that is her subject. At last, by focusing on the process of creation—artistic, physical, mythological—Plath explores that special domain of the artist. She examines poetically the nature and the products of artistic endeavor in various paintings and artifacts (Brueghel, Rousseau, de Chirico, Baskin) to understand better her role and function, however limited, in the creative process. As the title poem "The Colossus" shows, Plath gradually becomes aware of her futile efforts to construct a comprehensive imaginative vision. In fact, burdened with all her academic knowledge of technique, Plath's imaginative construction dwindles to *re*construction:

> Thirty years now I have labored
> To dredge the silt from your throat.
>
> I am none the wiser. [14]

One *Colossus* poem in particular, "The Eye-mote," describes the imaginative vision Plath reveres, yet also presents her limited grasp of the creative process at this stage in her poetic career. In the opening scene of "Eye-mote," the innocent poet gazes with a painter's eye at a scene that is an ideal emblem of the mental and emotional state she wants:

> Blameless as daylight I stood looking
> At a field of horses, necks bent, manes blown,
> Tails streaming against the green
> Backdrop of sycamores. (*Col.*, 12)

An instant of convergence in the pristine world balances the poet's perception ("I stood looking") with sharp details of the external world:

> . . . Sun was striking
> White chapel pinnacles over the roofs,
> Holding the horses, the clouds, the leaves
>
> Steadily rooted though they were all flowing
> Away to the left like reeds in a sea. . . . (*Col.*, 12)

Suddenly a splinter sticks in her eye, "needling it dark" and shattering the perfectly perceived aesthetic union with a reminder of the *imperfect* self. The ideal world gives way first to the dark, then to a caricature of the original that is now but a point of nostalgia for the speaker:

> A melding of shapes in a hot rain:
> Horses warped on the altering green,
>
> Outlandish as double-humped camels or unicorns,
> Grazing at the margins of a bad monochrome,
> Beasts of oasis, a better time. (*Col.*, 12)

The perfect imaginative moment has become a "place, a time gone out of mind," replaced by the immediate rude fact of the "red cinder around which I myself / Horses, planets and spires revolve." No fabled world of the imagination persists. A shrunken vision threatens any effort to "unseat the speck," and the poet-subject remains "fixed . . . in this parenthesis" somewhere between mythical past and desired future, "blind to what will be and what was."

In three respects, "Eye-mote" serves as a key to understanding Plath's imaginative arena throughout the *Colossus* poems. First, it sets forth a fixed, flat description of that emblematic world of opposites joined in a moment of simultaneity. Secondly, the presence of the cinder speck reminds the speaker of the necessary intrusion of the practical fact, a theme urged in earlier poems and one that will continue to plague the poet. Thirdly, "The Eye-mote" expresses the poet's desire for a way of seeing that is more comprehensive than the immediate realistic mode. "The Eye-mote" world moves timelessly, yet has the security of being anchored; it joins literary analogues with self-awareness ("I dream that I am Oedipus"); achieves great distance, whether historical, physical, or mythical, yet is localized in a single narrator ("fixed . . . in this parenthesis"). This world of simultaneity, however attractive, remains just out of reach of the *Colossus* poet, yet looms as an idyllic place to be recovered in imagination:

> What I want back is what I was
> Before the bed, before the knife,
> Before the brooch-pin and the salve
> Fixed me in this parenthesis;
> Horses fluent in the wind,
> A place, a time gone out of mind. (*Col.*, 13)

The Sea: "A world more full and clear than can be"

Plath's use of sea imagery recalls an historical tension in American letters between anthropomorphic and destructive forces ranging from Longfellow to Lowell.[15] Particularly influenced by Wallace Stevens, she focuses less on facets of death and destruction than on the sea as model for her imaginatively ideal state:

> I walk dry on your kingdom's border
> Exiled to no good.
> Your shelled bed I remember.
> Father, this thick air is murderous.
> I would breathe water. (*Col.*, 48)

The sea provided a curious ambience for Plath that continued to shape her poetic sensibility and provide her with a model for a complex, imaginative order throughout her career. According to her autobiographical essay, "Ocean 1212-W,"[16] her youth was dominated by the sea: Winthrop, Massachusetts on the bayside; Point Shirley, the home of her maternal grandparents, on the seaside. Even in her postcollege years she was attracted to England with its charm of having "no place more than seventy miles from the sea": "My childhood landscape was not land, but the end of land—the cold, salt, running hills of the

Atlantic. I sometimes think my vision of the sea is the clearest thing I own" (*O*, 102). Plath was continually lured by those first nine years of her life near the Atlantic, years that had "sealed themselves off like a ship in a bottle—beautiful, inaccessible, obsolete, a fine, white flying myth."

The myth of the sea, with its peculiar elements of contradiction, took root in Plath's psyche and shaped her poetic temperament for years afterward. At the same time that the sea suggested an unnatural black stillness, the breath of the sea was a pulsating "huge radiant animal": "Even with my eyes shut I could feel the glimmers off its bright mirrors spider over my lids. I lay in a watery cradle, and sea gleams found the chinks in the dark green window blind, playing and dancing, or resting and trembling a little" (*O*, 104). While the sea offered her tangible signs of "election and specialness," it also offered the poet sulphurous afternoons: "My final memory of the sea is of violence—a still, unhealthily yellow day in 1939, the sea molten, steely-slick, heaving at its leash like a broody animal, evil violets in its eye" (*O*, 108).

"With the typical good sense of the modern poet, Plath . . . endows the sea with the characteristics of her own mind," Charles Newman observes.[17] The familiar rooted-yet-flowing state is represented by her repertoire of sea figures and sea elements: the mythical marble-headed Lorelei in their "silver flux"; the battering waves eroding Point Shirley; an old Poseidon whose unknown origins add mystery to his rooted, labyrinthine tangle; or the Rock Harbor mussels that hang swaying in liquid suspension. Like the vanishing point in a painting to which all line, color, and perspective are magnetically drawn, Plath's "Man in Black" rivets together "three magenta breakwaters," the gray sea "to the left," the "cattle green / To the right," the snuff-colored sand cliffs and the white stones. The poet, too, would be such a pivotal and imaginative center, joining her nearly perfect syllabics (six per line) to the single, compelling sentence that forms this poem, the "unfisting" waves with the barbwired headland:

> And you, across those white
>
> Stones, strode out in your dead
> Black coat, black shoes, and your
> Black hair till there you stood,
>
> Fixed vortex on the far

Tip, riveting stones, air,
All of it, together. (*Col.*, 52–53)

Repeatedly in these poems, Plath's habit of vision is that of the artist: clearly illustrated compositional unity, perfectly balanced, perfectly inhuman—like the world of a ship in a bottle.

Once again she celebrates the contradictory qualities of the sea, humorous animism and rampant destruction, in the poem "Bull of Bendylaw," a masterful dialogue between form and narrative. In the poem a child's fable and its props—a king, queen, mulberry arbor, even a royal rose—are formed into a stiff, tight "playing card" world with "box-lined walks." Each stanza's repetitive rhyme and singsong metrics (two lines of tetrameter, one of trimeter) lend a nursery rhyme ambience to the simple storybook elements. Bendylaw is an orderly world that will "stay put," Plath claims. But in the narrative, the "bull-snouted sea" refuses to do so, much to the poet's dismay:

A blue sea, four horny bull-feet,
A bull-snouted sea that wouldn't stay put,
Bucked at the garden gate.
. . . .

The great bronze gate began to crack,
The sea broke in at every crack,
Pellmell, blueblack.

The bull surged up, the bull surged down,
Not to be stayed by a daisy chain
Nor by any learned man.

O the king's tidy acre is under the sea,
And the royal rose in the bull's belly,
And the bull on the king's highway. (*Col.*, 27–28)

If the sea introduced tumultuous chaos and violence, it also provided Plath with fantasies and real tokens of individuation. Its legacy included physical textures and imaginative myths, storybook bulls and tales of drowned sailors "gone straight to Davy Jones," as well as strewings of fan shells, egg stones, glass nuggets, and shivers of china bits. Plath delighted as much in the tangibility of the sea's wreckage and its steaming chowders as in its emotional nurture and myths of mermaids or the Spanish infanta.

Most importantly, the sea showed Plath a model of beautiful fusion with things of this world that she thought she had lost when, at the birth of her brother, she was forced to recognize

otherness: "The sea, perceiving my need, had conferred a bless-
ing." "When I was not walking alongside the sea, I was on it, or
in it," reunited with some impossible moment of dynamic flux.
She even learned to swim with "hands and feet milling in the
cold green," unanchored and literally absorbed in the sea's
contradictions. As model for her imaginative world, according
to George Stade, the sea "had come to saturate her sense of
identity . . . to represent for her the depths of poetry in which
literal losses underwent a change into symbolic recoveries."[18]

No wonder then that watery gods with their perfect union
of contradictory qualities dominate a number of the *Colossus*
poems. From both the stone maidens ("Lorelei") and the old
patriarch ("Full Fathom Five") we learn that the most vivid
danger to Sylvia Plath's ideal world is anything that is identified
with a distinct polarity, a precise fact, or one "scrutable" dimension. The exclusive precision of any such form violates a comprehensive, if tenuous, imaginative vision:

> . . . All obscurity
> Starts with a danger:
>
> Your dangers are many. (*Col.*, 47)

In her portrayal of the mythical figures, but especially in the
skillful "bickering" of form and narrative, "Lorelei" and "Full
Fathom Five" are excellent examples of Plath's longed-for imaginative world. With a grained face that "sheds time in runnels,"
the mythical old man in "Full Fathom Five" is half fact, half
archetype, aged yet timeless. He appears and disappears "as
the waves crest and trough," yet his "hair sheaves" and craggy
face are strangely solid:

> . . . white hair, white beard, far-flung,
> A dragnet, rising, falling, as waves
> Crest and trough. Miles long
>
> Extend the radial sheaves
> Of your spread hair, in which wrinkling skeins
> Knotted, caught, survives
>
> The old myth of origins
> Unimaginable. (*Col.*, 46)

Praised for his ambivalence, the old god warns of obscurity and
collision with blunt fact ("keeled ice-mountains"), yet beckons
to primitive, mythical sources (the "unbeaten channels of the
ocean").

While whirlpool and ridgepole are the physical referents for Plath's desired imaginative world, the well-wrought poetic devices and language are more tangible equivalents for her idyllic order than the puzzling old god. Words, deliberate not exploratory, are carefully placed, syntactically inverted in this poem. And the careful cresting and falling of the verse—the patterns of iamb and trochee—create a formal wave pattern that suggests both the old man's come-on and his danger:

> . . . sage humor and
> Durance are whirlpools
>
> To make away with the ground-
> Work of the earth and the sky's ridgepole.
> Waist down, you may wind
>
> One labyrinthine tangle
> To root deep among knuckles, shinbones,
> Skulls. Inscrutable,
>
> Below shoulders not once
> Seen by any man who kept his head,
> You defy questions;
>
> You defy other godhood. (*Col.*, 47–48)

Like the defiant Poseidon, the stony sirens of "Lorelei" embody Plath's ideal imaginative concurrence of opposites. Although they float upward toward the poet, their shapes at once light and fluid, they lure her downward, "limbs ponderous," "hair heavier / Than sculpted marble." They "trouble the face of quiet" with their ambiguities. The world promised by their song is a double-edged burden for the common ("whorled") ear:

> Yet these shapes float
>
> Up toward me, troubling the face
> Of quiet. From the nadir
> They rise, their limbs ponderous
>
> With richness, hair heavier
> Than sculpted marble. They sing
> Of a world more full and clear
>
> Than can be. Sisters, your song
> Bears a burden too weighty
> For the whorled ear's listening
>
> Here, in a well-steered country,
> Under a balanced ruler.
>
> . . . .

O river, I see drifting

Deep in your flux of silver
Those great goddesses of peace.
Stone, stone, ferry me down there. (*Col.*, 22–23)

By the poem's end, Plath the observer has moved from
description of quiet, mythical sources to a plea for direct
psychological and physical involvement in a realm of frightening contradictions: song-yet-silence, fear-yet-beckoning,
solidity-yet-flux. In the event of the poem an emblem has taken
a textured shape from the vague and amorphous. Specific elements of verse suggest this. Remarkably controlled syllabics—
seven per line—function as a check on the maddening harmony
of the Lorelei who beckon to their world of oblivion. A coy
interlocking rhyme scheme of "ghost" terza rima weaves its
physical equivalent to the sirens' gradual pattern of seduction.
The progression of verbals in the first two stanzas dramatizes
this: a "lapsing" black river in the first stanza yields to "drop-
ping" mists in the next three lines, and finally to fishermen
"sleeping" the death of the seduced. Again Plath's carefully
wrought craft captures the contradictory realm of the ladies,
their "unusual harmony," while their sphere remains
psychologically unattainable for the poet herself. The poet
moves beyond the "bland mirror sheen" to a disjunction where
a real voice in a real body forms a plea to enter that "world more
full and clear / than can be."

Such final disjunctions are common fare in a number of
Colossus poems, but in a curious way. Plath has created precise
images with a draftsman's eye and with an imagination whose
workings Alvarez sums up as "a gesture on the surface of the
poem," one that is not yet a "part of what she is actually
saying."[19] Each pictorial detail in her poetic tableau seems to be
a calculated, discrete item; each emblem "beyond the mundane
order" is a moment arrested in the flux of the poet-perceiver's
attention. While they represent some vague wish for duration,
such images do not last apart from their intellectualized moment
of description. As the poet rehearses these examples of
simultaneity—the rooted-yet-flowing field horses of "Eye-
mote," the "absolute landscape" of "Hardcastle Crags," or the
gull on the ridgepole holding the "whole flat harbor anchored in
/ The round of his yellow eye-button" in "A Winter Ship"—she
grows psychologically more distant from the momentary union

she describes. As she repeats these visionary emblems with a kind of verbal calisthenics borrowed from the early work, she is faced with her own separateness. Instead of imaginatively incorporating the metaphysical meaning of that explorer-crab ("Mussel Hunter at Rock Harbor"), the poet remains "one two-legged mussel picker" who poises on linguistic pivots, deflects feeling in exhaustive puns: "this relic saved / Face, to face the bald-faced sun." And at the end of "Lorelei," the poet is left making a high-pitched incantatory plea for her intellectual experience to be felt more directly: "Stone, stone, ferry me down there." Visual principles of perfection, it seems, precise serigraphs like the "Man in Black," have precluded the emotional primacy of the self with its searching voice, its exploring consciousness.

In a 1959 journal entry, Plath criticizes one of her short stories in words that accurately describe her failure to assimilate the idealized imaginative realm throughout *The Colossus* poems: ". . . a stiff, artificial piece . . . none of the deep emotional undercurrents gone into or developed. As if little hygienic trap-doors shut out the seethe and deep-grounded swell of my experience. Putting up pretty artificial statues."[20]

"Point Shirley" is perhaps her most ambitious attempt to texturally recreate the sea's contradictions as the source for her vision of simultaneity. Again the poem recounts Plath's failure. The evocative force of the sea's "bickering," the "gritted wave's" crash and collapse against the seawall, is echoed in the staggered and uneven meter and rhyme. Prosody captures the sensual and visual effect of the crashing retreat of the sea against shingles:

> From Water-Tower Hill to the brick prison
> The shingle booms, bickering under
> The sea's collapse.
> Snowcakes break and welter. (*Col.*, 24)

Natural elements introduce an emotional tension that is echoed in the formal structure of the lines and in the skillfully interwoven patterns of sound ("brick" and "bickering" are picked up by "snowcakes break"). Plath struggles to find the precise connective point between memory and object, between nostalgic impulse and time's subtraction of feeling. How does one reconcile enduring love for a dead relative with the eroding indifference

of the sea, its jumble of timbers, carcasses, and "quahog chips,"
the poet asks:

> This year
> The gritted wave leaps
> The seawall and drops onto a bier
> Of quahog chips,
> Leaving a salty mash of ice to whiten
>
> In my grandmother's sand yard. She is dead,
> Whose laundry snapped and froze here, who
> Kept house against
> What the sluttish, rutted sea could do.
> Squall waves once danced
> Ship timbers in through the cellar window;
> A thresh-tailed, lanced
> Shark littered in the geranium bed—
>
> Such collusion of mulish elements
> She wore her broom straws to the nub. (*Col.*, 24)

Such poetic anatomy of an emotion or an object in the
attempt to find a point of reconciliation is one of the most
distinctive traits of *The Colossus* volume. According to one critic,
Plath's "most serious question is 'how are the object and the
emotion interpenetrated, what effect has each on the other?' "[21]
Plath wants to grasp the origin and power of the creative impulse in physical objects, nostalgic settings:

> What is it
> Survives, grieves
> So, over this battered, obstinate spit
> Of gravel?
> . . . . .
> A labor of love, and that labor lost.
> Steadily the sea
> Eats at Point Shirley. (*Col.*, 25)

"Point Shirley" celebrates its own "collusion of mulish
elements." The tension between technique and imaginative
vision and the rapid shifts from nostalgic emotion to physical
debris, create a textural ambivalence. There is, nevertheless, a
terrible inevitability that undercuts the poem. The narrative
suggests that the grandmother, dead twenty years, fought a
losing battle not only against the sea, but against the disorder
and chaos of life itself. She wore "her broom straws to the nub"
in the futile, Sisyphean labor. The poet faces the same fore-

closed end in her attempt, once again through vain memory, to rescue and revive a childhood emotion of love from "dry-papped stones" to living passion:

And I come by
Bones, bones only, pawed and tossed,
A dog-faced sea.
The sun sinks under Boston, bloody red.

I would get from these dry-papped stones
The milk your love instilled in them.
The black ducks dive.
And though your graciousness might stream,
And I contrive,
Grandmother, stones are nothing of home
To that spumiest dove.
Against both bar and tower the black sea runs.
(*Col.*, 25–26)

The final stanza, a direct address to the grandmother, is significantly modal or provisional: "I *would* get," and "though your graciousness *might* stream." The desire, yet the doubt, in the verbal constructions suggests the vain attempt to recover the power or source of the grandmother's love, that experience of factual and emotional concurrence. The force of love and memory—that "spumiest dove"—fails, and vision again shifts to the black, diving ducks, the bar and tower, and the indiscriminately leveling sea. As in "Lorelei," the shortlived moment of perception is menaced by the "dog-faced" sea which has both the first and last word: its whimsical, dual nature remains the governing principle for the whole poem.

Several explanations come to mind for the poet's final disjunction from her idyllic world in the sea poems. For one, she selects remote, aesthetically distanced models to represent the ideal state: nodding, bald-headed ladies who smother with their curious silence ("Disquieting Muses"); vaporous old men from the archives of sea lore ("Full Fathom Five"); or shrill-songed sisters ("Lorelei") whose only directive to the poet is their vague "deranging harmony" or "ice-hearted calling."

But surely the world of *The Colossus* poems outlines a strangely atypical metaphysic. Absolutes are in flux, constantly metamorphosing, slipping away, evaporating. "Old despot" god figures, petulant children, or silent, inscrutable creatures assume protean shapes from watery mists, green flickerings, distant history, modern biology, even from the depths of memory. Snake charmers find their peculiar spheres to be water, not dust. The Lorelei's call is an ambivalent response—a burden and a promise—while an impersonal silence characterizes the "Disquieting Muses" or Lucina, the "bony mother":

> . . . laboring
> Among the socketed white stars, your face
> Of candor pares white flesh to the white bone.
> (*Col.*, 65)

Like "Faun," man becomes god in the Plath canon, but with great difficulty. Touchingly humanized, bumbling man exposes his cover and then absconds as if to underscore his ineptitude. Faun's metamorphosis is effected through dense verse fabric—consonance, assonance, kenning, and interlocking vowels—and an erratically rhymed five-line stanza:

> An arena of yellow eyes
> Watched the changing shape he cut,
> Saw hoof harden from foot, saw sprout
> Goat horns. Marked how god rose
> And galloped woodward in that guise. (*Col.*, 17)

Perhaps the most important function of Plath's godlike figures is their role as silent reminders to the poet of that grisly endurance required for the act of creation. A good example of the artist's defiance is the old patriarch of "The Hermit at Outermost House":

> Sky and sea, horizon-hinged
> Tablets of blank blue, couldn't
> Clapped shut, flatten this man out. (*Col.*, 56)

Or in "I Want, I Want," a crusty old god adopts a makeshift plan of "toughing it out":

> Dry-eyed, the inveterate patriarch
> Raised his men of skin and bone,
> Barbs on the crown of gilded wire,
> Thorns on the bloody rose-stem. (*Col.*, 39)

These figures assume increasing importance as Plath seeks to understand the limitations and commitments of the creative artist.

The Failure of Emblem: "a place, a time gone out of mind"

Richard Howard has summed up Plath's attempt to describe such perfect imaginative moments of equilibrium as self-canceling homeostasis in which the poet succumbs to a leveling off, a running down to nothing.[22] Failing to perceive the idyllic moments that fill Plath's *Colossus* world, Howard does nonetheless suggest a less dramatic but important occurrence in the volume: an effective menace by nature becomes increasingly apparent in the poems. As we have seen, Plath repeatedly finds herself helpless to sustain the emblematic visionary events as part of her direct experience. Exploring for mussels at Rock Harbor, for example, she comes to a pool bed where "it seemed / A sly world's hinges had swung / Shut against me":

> . . . I
> Stood shut out, for once, for all,
> Puzzling the passage of their
> Absolutely alien
> Order as I might puzzle
> At the clear tail of Halley's
>
> Comet coolly giving my
> Orbit the go-by. . . . (*Col.*, 70–71)

Poems such as "Medallion," "Mussel Hunter," "The Eye-mote," and "Hardcastle Crags" trace the poet's progress to a point where the moment of interpenetration—whether it be of place and emotion, present fact and distant memory, or simply the physical qualities of the rooted and the fluent—eludes her. Those shortlived moments of union she perceives do not animate her whole sensibility, so that by the end of *The Colossus* the poet has become her own "blunt, indefatigable fact." She is fixed in the parentheses of her pleas for imaginative entrance into an emblematic world: "What I want back is what I was," she laments. Or in "The Ghost's Leavetaking" she seeks an "ambrosial revelation" or "the hieroglyphs / Of some godly utterance," or simply:

> . . . the sign language of a lost otherworld,
> A world we lose by merely waking up.

Trailing its telltale tatters only at the outermost
Fringe of mundane vision. . . . (*Col.*, 43)

In "Point Shirley," her attempt to join distant memory with present passion, place with feeling, the grandmother's life with immortality, was merely a "labor of love and that labor lost." In "Lorelei," the poet remained earth-clotted in a "well-steered country / Under a balanced ruler," while she was left exiled on the shores of the dry kingdom in "Full Fathom Five."

Quite appropriately, "Manor Garden," the first poem in the volume, treats the difficult task of birthing as well as a life-giving myth, unaided by philosophies or supernatural systems. The subject of this poem (addressed to a newborn infant) is "convergence" or simultaneity—the biological, metaphysical, historical, and familial legacies that converge on the physically developing fetus. With this weight of inheritance, the poet suggests the difficulty of sustaining not just one's own imaginative life—a familiar issue for Plath—but the very fragility of the physical existence itself: "the spider on its own string / Crosses the lake."

The notion of convergence becomes increasingly complex as the poem weaves together several kinds of time—gestational, evolutionary, historical, psychological—in succinct imagery. As we move from ancient past ("the era of fishes") to the present moment (the "difficult borning"), from biological signature through the classical "crowns of acanthus" to personal history, the concept of birth-as-death becomes the most dramatic convergence in the poem. In the first stanza, the finality of death and desiccation ("roses are over") contrast with bursting sensuality ("pears fatten like little buddhas"). The simile is comforting, clever, and temporary. Those "broken flutings" of genetic promise are mollified, too, by the mock-epic humor of biological evolution:

You move through the era of fishes,
The smug centuries of the pig—
Head, toe and finger
Come clear of the shadow. History

Nourishes these broken flutings,
. . . . (*Col.*, 3)

For there is no deflecting from the truly "difficult borning": the child's acceptance of her personal, psychological legacy. Not even the smallest forms of existence can remove the threat and burden of this inheritance, more problematic than the physical birth itself.

Those humble physical existences in "Manor Garden"—the spider, the yellow stars, the small birds—introduce the growing threat from opaque nature that undercuts all that is tenuously human in *The Colossus*. (Recall again Richard Howard's comment that Plath, in attempting to describe imaginative moments of equilibrium, achieves only self-obliteration.) The menace—both from large, impenetrable elements and from murky threats beneath the surface—requires one to:

> . . . bear
> Dry witness
> To the gross eating game
> We'd wink at if we didn't hear
> Stars grinding, crumb by crumb,
> Our own grist down to its bony face.
> (*Col.*, 29)

Monotony, repetition, and neutrality gather force as distinct ingredients in Plath's poetic world of *The Colossus*. "This is not death, it is something safer. / The wingy myths won't tug at us any more," we are reminded. Air "ignites" while sea and sky are "horizon hinged," threatening to clap shut, flattening any human existence. Indifference is everywhere—in looming sandspits, "ochreous" salt flats, blue wastage of Egg Rock, "dry-papped stones," even the booming shingles of Point Shirley:

> . . . from Great Head's knob
> To the filled-in Gut
> The sea in its cold gizzard ground those rounds.
> (*Col.*, 25)

Nowhere is blunt impenetrability more evident than in the mute stoniness of "Hardcastle Crags." Petrifaction threatens human existence. The opaque prevails as the poet traces her own arrested development from the first flinty clatter of her feet through the very real threat of personal dissolution:

> All the night gave her, in return
> For the paltry gift of her bulk and the beat
> Of her heart was the humped indifferent iron
> Of its hills, and its pastures bordered by black
> stone set
> On black stone.

. . . .
. . . dairy herds
Knelt in the meadow mute as boulders;
Sheep drowsed stoneward in their tussocks of wool,
    and birds,
Twig-sleeping, wore

Granite ruffs, their shadows
The guise of leaves. (*Col.*, 15)

Pared down to a "pinch of flame" by the "long wind," the
granite crags and the stone pastures before her, the poet is no
match for that "absolute landscape." Nor does she find a point
of identification—no words, no "family-featured ghost," only a
"dream-peopled village"—in that opaque landscape. Only the
"sway of lymph and sap" moving timelessly against a "stony
light" describes the poles of that mythical realm:

. . . and the incessant seethe of grasses
Riding in the full

Of the moon, manes to the wind,
Tireless, tied, as a moon-bound sea
Moves on its root. (*Col.*, 14)

Finding herself too fragile, too threatened—but making this
discovery in a step-by-step progress that is the value of the
poem—the poet does an about-face to preserve a separate, if
humble, sense of self:

. . . but before the weight
Of stones and hills of stones could break
Her down to mere quartz grit in that stony light
She turned back. (*Col.*, 16)

It might be argued that the main character of the poem is not the
self-conscious perceiver who turns back, but the "whole landscape [that] loomed absolute as the antique world . . . unaltered
by eyes." This pristine world of opposites is sustained in the
textural dialectic of imagery throughout the poem: steel, stone,
boulder, and granite vie with flame, lymph, sap, and mist.

Petrifaction continues to threaten fragile humankind in the
poem "Departure." Nothing softens that impenetrable "jut of
ochreous rock," or those flatly insistent colors: green figs,
"brickred porch tiles," the town's "blue bay," the "leaden slag
of the world." No retrospective nostalgia changes the fact that
the "money's run out." Through the poem's series of imagistic
moments, prosody and verse form support the propositional

sense of nature "compounding her bitters," adding to human poverty:

Sun's brass, the moon's steely patinas,
The leaden slag of the world—
But always expose

The scraggy rock spit shielding the town's blue bay
Against which the brunt of outer sea
Beats, is brutal endlessly.
(*Col.*, 18–19)

In the same poem there is a counterworld set against this imposing landscape of indifference. A gradual movement toward insubstantiality lurks in the slowly corroding weather, in the sun shining on unripe corn. All the more insidious because it lacks bulky visibility, this threatening world is animate, alive, and covertly at work eroding any human images of imaginative concurrence. Surely the depleted atmosphere of "Departure" contrasts with the blatant drama of earlier poems where death (stasis, darkness, hardness, separateness) starkly contrasts with life (color, noise, movement, heat, radiance).

Always present in *The Colossus* poems is this world-in-the-forming that is partially visible. Menace is oblique; for example, the barren sound of "queer, crusty scrabble" of crabs rasping on seashells. A world glimpsed from the corner of the eye is unpeopled, brutal in its elemental guise. Metal is corroded by the sun's rays; stone is worn down gradually to "mere quartz grit"; the sea pulses "under a skin of oil," suspended activity masking the terror; ice is "knifed" imperceptibly by the sun's rays; mornings "dissipate in somnolence." Clearly, "the genius of plenitude / Houses himself elsewhere," but not among *The Colossus* images.

Qualities of withering and dissipating create a world of monotonous repetition, one moving toward final oblivion:

The insects are scant, skinny.
In these palustral homes we only
Croak and wither. (*Col.*, 68)

Fury is dissolved; a pall hangs about the world of the poems like the smoke of a fire, slyly choking. Scandals, never dramatic, "ooze" from "smoke-choked closets" like "blood spores" of the old tragedies.

Another note of resignation resounds in the imagery where "white bruises toward color, else collapses," and "Grub-white

mulberries redden among leaves . . . doing nothing." Insidiously, the whiteness of "Moonrise" is a mere void that becomes
a "complexion of the mind." The smell of death is hidden
beneath stones; or "white catalpa flowers tower, topple / Cast a
round white shadow in their dying." "All things sink / Into a soft
caul of forgetfulness" that recalls the weary neutrality of "Resolve," or the "bone pared free of fictive vein" in "November
Graveyard." The delicate tone of exhaustion is more dramatic
than any grand actions, more internalized than Plath's belabored imaginative cosmology. One is sensually immersed in a
world that is gradually sinking into nonexistence:

> Now coldness comes sifting down, layer after layer,
> To our bower at the lily root.
> Overhead the old umbrellas of summer
> Wither like pithless hands. There is little shelter.
>
> Hourly the eye of the sky enlarges its blank
> Dominion. The stars are no nearer.
> . . . all things sink
> Into a soft caul of forgetfulness.
> This is not death, it is something safer.
> The wingy myths won't tug at us any more.
> (Col., 80–81)

The tone of resignation, of the spent imagination, resounds
throughout *The Colossus* poems, more convincing and more
personal than the "deranging harmony" of the visionary
Lorelei:

> And we shall never enter there
> Where the durable ones keep house.
> The stream that hustles us
> Neither nourishes nor heals. (Col., 77)

Plath continues her drama of systematic degeneration in
elemental terms distinct from both the later mindscapes of
Winter Trees poems and her earlier syntactical war of abstractions. "The Thin People" are presented as quiet and obsequi-
ous, yet a growing threat. Relegated to the distant past of
childhood or another generation of history, dismissed as harm-
less gray figures in a dull newsreel, these characters learned a
power to endure, not to prevail. These one-dimensional sufferers demonstrate a negative capability in their "thin silence":

> They
> Are unreal, we say:

It was only in a movie, it was only
In a war making evil headlines when we

Were small that they famished and
Grew so lean. . . .
. . . .
It was during the long hunger-battle

They found their talent to persevere
In thinness, to come, later,

Into our bad dreams, their menace
Not guns, not abuses,

But a thin silence.
Wrapped in flea-ridden donkey skins,

Empty of complaining, forever
Drinking vinegar from tin cups: they wore

The insufferable nimbus of the lot-drawn
Scapegoat. (*Col.*, 32–33)

The poem, an accumulation of thin couplets, dramatizes the obstinate force of these people in continuous run-on lines. Paradoxically, their physical force is negligible, but their "thin-lipped smiles" embed themselves in memory and imagination. Their power in passivity topples even the strongest defenses:

They persist in the sunlit room: the wallpaper

Frieze of cabbage-roses and cornflowers pales
Under their thin-lipped smiles,

Their withering kingship.
How they prop each other up! (*Col.*, 34)

The force of the poem is that the thinness is merely implied, never defined: it gathers force in cumulative appositional clauses. Supported by images of withering, shrinking, and splitting, and bolstered by those major metaphoric shifts in the poem—night to day; grayness to color; unreality to reality; movie screen to sunlit room—thinness grows animate. Like the musty frieze of cabbage-roses, the thin people's presence comes to dominate through nonreaction ("not even moving their bones"): their grayness invades the imagination.[23]

The Art of Reconstruction: "an old beast ended in this place"

Another provisional stance against a failed imaginative order is Plath's poetic exploration of certain works of graphic art.

In 1958, she wrote her mother about her new source of creativity:

> These are easily the best poems I've written and open up new material and a new voice. I've discovered my deepest source of inspiration, which is art: the art of primitives like Henri Rousseau, Gauguin, Paul Klee, and de Chirico. . . . I feel like an idiot who has been obediently digging up pieces of coal in an immense mine and has just realized that there is no need to do this, but that one can fly all day and night on great wings in clear blue air through brightly colored magic and weird worlds. (*LH*, 336–37)

Plath draws from the simple emotional world of the primitive painters, from Pieter Brueghel's "panorama of smoke and slaughter," and the sculptures of Leonard Baskin. She does so less to "fly . . . on great wings," that is, to borrow the ready-made shape and order of graphic art, than to look closely at the nature and the products of artistic creation for some clue to her own deficiencies.[24]

The unnatural vision that characterized the work of so many of the primitives found its roots in the Romantic cult of emotion. This cult not only glorified subjective experience, particularly aspects of privacy and noble savagery, but also suggested the sinister. One thinks of the empty van and the portentous shadow that await the girl with the hoop in de Chirico's *Mystery and Melancholy of a Street*, or the playful ominousness of Paul Klee's *Twittering Machine*. In both paintings the quality of foreboding grows out of the precise economic simplicity of the visual facts.[25] Thus, we find that the sinister earthly paradise of Rousseau, or the unspoiled Brittany peasant faith of Gauguin, or the gloom in Klee's children's drawings are present also in Plath's poetry about painting. Her bald-headed muses overpower a child's storybook fictions with their terrible bulk and silence ("Disquieting Muses"). The "tame cygnets," the "thumb-size" birds and the "hedging meadows of benign / Arcadian green" in "Watercolor of Grantchester Meadows" barely manage to disguise the water rats and the spines of the "blood-berried hawthorn." And the snake charmer's realm, however comical, is the dark creation of a snake-rooted mind, while the explorer-crab at Rock Harbor has a face etched like a "samurai death mask done / On a tiger tooth, less for / Art's sake than God's."

Although there appear to be simple equational similarities in any discussion of poetry and painting, John Berryman has offered a warning and a guideline for comparing the two disciplines. Berryman insists that the poem need not be viewed as the verbal equivalent of the painting that inspires it, nor as a strict interpretation of that picture. What aestheticians fail to do, according to Berryman, is to interpret "the event of the poem" itself, a task that often proves the painting to be merely extraneous material for—or a springboard to—a different poetic meaning.[26]

Always the tinkerer with an impulse to improve her "making," Plath explores the divergence of the private and public realms in art, the motivation of the artist, the role of the creator, and the limits of "reconstructive" creation in such poems as "Two Views of a Cadaver Room," "Colossus," and "The Burnt-out Spa."

Brueghel's painting *The Triumph of Death*[27] holds the extremes of life and death, illusion and desolation, in a tensive balance, precarious yet protected. A little romantic scene in the righthand corner of the painting pictures two lovers who show no concern for the "carrion army" that sweeps through all strata of life. Oblivious to the fact that they are overshadowed by death's head, they court each other to musical accompaniment in a little country "stalled in paint."

Triumph of Death departs from Brueghel's more famous ironic view of human suffering in *Landscape with the Fall of Icarus* where, according to the poetic interpretation of the painting by W. H. Auden, suffering is ironic, no doubt because it is unnoticed and unexpected:

> They never forgot
> That even the dreadful martyrdom must run its course
> Anyhow in a corner, . . . [28]

Instead, *Triumph* celebrates the human capacity for forgetfulness or illusion in the face of inevitable death. This theme, less than the irony, would be likely to attract the attention of Sylvia Plath.

Plath employs the structural and prosodic elements of "Two Views of a Cadaver Room" to cultivate a similar kind of wry oblivion, and at the same time to suggest that death and dismemberment are commensurate with a mature and comprehensive vision of life. The poem's two-part structure is itself an aesthetic "stalling," a formal representation of the Brueghel work where death oversees the romantic-artistic collusion in the corner. This structure suggests that neither clinical disinvolvement (the autopsy) nor romantic illusion (the impervious courtship) is an adequate response to the complexity of life. The first kindles no imaginative vision beyond that fact of half-strung cadavers or babies floating in formaldehyde; the second is an irresponsible illusion, a "foolish and delicate" posturing that is at best only a temporary stay against destruction:

> He, afloat in the sea of her blue satin
> Skirts, sings in the direction
> Of her bare shoulder, while she bends,
> Fingering a leaflet of music, over him,
> Both of them deaf to the fiddle in the hands
> Of the death's-head shadowing their song.
> These Flemish lovers flourish; not for long.
>
> Yet desolation, stalled in paint, spares the little
>   country
> Foolish, delicate, in the lower right-hand corner.
> (*Col.*, 6)

The aura of vinegary sterility and the rubble of the cadaver room in the poem's first half merely exaggerate the anesthesia of romance in the second. Meticulous prosodic crafting makes the contrast even more stark: the lilting, rising meter, the alternate liquid and sibilant sounds (*l* and *s*), and the run-on lines checked by the abrupt vernacular, "not for long." Blunt reification threatens in the first half: hearts like "cracked heirlooms," the vinegary fumes, unstrung bodies with caved-in heads and blackened skin. Amidst such decay, the poet's defense against a failed imaginative vision, is, within formal limits, a crevice, or protective hollow. Ironically, that "desolation stalled in paint," the Brueghel painting, provides only a feeble stay against death and mutability. It is the poem itself—the more comprehensive artwork—that becomes the small country with the unitive vision of the poles of existence: the metaphysical (the interrelationship of life and death, blue satin charms and the death's-head); the technical (the poem's two-part structure); and the aesthetic (the narrative description of the Brueghel painting).

"The Colossus" and "The Burnt-out Spa" narrate the process of renovating broken or decaying objects. Central to both poems is Plath's description of her changing relation to the theory of the imagination that she has idealized throughout *The Colossus*. If, as one critic has claimed, a "sense of the huge and continuing" dominates Plath's sensibility, then it must be observed that such monuments of hugeness as the stone statue and the old spa in these poems exist in a state of disintegration; they require active repair or reclamation.[29]

The metaphor of the title poem, "The Colossus," invites a variety of interpretations. Among these the most immediate, but perhaps least satisfactory, is the autobiographical. In the act of repairing the huge statue, Plath struggles to come to terms with her childhood. By forming the gestalt (the father "put together entirely") she gains release from the painful, piecemeal memory of her authoritarian father, Otto Plath, who died suddenly when she was nine. Another approach to the central metaphor sees the poet striving to reconcile her living sensibility with the sentiments and traditions of past generations—the situation in "All the Dead Dears" where museum-cased mummies serve to remind her of the interrelationship of life and death, fact and memory. A more general interpretation, borrowing from T. S. Eliot, reads the poem as a dialogue between the man who suffers and the mind that creates.

But perhaps the most forceful interpretation—and the one closest to Plath's artistic concerns in this volume—takes the statue-renovating metaphor as a dramatic description of the poet's relation to her present aesthetic as well as of the eventual failure of her integrative process. Unable to grasp the imaginative shape of the whole venture, she fails to reclaim the discrete parts:

> I shall never get you put together entirely,
> Pieced, glued, and properly jointed.
> Mule-bray, pig-grunt and bawdy cackles
> Proceed from your great lips.
> It's worse than a barnyard.
>
> Perhaps you consider yourself an oracle,
> Mouthpiece of the dead, or of some god or other.
> Thirty years now I have labored
> To dredge the silt from your throat.
> I am none the wiser. (*Col.*, 20)

Three aspects of the poem seem particularly significant: the poet's role, the futility of her labor, and the final, provisional stance she adopts toward her overly ambitious task. Literally, the poet's chore is an unending labor of reconstructing a formerly grand, even mythological image that has deteriorated to a crumbling mass of broken parts; like its historical predecessor, that bronze Colossus of Rhodes, it seems to be shattered irreparably. While the "huge and continuing" may once have dominated Plath's sensibility, here the poet's world is leveled to a series of small, separate gestures that attempt to put together a single, coherent identity. She is at once patcher, mender, renovator, dredger of silt, debunker of false grandeur, and recipient of a small and dubious reward: the labor is *reconstructive*. As in that patchwork task of composing her early poems—inching laboriously over words and phrases, juggling syllabics and rhyme schemes—the poet wields gluepots and pails of Lysol here, not her thesaurus.[30] Ironically, she meets her match in stubborn clay and silt that bulk and clog like those poetic forms and borrowed cadences of her early poetry.

The initial imbalance between the gigantic task, the dismembered colossus confronting the poet, and her own ability to clear and reassemble the pieces is enormous, even ludicrous. As the poet labors on, the integrative process grows at once more taxing and more futile. Decay is all-pervasive; facts are insistent; imaginative gestalt is missing; the once classical theories of art—"pithy and historical"—are now reduced to unintelligible animal grunts and cackles:

> Your fluted bones and acanthine hair are littered
> In their old anarchy to the horizon-line.
> It would take more than a lightning-stroke
> To create such a ruin. (*Col.*, 21)

According to one critic, there is a kind of "symbolic ossification" going on throughout *Ariel* and *The Colossus* that reduces the individual to a thing: "a calcification or some other type of physical or mental hardening—the deadening of sensitivity and loss of ability to feel tender or loving—a process which reverses the original softening of the hard stones and the implacable gods."[31] Hardness and ossification grip "The Colossus" in the form of fluted bones, weathered forums, pillars, stones, and shadows. In their presence, the poet-laborer finds the risk of total reconstruction unproductive, if not altogether hopeless, and, taking shelter in a part of the statue, decides on a more limited goal. This retreat to a simple, physical haven is a departure from Plath's original ideal vision:

> Nights, I squat in the cornucopia
> Of your left ear, out of the wind,
> Counting the red stars and those of plum-color.
> The sun rises under the pillar of your tongue.

My hours are married to shadow.
No longer do I listen for the scrape of a keel
On the blank stones of the landing. (*Col.*, 21)

Forced to take a more provisional stance, the poet no longer seeks a whole, integrated identity, whether in the reconstruction of her aesthetic (physical fact integrated with imaginative vision) or in her own sensibility. Gaining a wry sense of distance she squats in a crevice out of the wind. But will this leveled vision be more than a temporary shelter against a menacing world that threatens to thwart any reunion of fact and imagination?

Within this metaphor of an unreconstructed state of art, what is the plight of the poet's self? What is her future? Timorous ("an ant in mourning"), distracted by cosmic concerns (the sun, plum-colored stars), her future promise now "married to a shadow," mouthpiece for hollow literary echoes, despairing about release from her chore ("No longer do I listen . . ."), the poet is alarmingly silent. Weeds and white tumuli cloud her vision, settling silt clogs "oracular" pronouncements. As in the other poems in the volume, insinuating nature, culling all into obscurity if not oblivion, triumphs over the *Colossus* aesthetic. One might say of both *The Colossus* poems and of the poet's revered imaginative vision that "an old beast ended in this place."

In "The Burnt-out Spa" the poet labors—amidst charred "rafters and struts," the "rubbish of summers, the black-leaved falls"—for the smallest glimmer of understanding about the failure of her artistic theory. Instead of attempting a lofty aesthetic reconstruction, she gleans only an ironic awareness of nature's predatory reversal:

I pick and pry like a doctor or
Archaeologist among
Iron entrails, enamel bowls,
The coils and pipes that made him run.

The small dell eats what ate it once. (*Col.*, 77)

The blunt force of coil and pipe is overwhelmed by a subtle, almost imperceptible power of nature:

Now little weeds insinuate
Soft suede tongues between his bones.
His armorplate, his toppled stones
Are an esplanade for crickets. (*Col.*, 76)

If this broken piece of machinery is the landscape of the imagination, everything is in a state of decay, breakdown, or ossification. Liquid has hardened to "lumps / Of pale blue vitreous stuff, opaque / as resin drops"; everything is rubble, "iron entrails, enamel bowls." Yet in spite of its weedy overgrowth, rusty entrails, and "sag-backed bridge," the spa surprisingly produces a flowing "ichor" that runs "clear as it ever did / From the broken throat, the marshy lip."

It is in the face of this triumph against odds—the availability of a real voice in the midst of imaginative dross and dysfunction—that the poet realizes most clearly her own failures, her own betrayals in the *Colossus* poems. For in place of a convincing voice with a full range of tones and nuances, the poet finds only a "blue and improbable" self-image. Fixed and static, aesthetically framed ("a basketwork of cattails"), her visage muffles her voice in these flat, pictorial poems:

> Leaning over, I encounter one
> Blue and improbable person
>
> Framed in a basketwork of cattails.
> O she is gracious and austere,
> Seated beneath the toneless water!
> It is not I, it is not I. (*Col.*, 77)

At the end of the poem, reconciled to a bland neutrality, the poet knows that she is neither physically nor artistically one of the "durable ones." Through the practice of her poetic trade—the syllabics, slant rhymes, ghost rhythms, carefully crafted emblematic moments fixed on a mythical world—she has failed to achieve a sense of wholeness:

> No animal spoils on her green doorstep.
> And we shall never enter there
> Where the durable ones keep house.
> The stream that hustles us
>
> Neither nourishes nor heals. (*Col.*, 77)

The Poet as Creator: "the vase, reconstructed"

The end of *The Colossus* supposedly heralds a new departure in Plath's art, one identified as:

> the confrontation between . . . the lithic impulse—the desire, the need to reduce the demands of life to the unquestioning acceptance of a stone, "taciturn and separate . . . in a quarry of

silences"—and the impulse to live on, accommodating the rewards as well as the wrecks of existence so that "the vase, reconstructed, houses / The elusive rose."[32]

It is on this "vase, reconstructed," the various and provisional
images of the artist as creator, that Plath focuses her energies. As
she analyzes the methods and motives of the artistic process
("Yadwigha, on a Red Couch, Among Lilies; A Sestina for the
Douanier," "Blue Moles," and "Sculptor"), she gains a better
grasp of the commitments and limitations of creating. Through
the personae of her off-beat creators ("Snakecharmer" and
"Hermit at Outermost House"), she forges a myth of the
creator-god as individualist. A fine irony is suggested by the
hermit who sits on his doorsill and, against all odds, laughingly
creates. The power of this solitary figure is not of the usual
metaphysical sort. Both his visage and expertise mock the traditional dour gods—"Stone-Head" and "Claw-Foot"—gloomy,
winded, and petulant old despots. Lacking divine mandates, an
iron fist, or bombastic words, the hermit is strong in his apparent powerlessness. His skill lies in his curious manner of
creating. His bravado is far more understated than the biblical
fiat, "Let there be light," might suggest.

In contrast, this old chap "thumbs out" an idiosyncratic
creation. Impervious to a world of physical objects and to the
menace of a sea and sky clapping shut on him, the hermit has a
greater immunity to cosmic clashes than do the old gods. He
prevails by refashioning the old dodderers and the world to his
idea:

> Still he thumbed out something else:
> Thumbed no stony, horny pot,
>
> But a certain meaning green. (*Col.*, 57)

Both Stone-Head and Claw-Foot only "verged on green," we
are told; this hermit interprets and makes sense of it! His power
reminds one of those thin sufferers who also prevail, or of the
poet's disquieting muses who, during her childhood and
adolescence, gradually absorbed her with their nagging silence.
Resisting all sharp consonants with only fluid, stalling sounds (*u*
and *l*), the texture of the poem is as idiosyncratic as the hermit
himself. Staid syllabic tercets, seven syllables in each line, are
checked by elements of alliteration, assonance, and consonance. In most stanzas off-rhymes replace the traditionally

rhymed tercets. The prosodic texture, unlike the regular "brain count" dictates of syllabics, actually dramatizes the hermit's peculiar process of creation.

Just as the "gods began one world, and man another," so too the poet-creator invents—ever so gradually—an imaginative sphere in "Snakecharmer":

> He pipes. Pipes green. Pipes water.
>
> Pipes water green until green waters waver
> With reedy lengths and necks and undulatings.
> And as his notes twine green, the green river
>
> Shapes its images around his songs.
> He pipes a place to stand on, but no rocks,
> No floor: a wave of flickering grass tongues
>
> Supports his foot. He pipes a world of snakes,
> Of sways and coilings, from the snake-rooted bottom
> Of his mind. And now nothing but snakes
>
> Is visible. The snake-scales have become
> Leaf, become eyelid; snake-bodies, bough, breast
> Of tree and human. And he within this snakedom
>
> Rules the writhings which make manifest
> His snakehood and his might with pliant tunes
> From his thin pipe. (*Col.*, 54–55)

The poem is a cleverly ironic comment on inherited literary influences and ready-made forms as well as on the traditional mode of creation portrayed in Genesis. Here the creator projects a world that reflects an individual mental geography: undulating, wavering, flickering—images in-the-forming that take shape from "the snake-rooted bottom of his mind." Not ex nihilo, not from a literary hall of fame, not from antiquity, not even from dust does the snake charmer create. The mouth pipe is his tool; the moony eye his imaginative vision; swayings and coilings his product.

The craft of the poem provides a formal statement of the process of focusing, forming, and then dissolving the creation. Line enjambment couples with interlocking slant-rhymes to move from isolated elements—"pipes green"; "pipes water"— to whole sentences in stanzas five and six. Whimy in verse texture complements the poet's mocking subject matter: an atypical creator. In contrast to the mode of creation in Genesis, the snake charmer's power here is merely a thin reed pipe. His

rationale for dissolving water, grass, and snakes is not a master
plan for usage, but sheer boredom:

> And snakes there were, are, will be—till yawns
>
> Consume this piper and he tires of music
> And pipes the world back to the simple fabric
> Of snake-warp, snake-weft. Pipes the cloth of snakes
>
> To a melting of green waters, till no snake
> Shows its head, and those green waters back to
> Water, to green, to nothing like a snake.
> Puts up his pipe, and lids his moony eye. (*Col.*, 55)

According to one critic, the poem is based on a description
of Rousseau's *La Charmeuse de Serpents*. But unlike the painting,
the poem omits certain ingredients: "the pink and white tropical
bird to the left, the pale reddish flowers among the bushes, the
yellow-edged blades of the reeds and the blue exotic flowers
above the reeds to the right."[33] It seems that in omitting these
decorative features, Plath wanted to focus on the creator's act of
making and on the "simple fabric" of his ingredients in the
forming.

Shortly before the appearance of *The Colossus*, Plath published another poem based on a controversial Rousseau painting, "Yadwigha, on a Red Couch, Among Lilies."[34] The subject
is, quite simply, a red couch. When Rousseau's work showing a
naked woman on a red couch in the middle of a jungle was
exhibited at the Salon des Independents in 1910, the subject
matter was called "intolerable *naif*" by one critic. Controversy
followed the artist's response to the critics, for the explanation
that he gave in public was not the one he uttered in private.
Privately he said, simply, that he liked the color red.[35]

> But to a friend, in private, Rousseau confessed his eye
> So possessed by the glowing red of the couch which you,
> Yadwigha, pose on, that he put you on the couch
> To feed his eye with red: such red! under the moon,
> In the midst of all that green and those great lilies!

In this sestina, as in all of Plath's "meta-creative" poems,
the motives of the creator and the materials of creation are
explored and challenged. The poet knows that the artifact under
discussion, the conspicuous red couch, stands stubborn against
a world that barrages it with "monstrous lilies" and "fifty
variants of green." The couch remains separate both from the

public explanation of its origin and from the artist's motivation, a fact stubbornly resistant to the fictive vein. She also
recognizes that, apart from lofty theories, the simple physical
fact of the color motivated the artist.

Perhaps she is moved by Rousseau's unabashed, if private,
source of inspiration in the color red. In several of the *Colossus*
poems Plath indicates the primary force of physical matter, not
inspirational ideas, in the creative process as a way of "captur-
ing real, extant things, before any mythic significance is
exhumed."[36] As Charles Newman has observed: "Emily [Dick-
inson] is in many ways the beginning, and Sylvia the culmina-
tion of the movement whereby the imagination, sated with the
abstraction of myth, is driven back to the concrete."[37] Ted
Hughes, too, has claimed—and the *Johnny Panic* selections
confirm—that Plath's best early writing is often her simply
objective records of people and places in her notebooks, un-
tainted by the "artful shaping" of fantasy or the invention of plot
(*JP*, 7).

In the poem "Sculptor" (a reference to Leonard Baskin),
physical matter asserts itself over flimsy, vain images of light
and air. If we consider the analogy between poetry and
sculpture, we might view the poem as a kind of monument of
the moment, a surface presenting the volume of an entire life
experience: "Rodin said that a sculptor must never think of a
surface except as the extension of a volume. Everything pushes
up from under, against the taut surface of the world . . .
[poems] remain words but they become material we walk into
and lie down in."[38] Plath's craft—represented in the densely
wrought verses of *The Colossus*—is surely as demanding as the
sculptor's work with tensive, physical volume. Syllabics of the
first stanza, interlocked by slant-rhyme, are perfect until a last
extra syllable ("weighty" in the final line, for example) formally
indicates the "obdurate" dominance of sheer matter:

> To his house the bodiless
> Come to barter endlessly
> Vision, wisdom, for bodies
> Palpable, as his, and weighty. (*Col.*, 78)

"Sure stations in bronze, wood, stone" take sculpted shape, as
the sounds of the diction (*u*, *b*, and *d*) become increasingly
resistive:

Obdurate, in dense-grained wood,
A bald angel blocks and shapes
The flimsy light; arms folded
Watches his cumbrous world eclipse

Inane worlds of wind and cloud.
Bronze dead dominate the floor,
Resistive, ruddy-bodied,
Dwarfing us. (*Col.*, 78–79)

Throughout this poem, the verbal progression presents the gradual "eclipsing" of conceptual reality by matter. Movement is from endless "barter" between idea and volume to that which "blocks and shapes," from eclipsing to dominating and, finally, to the assertion of matter over concept.

The new departure hailed at the end of *The Colossus* is no mere verbal chant rehearsed in the face of romantic disillusionment, no tempering of metaphoric acrobatics with clever adjectival reminders of the physical world. Now, after *The Colossus*, the poet has not only a clear sense of the erosive, neutralizing threat from the physical world, but also a better understanding of her imaginative and creative powers and limitations in the face of sheer matter. She knows her labor is like the work of the "Blue Moles," conspired against by a wry, Hardian universe where everything is neutralized by "blind nature":

Outsize hands prepare a path
They go before: opening the veins,
Delving for the appendages
Of beetles, sweetbreads, shards—to be eaten
Over and over. And still the heaven
Of final surfeit is just as far
From the door as ever. (*Col.*, 50)

But knowledge of limitations gives way to a "wry complaisance." The poem "Companionable Ills" best illustrates this ironic acceptance that lives on to accommodate the rewards, as well as the wrecks, of existence:

The nose-end that twitches, the old imperfections—
Tolerable now as moles on the face
Put up with until chagrin gives place
To a wry complaisance—

Dug in first as God's spurs
To start the spirit out of the mud

It stabled in; long-used, became well-loved
Bedfellows of the spirit's debauch, fond masters.
(*Col.*, 63)

Brief, elliptical phrases communicate the gradual dominance of these "fond masters," the old imperfections. The poet must be obliging, accommodating.

In the final poem of the volume, "The Stones," Plath "arrives at her own center of gravity."[39] She places self at the center of the metaphor, which is here a surgical procedure to restore the speaker to wholeness. While the poem's craft recalls the early work, the self-deprecatory tone and dramatic metamorphosis of the speaker anticipate the best poems of *Crossing the Water*:

This is the city where men are mended.
I lie on a great anvil.
The flat blue sky-circle

Flew off like the hat of a doll
When I fell out of the light. I entered
The stomach of indifference, the wordless cupboard.
The mother of pestles diminished me.
I became a still pebble. (*Col.*, 82)

As the poet struggles with the integrative process, it is the self she is trying to construct now, not a poetic theory or an ideal imaginative emblem from a bit of seascape or a crag of land. The only geography is that of the self in this "city of spare parts."

After failing to adopt the impersonal imaginative perfection that she addresses with such insistence in *Colossus*, the poet must now retreat to a "wordless cupboard," to a preverbal "stomach of indifference." Here she becomes as inanimate as a still pebble. She is a part of that stubborn and unflinching objective world that menaced the artistic imagination. She is bereft of literary mentors, borrowed forms, hyperintellectualized imaginative realms.

The self is separated into a series of tiny, ossified parts—as "taciturn and separate" as hunted stones—that await the precision tools and chisel of the doctor. These will quarry, prod, agitate, and finally shape her into an image of vitality and individuality where impersonal reconstruction of the kind Plath described in *Colossus*—kids trading "hooks for hands" on Fridays or anonymously depositing eyes—is no longer useful:

The food tubes embrace me. Sponges kiss my lichens away.

The jewelmaster drives his chisel to pry
Open one stone eye.
. . . .
The grafters are cheerful,
Heating the pincers, hoisting the delicate hammers.
A current agitates the wires
Volt upon volt. Catgut stitches my fissures. (*Col.*, 83)

Perhaps the poet of *The Colossus* and the early poems is the doctor in "Stones," the "jewelmaster" perfectionist who now must use her craft to fashion a self-image that is—for her poetic purposes—a serviceable vessel, "the vase reconstructed." Now in disingenuous tones, and with a clear sense of personal metamorphic power to map out a mobile self-image, the "good as new" speaker says:

Love is the uniform of my bald nurse.
Love is the bone and sinew of my curse.
(*Col.*, 83–84)

Plath has tumbled from the verbal calisthenics of the early poems to the inhuman "wordless cupboard." Reluctantly, she abandons those multiple emblems of simultaneity she so admired in *The Colossus*. Her powers of the imagination, employed once to recreate that union of contradictory qualities in the realm of art, are now exhausted. Her models of the artist-creator and her grasp of the aesthetic process demanded a capacity for psychological integration that she could not manage throughout *The Colossus*.

What is evident in "The Stones" is the restlessness of a poet no longer content with impersonal reconstruction. The "elusive rose" is the poet's emblematic vision, that entire mode of perception that has teased, but finally escaped, her through this volume. Plath does not yet have the dramatic power to define and portray the self, nor has she found a balance between self-revelation and artistic form. Simply, she does not have the expressive means—the pure act, not pure art—to say what is happening to her. She betrays her discontent both in terms of the allegory in "Stones" ("my mendings itch") and by the tone of false bravado mingled with ambivalence that is captured in the trite end rhymes of the final two lines: "There is nothing to do. / I shall be good as new." The challenge of this voice—its tonal possibilities and new forms for expression—is one Sylvia Plath will take up in *Crossing the Water*.

III.

Crossing the Water: Transitional Poems
"one too many dimensions to enter"

Introduction

When *Crossing the Water: Transitional Poems*[1] appeared in 1971, a substantial number of critics and reviewers approached the poems only in relation to the tragic unity of *Ariel*. Aware of the frenzied spate of creativity during the last few months of Sylvia Plath's life, and of the posthumous popularity of the *Ariel* poems, critics saw the poems as "raw musings," way stations on the stylistic footpath that connected the *Colossus* and *Ariel* volumes. In the words of one reviewer:

> What struck me most after reading *Crossing the Water* was not just that it was so good, or that none of the poems there had been thought good enough for *Ariel*, but that *Ariel* itself represents such a unified stretch of work, such a strong and tragically magnificent working out of a single complicated theme.[2]

Ariel was a sirenlike cry from the heart, luring readers away from several other important voices of Sylvia Plath and underscoring the sad truth stated by Helen Vendler: We have not discovered a way of appreciating Plath's quieter and more muted verses—such as those of *Crossing the Water*—that combine both formal toughness with later aspects of self-intensification.[3]

Two factors may have encouraged the retrospective—and reductive—view of *Crossing the Water*:[4] the disparate selection of poems included in this volume, and collector Ted Hughes's comments on the state of Plath's art. Despite the subtitle, the poems do not form a definitive chronologically ordered collection. Although most of the poems were written during the three years between 1959 and 1962, the volume ranges from "Two Sisters of Persephone" and "Black Rook in Rainy Weather" (1957) to "Mirror" (1963). Included are clusters of poems published in journals and magazines in 1961 and 1962: poems from small limited editions, such as *Crystal Gazer*, and

Uncollected Poems, and ten other poems, omitted from the American *Colossus*, that were included in the British publication.[5]

To further complicate interpretation of this range of poems, Ted Hughes has suggested a puzzling chronology that emphasizes "a single center of power and light."[6] He insists that Plath's works are really one long poem that records her progress toward a mythically foreclosed universe, rather like a Greek tragedy locked into its own imagistic and ideological system: "The poems are chapters in a mythology where the plot, seen as a whole and in retrospect, is strong and clear—even if the origins of it and the dramatis personae are at bottom enigmatic . . . the whole scene lies under the transfiguring eye of the great white timeless light" (*N*, 81). By attempting to shape individual works into a simple mythical statement, Hughes lends support, perhaps unwittingly, to the interpretation of the poems as "mutants": "What she was after was the new poetic world she had glimpsed in the poem titled, 'Stones,' printed at the end of *The Colossus*, and of course when she got back there, early in 1962, with poems like 'Elm' and 'The Moon and the Yew Tree,' everything before that became unimportant."[7]

His portrait of Plath as a yet undeveloped figure, a "muse full of contradictions" who makes several different sorts of interim appearances (*R*, 172), has invited widely divergent criticism of the volume. Praise is either for Plath's crisp metaphoric observation or for her boisterous theatrics. Language is "half formal, half-vernacular . . . capable of bearing the full weight of the grand style while staying true to the sharpest observation."[8] The precise control, depth, and strength of perception in the vocabulary itself leads the way to true discovery of style in this volume full of "perfectly realized works." Other critics cite Plath's strong narrative candor and her budding flare for theatricality: "a setting up of scenery, a pulling in or a mouthing of set-piece monologues."[9] The fact that each critical approach—emphasis on craft or on self-display—ignores the other reminds us that the truly original achievement of these poems and the complexity of the poet have gone unremarked.

Immediately evident is Plath's technical, thematic, and imaginative coming of age in the *Crossing the Water* poems. She has learned a new vernacular, introduced in "Stones" and now manifest in slant-rhyme couplets, variations on the staid tercet and quatrain, idiosyncratic rhythms, and cleverly cumulative image patterns. The point is not that Plath's technical artistry is apparent for the first time in *Crossing the Water*. Youthful Plath was surely a prosodic acrobat on her tightwire of form. But the persistent use of leaden philosophical themes, the insistent overkill in graphing imaginative states, and her clever pirouettes with traditional form are now modulated by—and less powerful than—the developing irony of the speaking voice ("Maenad," "Mirror," "Zookeeper's Wife"). This voice has a whole repertoire of passions, among them a powerful nostalgia that erodes the boundaries between self and nonself and becomes a form of consciousness. Losses are poignant, savored; memories recede, "untouchable as tomorrow."

> I come to wheel ruts and water
> Limpid as the solitudes
> That flee through my fingers. (*CW*, 2)

In "Candles" a mother indulges "false, Edwardian sentiments" as she muses over her infant's crib:

> In twenty years I shall be retrograde
> As these drafty ephemerids.

> I watch their spilt tears cloud and dull to pearls.
> How shall I tell anything at all
> To this infant still in a birth-drowse? (*CW*, 25)

The speaker in "Private Ground" feels the grasses "unload their griefs on my shoes": "The woods creak and ache, and the day forgets itself. . . . Morgue of old logs and old images" (*CW*, 21).

In *Crossing the Water* Plath begins to examine the legacy of women's myths in such poems as "Witchburning," "Two Sisters of Persephone," "Stillborn," and "Magi." She is particularly interested in personalizing the myth that links voluntary and involuntary creation. By testing out her metamorphic talents against some cultural mandates of women's heritage, the poet exercises a new tonal authority. Usually her authority is paradoxical, forceful in self-deprecating irony, powerful in passivity ("I Am Vertical"), or prankishly humorous in the celebration of inverted romantic love myths ("Love Letter").

Most startling, however, is the fact that a protean self-image coexists with the poet's continuous critique of her art in *Crossing the Water*. By no longer simply describing but enacting the growing mobility of her own consciousness at the same time that she evaluates the development of her poetry, Sylvia Plath emphatically contradicts those charges that hers is a formulaic confessional art. She avoids stifling self-exploration and myopic personal derangement by searching each poetic context for a frank, literary version of the emotional growth that she is experiencing.

In *The Colossus*, artistic form was fixed and repetitive, the language still formal and slightly archaic, the imaginative vision static and distanced in natural elements, myth, and antiquity. The process of visualizing such a perfect, emblematic world required little human participation. Where previously Plath had learned an element of control in the external world of detached description, she now "puts the outer world inside her mind, inside her poetry."[10] "Give me back my shape," she demands of the desiccating formalism of her earlier work; or she asks, "Lady, what am I doing / with a lung full of dust and a tongue of wood, / knee-deep in the cold and swamped by flowers?" Now "competing sensibilities" and "competitive pains" in form and feeling characterize the *Crossing the Water* poems: "the particularity and the generalization run together in equal balance, asking questions of each other, eroding each other, unifying in true imaginative modification."[11] Suddenly Plath has little need of resolution, closure, or conformism to identify and explore all dramatic possibilities for the self. To borrow the words of Adrienne Rich, Plath wants to not just revise the content, but also remake the very forms of knowing in these transitional poems.[12]

Invigorated by a new imaginative power, Plath shows an equally strong tendency to diminish self to the domesticated and the palpable and then to reveal the self boisterously in the guise of various personae. What she values is the act of dramatic metamorphosis, devised by her own poetic imagination, not borrowed from her literary or cultural mentors. She frequently dramatizes a carefully cultivated passivity, assuming the illusionless existence of a shell, a mere husk that is groping for definition:

> Should I stir, I think this pink and purple plastic
> Guts bag would clack like a child's rattle,
> Old grievances jostling each other, so many loose teeth.
> (*CW*, 38)

"Mother, keep out of my barnyard, / I am becoming another," she warns. Elsewhere she pleads, "Lady, tell me my name," or announces, "Empty, I echo to the least footfall." At the same time that she is "tiny and inert as a rice grain," cowering among minerals and roots, the poet imagines becoming "Mother of a white Nike and several bald-eyed Apollos." She floats through the air, godlike in her "soul shift," or soars heavenward in triumph:

> My ankles brighten. Brightness ascends my thighs.
> I am lost, I am lost, in the robes of all this light. (CW, 53)

In her act of discovering a self-image by exposing the investigative process, Plath records her playful belittling only to exaggerate within the poetic texture her newfound dramatic impulse. Boasting of this discovery, Plath expresses its power with lively, if disingenuous, wit:

> And I slept on like a bent finger.
> . . . .
> I shone, mica-scaled, and unfolded
> To pour myself out like a fluid. . . .
>
> . . . .
> My finger-length grew lucent as glass.
> I started to bud like a March twig:
> An arm and a leg, an arm, a leg.
> From stone to cloud, so I ascended.
> Now I resemble a sort of god
> Floating through the air in my soul-shift. . . . (CW, 27–28)

Plath's point is that any single image of the self must be considered within the process of the poem, for the speaker's manner of becoming is the key to Plath's transitional poetry. It is the developmental nature of the *Crossing the Water* poems— candid evaluations in process—that suggests that they are an investigative resource for the poet's identification of her newfound emotional possibilities. The words of critic Don Geiger apply to Plath's exploring, speaking self: "The poem's language context as it evolves comprises a changing of meanings containing various but not limitless potentialities for further ordering."[13] And Plath glories in her newfound possibilities for "further ordering."

One distinct critical problem accompanies the new freedom in *Crossing the Water*: can the poet reconcile her state of coy passivity with wild self-display? Can she convince us that the witch and maenad are one and the same person as the twig or owl pellet? Any attempt to connect these images raises the question of how comprehensive the poet's awareness of herself in the context of the poem's meaning actually is. Can she consciously preserve the memory of one state when in the throes of another? Helen Vendler thinks not. She is disturbed by her sense that Plath opts for "partial and despairing truths," each of a shorter memory than her whole expansive consciousness: "The person who wrote the one set of poems scarcely knows the person who wrote the other set. Does the corpse know the witch? Does the patient know the revenant? Does the victim know the murderer? Does the pellet know the maenad?"[14]

Surely it is a betrayal of the poem's imaginative range and the poet's extraordinary technical skills to assume that Plath's sense of self as not one, but two or more selves is a preface to madness, falseness, schizophrenia, or eventual death—the old saws of most early confessional poetry analysis. We must not mistake Plath. Hers is not a pejorative ambivalence in presenting the self. Nor was it in the Cambridge Manuscript poems where knowing that "the choice is always to be made" was more important than a glib partisanship on behalf of either the intellect or the imagination. As it has developed, Plath's poetry is not concerned with determining false or true selves (either psychologically or sociologically), or with erasing that double bind of the woman-poet by coordinating her warring alternatives. Nor does Plath cower in a host of reconstructed artifacts to protect herself from her own reality as Ted Hughes suggests (R, 169). As she tries on several provisional, and often contradictory, selves, Plath flaunts the protean nature of her consciousness, the jaunty colloquial voice:

> Not easy to state the change you made.
> If I'm alive now, then I was dead,
> Though, like a stone, unbothered by it,
> Staying put according to habit. (CW, 27)

"Touch it: it won't shrink like an eyeball," she jeers about the perfectly ordered, rational image of a life:

> Nobody in there looks up or bothers to answer.
> The inhabitants are light as cork,
> Everyone of them permanently busy.
>
> At their feet, the sea waves bow in single file.
> Never trespassing in bad temper:
> Stalling in midair,
> Short-reined, pawing like paradeground horses.

Overhead, the clouds sit tasseled and fancy

As Victorian cushions. (CW, 54)

Yet in this same poem she offers a view of existence that is no
"egg-shaped bailiwick," but a mental geography, starkly frank
and illusionless:

A woman is dragging her shadow in a circle
About a bald hospital saucer.
It resembles the moon, or a sheet of blank paper
And appears to have suffered a sort of private blitzkrieg.
. . . .
She has one too many dimensions to enter. (CW, 54–55)

Perhaps the best transition from *The Colossus* to *Crossing the
Water* is "Disquieting Muses," a poem in which Plath
reexamines women's myth heritage—specifically the legacy of
mother to daughter—as she displays new emotional energy for
the speaker. The poem anticipates in technique and theme
many poems characteristic of *Crossing the Water*: self-
disparaging irony; female—even familial—subject matter; the
hint of a child's fantasy narrative;[15] the self-conscious anatomy
of the poet's vocation; the unresolved ending. Since a de
Chirico painting is the catalyst for the speaker's description of
her relationship to the aesthetic process, "Disquieting Muses"
also maintains a link with its companion poems in *The Colossus*.

In her unpublished discussion of Plath's complex attitudes
toward—perhaps even reluctance to accept—the cultural inheritance of the modern woman, Helen Vendler has described
the new tonal achievement of "Disquieting Muses":

What is most personal . . . is her staking out new territory for the
female voice, which has been known in learned literature chiefly
for saying things like "If ever two were one, then surely we," or
"How do I love thee? Let me count the ways." It is no small step
that a woman poet can now say, "If I've killed one man, I've killed
two," or "Meanwhile there's a stink of fat and baby crap," or
"Bastard, masturbating a glitter." . . . What matters is that . . .
they suggest new ways in which certain emotions in life, eternally
present but formerly only furtively suggested in poetry, can be
brought defiantly to light.[16]

Plath spent many years trying to shape the "early alien distinct-
ness" she felt as a child into the "vocation of poetry," Vendler
tells us. In its mastery of the self-deprecatory tone, "Disquieting
Muses" dramatizes a young girl's reluctant admission of her

separateness from other women, yet her recognition of the curious necessity of the female tradition in her development.

The poem recounts the passage of a young girl through the difficult stages of becoming a conscious woman. Catalyzed by her mother's fairy-tale world, she must accept both the disillusionments of her individual life and the burdens of her mission as female artist: "And this is the kingdom you bore me to, / Mother, Mother." The force of the poem derives from the fact that Plath assumes the persona of a credulous young girl bewildered at the presence of unforeseen elements in her life:

> Mother, mother, what illbred aunt
> Or what disfigured and unsightly
> Cousin did you so unwisely keep
> Unasked to my christening, that she
> Sent these ladies in her stead
> With heads like darning-eggs to nod
> And nod and nod at foot and head
> And at the left side of my crib? (*Col.*, 58)

Stanza by stanza, the willfully ignorant speaker rehearses events from her childhood and adolescence. She finds an increasing gap between her mother's comfortable world—a world whose "witches always got baked into gingerbread"—and the grisly consciousness taught by her silently nodding mentors: "I learned, I learned, I learned elsewhere, / From muses unhired by you, dear mother." Only very gradually does the speaker realize that her peculiar talents cannot be developed by practicing arabesques and trills on the piano, or by "singing the glow-worm song" in a twinkle dress:

> I woke one day to see you, mother,
> Floating above me in bluest air
> On a green balloon bright with a million
> Flowers and bluebirds that never were
> Never, never, found anywhere.
> But the little planet bobbed away
> Like a soap-bubble as you called: Come here!
> And I faced my traveling companions. (*Col.*, 59–60)

In a tone of confident unawareness, the naïf indicts the informed: daughter chides mother for being an unacceptable model of womanhood. Interestingly, the daughter's real muses are never defined within the poem, but remain unfleshed and unnamed. Yet they are the chief characters. The effect of their repetitious silence starkly contrasts with the mother's fantasy world of avoidance. During the narration of the speaker's personal history they take on an increasingly macabre and active role. At first they merely nod, "mouthless, eyeless, with stitched bald head." Then, as the mother feebly chants songs to Thor, these "dismal-headed godmothers" smash the windowpanes during a storm. Soon their shadows lengthen, stretch, and envelop the speaker as they assume their permanent vigils, united with her in a world of art, here a timeless realm of stone:

> Day now, night now, at head, side, feet,
> They stand their vigil in gowns of stone,
> Faces blank as the day I was born,
> Their shadows long in the setting sun
> That never brightens or goes down. (*Col.*, 60)

These sinister figures—modeled on de Chirico's "Les Muses Inquietantes"—are touchstones against which we measure the degree of transformation in the speaker. They change in the daughter's perception from vengeful wedding furies (slighted according to fairy-tale protocol), to unwitting mentors, insistent guides, and finally, reluctantly, to traveling companions.

Plath's mode of irony here is singular in its emotional punch and its economy of means. The simple feigned innocence of the speaker, couched in a fairy-tale framework and bolstered by the troubled questions of the young girl, encourages the possibility of greater dramatic metamorphosis. The burden of growth is placed on the speaker, not on the muses' or the mother's tutelage. By understating herself with a convincing naiveté in the beginning, the speaker permits us to witness the whole range of emotions that accompany developing consciousness within the investigative process of the poem. Such "willful unawareness" only emphasizes the gulf between the worlds of mother and daughter, marking the daughter's painful but requisite separateness.

The final two lines are tonally perfect, the poem's consummate achievement. They offer another tribute to Plath's sophisticated emotional range as well as to her ability to risk nonresolution in the *Crossing the Water* poems. At a point where it might be convenient to offer a pat, rhetorical statement on behalf of the grisly muses, the young woman remains detached, understated, perhaps wary. Instead of flaunting her newfound relationship, the speaker manages a deft and mature ambivalence that communicates precisely the difficulty: her reluctance toward, yet the necessity of, allegiance to those unsavory muses:

> And this is the kingdom you bore me to,
> Mother, mother. But no frown of mine
> Will betray the company I keep. (*Col.*, 60)

A Rook's Task of Poetic Construction: patching together "a content of sorts"

Not only in "Disquieting Muses," but throughout *Crossing the Water*, Plath offers a commentary on her changing art of poetry. She does this within the context of the poems and by means of reviewing certain stereotypical female truths. In particular, she expands her definition of poetic construction, those attempts to "patch together a content of sorts" in the transitional work. Plath seems to insist that the processes are interdependent, that understanding the woman artist within the female tradition is interwoven with her development as a highly conscious and deliberate craftsman. Several poems provide a nexus for understanding the shape of the entire volume of transitional work. "Stillborn" and "Ouija," for example, reexamine female subject matter to describe, respectively, the shortcomings of her existing oeuvre and her requirements for a satisfactory, if not ideal, poetic.

Another poem, "Black Rook in Rainy Weather," asks certain preliminary questions about the nature of poetry that apply to other poems: what is the relationship between the poet's task in creating and the inspirational poetic moment? Or where does the convergence occur between charged, alert self-observation and the dispassionate arranging of themes? The central image in this poem, a wet black rook arranging its feathers, represents for the poet a symbol of cautious expectation from life and from art:

> On the stiff twig up there
> Hunches a wet black rook
> Arranging and rearranging its feathers in the rain. (*CW*, 41)

Embarrassed by lofty passions, the poet, like the rook, avoids "largesse, honor, / One might say love":

> I do not expect a miracle
> Or an accident
>
> To set the sight on fire
> In my eye, nor seek

> Any more in the desultory weather some design,
> But let spotted leaves fall as they fall,
> Without ceremony, or portent.
>
> Although, I admit, I desire,
> Occasionally, some backtalk
> From the mute sky, I can't honestly complain. . . .
> (CW, 41)

The tone urges the scaling down of visionary hopes to the ordinary tedium of waiting, a theme characteristic of Plath's earliest poems but now one that also provides a critique of her developing creative process:

> At any rate, I now walk
> Wary (for it could happen
> Even in this dull, ruinous landscape); sceptical,
> Yet politic; ignorant
>
> Of whatever angel may choose to flare
> Suddenly at my elbow. (CW, 41–42)

Like "Black Rook," a number of poems in Crossing the Water distinctly counsel avoidance of the grand and bombastic in life. They do so through qualifying language (here a nexus of adverbs), not by rhetorical polarities. These poems characterize an approach that at once looks backward to the neutrality of limited visions in her Smith and Cambridge poems, yet anticipates the very earthy philosophy of Plath's remarkable late poems to her children in Ariel and Winter Trees.

The theme of illusionless existence is apparent particularly in her approach to nature, and markedly contrasts with the process of dramatic change in the self she records. Quiet meditative poems about rock dumps, a pewter sea, "drafty half lights," bald hills, and ephemeral distances are familiar territory in this volume. The two people of the title poem live in a graphic, shadowy world of the imagination that lacks substance: "black lake, black boat, two black cut-paper people." In addition to representing simple neutrality, this world is at times a radical inversion where even the reflection in a mirror has flattened out and "stars open among lilies." Only a "little light is filtering from the water flowers." Silence is the only utterance, black the color, flatness the single dimension. In "Crossing the Water," the senses, once reliable, are purposefully confused and jumbled: "Are you not blinded by such expressionless sirens?"

Such poems of landscape in Crossing the Water are less pure

description, as in *Colossus* the clinging to the "contours of things for their own sake—" than a kind of restless symbolism that proposes one allegory after another as vehicle to the poet's sensibility (Z, 16). The diminished quality of life they suggest has been absorbed by the speaker in a way never accomplished in the previous poems. In "Wuthering Heights," for example, the poet gently toys with becoming part of a world of heather roots, ruts, puddles, and sheep as "grey as the weather." Nature invites the poet, "the one upright / Among all horizontals," to "whiten her bones" in the oblivion of its quiet force. It has the upper hand in the war of effacement with fragile humankind. Even the barest traces of human life become faint memories, mere reminiscences to be "leaned on" or "funnelled away." They are jeopardized by the threat of annihilation from the simple, enduring elements of wind, sky, grass, and stone. But it is not the threat of effacement that is central here (as in *Colossus*), but simple nostalgia for the human voice:

> Of people the air only
> Remembers a few odd syllables.
> It rehearses them moaningly:
> Black stone, black stone. (CW, 2)

As the poet continually minimizes, contracts, and domesticates a world of nature in her transitional poems, she wants a familiar animation, an imagistic precision, a clear-cut significance that finds the night sky like a "piece of carbon paper," or gulls as tangible as the "hands of invalids." While she praises a simplified state of existence, she shows a singular kind of empathy in describing places. Nature—fleeting, ephemeral, eroding—no longer threatens human beings, but incorporates their desires, promises, and visions. Nature is one with wistful images of human death, infirmity, and disintegration: rocks have "bald eyes," petals "unlatch," drained ponds are discovered "collapsing like lungs," grasses "unload griefs" on shoes, and the land's end is described as "knuckled and rheumatic / Fingers cramped on nothing." Mists "go up without hope like sighs." As the poet says, "I walk among them and they stuff my mouth with cotton. / When they free me, I am beaded with tears." Cliffs, too, are "edged with trefoils, stars and bells / Such as fingers might embroider close to death" ("Finisterre," CW, 3).

One explanation for the particular mode of empathy derives from Plath's ambivalence about the simple life that she seems to admire. In "Wuthering Heights," the constructive urge of a life of the mind is in tension with the pained sensibility that seeks refuge in a numbed existence. Such description might well serve as an appropriate summary of the entire transitional volume. Although Plath admires a life of simplicity—the wind pouring by "like destiny, bending / Everything in one direction," the smug indifference of sheep who accept their "grey neutrality," the homely existence of stone—she cannot force herself to accept limits of the same destiny. Her fate is to admire, not adopt, a life of purposeful directness. Her imaginative life will not be quelled.

Despite the lure of dumb simplicity, an important irony undercuts "Wuthering Heights." The poet knows that there is, indeed, a life beyond the muteness of sheep, an existence higher than the grasstops, and a destiny unbent by the wind's coercion. Her only defense against the dumb but cajoling world of nature that threatens her with oblivion is retaliation through language, the imagination, and the process of dramatic change. The poem "Mirror" introduces such a process of change by showing a life without illusion in two images of replication, a lake and a mirror:

> I am silver and exact. I have no preconceptions.
> Whatever I see I swallow immediately
> Just as it is, unmisted by love or dislike.
> I am not cruel, only truthful. . . . (CW, 34)

The ideal world here is one of unaltered replication, unemotional accuracy, and bland coloring. But in this ideal state the poet cannot sustain for long the perfect fusion of self and outer world. The mirror's simple reproduction of the adjacent wall ("pink, with speckles") is soon disturbed. "It flickers," the poet tells us: "Faces and darkness separate us over and over."

The point—one crucial to the speaker's awareness throughout these poems—is that the complication of human emotion gets in the way of one's attempts to be "silver and exact." Precision without illusions or preconceptions is impossible for the poet. Perhaps the only lasting image is the inevitable process of changing. In the second half of the poem, a woman searches that "faithful reflection" of herself in a lake for "what she really is." But she finds there a different visage each day:

> Now I am a lake. A woman bends over me,

Searching my reaches for what she really is.
Then she turns to those liars, the candles or the moon.
I see her back, and reflect it faithfully.
She rewards me with tears and an agitation of hands.
I am important to her. She comes and goes.
Each morning it is her face that replaces the darkness.
In me she has drowned a young girl, and in me an old woman
Rises toward her day after day, like a terrible fish.
(CW, 34)

If the theme counseled by "Black Rook" and echoed throughout other transitional poems is a cautious expectation from life, such advice also applies to the formal aspects of Plath's poetry. With her craft, the poet is involved in the same insignificant action as the rook in the tree branch sorting his feathers. The burden of making poems, Plath suggests, is a task as solitary and repetitive as the rook's: it requires a disciplined action of ordering—and more importantly, reordering—mere words and images, the tools of her trade. Yet the moment of creative inspiration itself, one of those "spasmodic tricks of radiance," is not catalyzed by any effort or skill of the poet. Gratuitously bestowed, it becomes "whatever angel may choose to flare / Suddenly at my elbow."

"Black Rook" dramatizes a tension between the brevity of the poetic moment and the tedium of waiting for its appearance, that "rare, random descent." All that is mute, dull, obtuse, inconsequent, and even carefully hypothetical ("one *might* say love"), provides a foil for those rare, assertive moments of fire which seize the senses with pure passion and haul the eyelids upward. Halting rhythm, as well as the cautiously distanced language, suggests the poet's psychic and emotional reticence. She waits for the incongruous happening, that "unicorn thing," a state of mind signaled in her arrangement of words and metaphors. Suddenly it seizes those humble everyday realities, even the most obtuse objects, such as kitchen chairs, tables, and falling leaves. But the event does not outlive the moment when it captures and consumes. The poetic moment is merely a "brief respite from fear / Of total neutrality."

"Black Rook" makes a peculiarly succinct textural statement of waiting and cautionary suspense by its patterns of end-rhyme, stanzaic structure, and well-tempered diction. Language alternates between the tempering and qualifying on the one hand (adverbs and adverbial phrases, such as "otherwise," "now and then," "at any rate," "even," "although," and "anymore"), and the mystical flaring on the other (things "leap incandescent" or are consumed in a "celestial burning"). The tempered language dulls like the dim light and "desultory weather" described in the poem. It portrays the infinitely weary-ing sense of waiting:

> Although, I admit, I desire,
> Occasionally, some backtalk
> From the mute sky, I can't honestly complain. . . . (CW, 41)

The five-line stanzas are repeated eight times, creating the sense of a suspended, limited hope, certainly no miraculous progress. Yet the unique rhyme scheme (a b c d e), also repeated in each stanza, creates the tension—here an illusion—of restless movement and the feeling of being drawn forward in inspira-tional progress. Stanzaic design begins with a few syllables, expands in the third or middle line, and then contracts in the fifth line with a series of brief ideas, each resounding with a certain formality and psychological distance (stanza two: "with-out ceremony or portent"; stanza four: "otherwise incon-sequent"; or stanza five: "sceptical, yet politic").

Within the poem, the poet's sensibility equivocates be-tween a state of readiness and a limited hope of lasting signifi-cance; between the tedium of the "long wait" and the energy of total seizure; between the aggressively sexual "sinking a shaft down into oneself" for words and ideas, and passive waiting:

> With luck,
> Trekking stubborn through this season
> Of fatigue, I shall
> Patch together a content
>
> Of sorts. Miracles occur. . . . (CW, 42)

The formal equivocation expressed in "Black Rook" suggests the dramatic dynamics of the poet's protean self-image in the *Crossing the Water* volume. The willfully small and inert self-images show a paradoxical power for unexpected growth. And, in poem after poem, Plath becomes dutiful cataloger of such growth.

"Black Rook in Rainy Weather" also suggests characteris-tics of rhyme and rhythm that are more generally developed throughout these transitional poems. "Retreat from harm and sing to it," is the poet's guideline in this volume, according to Ted Hughes (R, 171). Rhythmically, Plath is at her startling best, weaving—singing—subtle sound patterns in abrupt neologisms and hortatory phrases ("Beast," "Dark House," or "Zookeeper's Wife"). At the same time she boldly explores new areas of consciousness, new losses, nostalgias, reminiscences, and desires, with a surprising lyric fluidity:

> While the heath grass glitters and the spindling rivulets
> Unspool and spend themselves. My mind runs with them,
>
> Pooling in heel-prints, fumbling pebble and stem.
> (CW, 8)

Accentual or syllabic "finger counting" is abandoned in *Crossing the Water* for a new rhythmic mode extending the poet's psychic energies through colloquial expression. "Now she's done for, the dewlapped lady . . . old sock-face sagged on a darning egg." Or of the "Magi" she jeers: "They're / The real thing, all right: the Good, the True." Plath, we're told, placed a high value on rhythm: "The poets I delight in are possessed by their poems as by the rhythms of their own breathing. Their finest poems seem born all-of-a-piece, not put together by hand," she said.[17] One critic summed up Plath's own developing organic style in the following way:

> The flow of sound in these lines from "Parliament Hill Fields"—so precise yet so powerful; the slant rhyme couplets in "I Am Vertical"; her many capable variations on the tercet and quatrain; the interlocking stanzaic rhyme of "Black Rook in Rainy Weather"; the purposeful modulation of metrics in "Wuthering Heights"; all attest to the maturation of her technical artistry.[18]

A newfound technical skill in knitting and girding image patterns recalls the rook's arranging and rearranging his feathers in *Crossing the Water*. "Code images," some quite hermetic, are repeated in clusters of interlinked thought throughout this volume. Plath's permeable vocabulary shows a developing sense of order as it imitates the dramatic changes of her protean self-image:

> She uses what the child psychologist Piaget has called transductive thought, a syncretic approach in which qualities are associated, not substances or concepts. . . . This leads to underlying associations and derived meanings which can be extremely cryptic if one is not aware of their derivation. . . . Thus the obscurity of some poems never springs from the fact that we do not know what personal experiences were their immediate cause (even when it is plain that there were such experiences) but from our inability to

grasp the central structure according to which the clusters of
images are arranged. [19]

Whiteness, for example, weaves together a dramatic force
from an entire continuum of associations in *Crossing the Water*:
blank abstraction, immobility, precision, sterility, even death
and decay. The "Magi" are white abstracts that "hover like dull
angels," distinct from the everyday concerns of laundry or milk.
A soul ("Surgeon at 2 A.M.") recedes "like a ship's light" in a
weakening whiteness, while the poet herself is "Mother of a
white Nike and several bald-eyed Apollos." The white opacity
of a "bald hospital saucer" is like "the moon, or a sheet of blank
paper," while a hill is "faceless and pale as china."

Whiteness is often most frightening when it is associated
with a simple neutrality or sterility. A woman's life is portrayed
as a landscape where "light falls without letup, blindingly."
Flowers and faces "whiten to a sheet" ("Last Words") or sea
mists suffocate, stuffing a mouth with cotton ("Finisterre").
"Tight white mummy cloths" cover a clinical anonymity in
"Face Lift." A "bone-white light like death" behind all things
gains a threatening neutrality in "Insomniac." In this poem
whiteness at first appears only as light through "peepholes,"
then as a "heat-lightning flicker" linked to sleeplessness, the
granite stiffness of mortuary stone, the "white disease" of day,
and finally people's "mica-silver," "blank" eyes.

> Nightlong, in the granite yard, invisible cats
> Have been howling like women, or damaged instruments.
> Already he can feel daylight, his white disease. . . .
> . . . .
> And everywhere people, eyes mica-silver and blank, . . .
> (*CW*, 11)

By contrasting color patterns (red and white) that breed and
tangle transductively within the poem, Plath dramatizes the
difficult night tasks of a doctor who has to sever a patient's limb
in "Surgeon at 2 A.M." In the first image, a white light that is
"artificial, and hygienic as heaven" is aseptic but deadly:

> The microbes cannot survive it.
> They are departing in their transparent garments,
>   turned aside
> From the scalpels and the rubber hands. (*CW*, 30)

Next, "the scalded sheet is a snowfield, frozen and peace-
ful" emphasizes the obscuring quality of whiteness. In the third

image, the patient is faceless, anonymous, "a lump of Chinese white / With seven holes thumbed in." At last the spiritual aspect of whiteness becomes imperceptible to the surgeon, for "tonight [the soul] has receded like a ship's light."

The white image pattern, with its interdependencies of meaning, contrasts with the surgeon's description of the body: an overgrown garden, filled with stenches and oozings, a place where he must "worm and hack in a purple wilderness":

> It is a garden I have to do with—tubers and fruits
> Oozing their jammy substances,
> A mat of roots. My assistants hook them back.
> Stenches and colors assail me.
> This is the lung-tree.
> These orchids are splendid. They spot and coil like
>   snakes.
> The heart is a red bell-bloom, in distress. (*CW*, 30)

Paradoxically, red gradually takes on the clinical neutrality of whiteness ("blood is a sunset," or the "clean pink plastic limb"), absorbing its threatening, flat repose. Such dramatic commingling of images captures perfectly the surgeon's impersonal, yet malignantly violent, actions against all that is vital and natural. He, too, is reduced to the neutrality of limited vision:

> I walk among sleepers in gauze sarcophagi.
> The red night lights are flat moons. They are dull
>   with blood.
> I am the sun, in my white coat,
> Grey faces, shuttered by drugs, follow me like
>   flowers. (*CW*, 31)

So, within the nexus of her code images in *Crossing the Water*, Plath creates another pattern of dramatic change, another example of the dynamic process of becoming she respects as a crucial part of the poetic trade.

A Woman's Legacy: from "fair chronicle" to "foul declension"

Taunted by those distanced yet demanding muses of *The Colossus*, Plath began to draw upon a distinctly personal subject matter in *Crossing the Water*—a cache of women's myths. She employs intimate metaphors of women's blood consciousness—pregnancy, stillbirth, abortion, aging, courtship, even widowhood—to scrutinize her aesthetic development. In her search for more representative and elastic forms, she wryly inverts some prominent myths in the women's heritage. She undoes preconceptions about her own emotional and intellectual nature, and about her previous aesthetic aims.

In "Wuthering Heights," she cleverly imagines a whole sisterhood of women with a common legacy. They become for her a pack of matronly sheep maundering about, nonchalantly accepting their mutual destiny:

> The sheep know where they are,
> Browsing in their dirty wool-clouds,
> Grey as the weather.
> The black slots of their pupils take me in.
> It is like being mailed into space,
> A thin, silly message.
> They stand about in grandmotherly disguise,
> All wig curls and yellow teeth
> And hard, marbly baas. (CW, 1)

To them it is all quite simple: knowing *where* they are implies knowing *who* they are. But for the poet who fights the social inheritance of the mother's soap-bubble world and the biological myths of bloodwise women, the matter of identity is not so easy. She sees herself as a mere reflection of the sheep's existence in the poems, and dependent upon such comical, metaphoric status ("a thin, silly message"), a fact she battles continually after *The Colossus* poems. Plath moves from the "arbitrary creation of non-personal myths" to the intimately personal truths, according to Helen Vendler (Z, 8). As she does this, she enlarges her emotional range, hones her critical powers, and redirects her sense of metaphor. In "Heavy Women," for example, she mocks the brooding physical contentment of pregnancy through a series of deflating etaphors that employ art history as well as Christian tradition for their debunking effect:

> Over each weighty stomach a face
> Floats calm as a moon or a cloud.
>
> Smiling to themselves, they meditate
> Devoutly as the Dutch bulb
> Forming its twenty petals.
> . . . .
> Pink buttocked infants attend them.
> Looping wool, doing nothing in particular,
> They step among the archetypes. (CW, 9)

In another poem, "Dark House," she describes the quiet

brag of unwitting creation. At first it seems as if Plath wishes to espouse a comfortably stereotyped notion of pregnant women absorbed in self-confinement:

> This is a dark house, very big.
> I made it myself,
> Cell by cell from a quiet corner,
> Chewing at the grey paper,
> Oozing the glue drops,
> Whistling, wiggling my ears,
> Thinking of something else. (CW, 50)

"I am round as an owl, / I see by my own light," she boasts, until an animallike force intrudes upon her solitude. Upon closer look, the speaking embryo is a writer-in-training. Instead of cowering in her blood-truth, she turns biological inadvertence (the embryo in the "marrowy tunnels") into a plea for imaginative description through the constructive powers of language: "so many cellars . . . *I must make more maps*" (emphasis added).

Plath does not opt for simple female concretion over male abstraction, as we see in "Magi":

> The abstracts hover like dull angels:
> Nothing so vulgar as a nose or an eye
> Bossing the ethereal blanks of their face-ovals.
>
> Their whiteness bears no relation to laundry,
> Snow, chalk or suchlike. (CW, 26)

With slangy diction, she mocks the sanitary irrelevance of those "papery godfolk" who are removed from the sensual immediacy of a woman's world:

> They're
> The real thing, all right: the Good, the True—
>
> Salutary and pure as boiled water,
> Loveless as the multiplication table. (CW, 26)

By the end of the poem she has parodied both sets of assumptions: the young girl whose "heavy notion of Evil / Attending her cot is less than a belly ache," as well as those aspiring male "lamp-headed Platos." Like so many *Crossing the Water* poems, "Magi" taunts coyly with its final, double-edged question: "What girl ever flourished in such company?" The speaker dares the reader to either reduce the female to a passel of blood truths or impersonalize her experience by equating it with ethereal male blankness.

Examples of Plath's revisionist eye for myths multiply. The use of the female tradition seems to suggest Plath's self-consciousness about some very old stereotypes—passivity, formlessness, confinement, materiality, and compliancy—qualities that might reinforce the all-too-comfortable identification of sexual and intellectual faculties.[20] But repeatedly Plath reviews and reevaluates women's themes by reexamining her poetics. She brings a personal revisionist force to the commonplace assumptions about women as well as to the practice of the poetic art. She does what Adrienne Rich claims most discriminating contemporary women critics are doing:

> Re-vision—the act of looking back, of seeing with fresh eyes, of entering an old text from a new critical direction—is for us more than a chapter in cultural history: it is an act of survival. Until we can understand the assumptions in which we are drenched we cannot know ourselves.[21]

Her irreverence toward sexual custom, if not her out-and-out inversion of some common stereotypes, often takes the form of sexual self-mockery. In "Zoo Keeper's Wife" she imagines herself "wooed and won" in a disastrous courtship and marriage. The event has been conducted in "tindery cages" by a bog-breathed zookeeper. That hoarder of bizarre animals dupes her into giving up her sensitive human identity so that she might join his menagerie of the quietly desperate:

> You wooed me with the wolf-headed fruit bats
> Hanging from their scorched hooks in the moist
> Fug of the small Mammal House.
> . . . .
> I remembered the bloodied chicks and the quartered rabbits.
>
> You checked the diet charts and took me to play
> With the boa constrictor in the Fellow's Garden. (CW, 38–39)

Like the dozing, bald armadillo or the "bear-furred" spider, she has become passive and motionless, even copulating from sheer lethargy. By her literally spineless behavior she has betrayed her sisters and must now prey upon their existences for her parasitical livelihood:

> I can stay awake all night, if need be—
> Cold as an eel, without eyelids.
> Like a dead lake the dark envelops me,
> Blueblack, a spectacular plum fruit.
> No air bubbles start from my heart. I am lungless

And ugly, my belly a silk stocking
Where the heads and tails of my sisters decompose.
Look, they are melting like coins in the powerful juices— . . .
(CW, 38)

Despite the mock-epic levity in the Garden of Eden and ark imagery, the zookeeper's world and his control are ominous. At the poem's end, however, she has finally caged herself both mentally and emotionally, for she has let him invade her dreams and fantasy life:

Nightly now I flog apes owls bears sheep
Over their iron stile. And still don't sleep. (CW, 39)

The story line tells of victimization, while the imagery celebrates the raucous biological escape through clever, comic metaphors.

Plath's triumph is her overwhelming power to "construe," and thereby overturn, victimization in romantic love by her sheer poetic inventiveness:

I pretended I was the Tree of Knowledge.
I entered your bible, I boarded your ark
With the sacred baboon in his wig and wax ears
And the bear-furred, bird-eating spider
Clambering round its glass box like an eight-fingered
    hand. (CW, 39)

Mary Ellmann describes this broadened emotional range which risks fresh wit and play as one of the rarest skills in the contemporary woman writer:

Self-mockery, particularly sexual self-mockery, is not expected in a woman, and it is irresistible in the criticism of women to describe what was expected: the actual seems to exist only in relation to the preconceived. . . . The emphasis is finally macabre, as though women wrote with breasts instead of pens—in which event it would be remarkable . . . if one of them achieved ironic detachment.[22]

Finding forms to properly express the rhythm and pace of such newly discovered emotional possibilities is largely a matter of Plath's becoming aware of the limitations of the old forms. Two poems in particular from Plath's transitional work dramatize the conflict between the claims of the old and new poetic modes. Both "Ouija" and "Stillborn" criticize Plath's existing oeuvre by reevaluating—re-viewing—particularly intimate subject matter: the myth of romantic love and the link between voluntary and involuntary creation.

"Ouija" ostensibly describes a failed courtship between an antiquated god and a bawdy queen of sex and death but is actually a casebook study of ingredients necessary to the new poetry. The Ouija board, used in spiritual seances to receive messages, is ironic here, for like her saffron-haired queen, the poet is very much in control of her art. An old god is summoned to the glass window where poetic images ("those unborn, those undone") are clustered, splendidly ornamented, but somehow incomplete and begging for a kind of vitality:

> Vermilions, bronzes, colors of the sun
> In the coal fire will not wholly console them.
> Imagine their deep hunger, deep as the dark
> For the blood-heat that would ruddle or reclaim. (CW, 44)

The qualities of the old poetry criticized here refer to more than the distanced psychological disturbance cited by Alvarez, or the stylistic "fops and gauds" pointed out by George Stade:[23]

> The old god, too, writes aureate poetry
> In tarnished modes, maundering among the wastes,
> Fair chronicler of every foul declension.
> Age, and ages of prose, have uncoiled
> His talking whirlwind, abated his excessive temper
> When words, like locusts, drummed the darkening air
> And left the cobs to rattle, bitten clean. (CW, 44)

The old aureate poetry hides behind the language of euphemism and detachment, like the abstract theories of the "papery godfolk" in "Magi." The old god is a waster of words, a perennial optimist, a useless aesthete. Mincingly, he chronicles or simply renarrates, he does not create, does not take imaginative risks. A dispassionate deflection characterizes the weak efforts of the old dodderer:

> I see him, horny-skinned and tough, construe
> What flinty pebbles the ploughblade upturns
> As ponderable tokens of her love.
> He, godly, doddering, spells
> No succinct Gabriel from the letters here
> But floridly, his amorous nostalgias. (CW, 45)

His poetry is outmoded, lethargic, verbose (a "talking whirlwind"), unnecessarily sentimental, and ignorant of all the ragged, impolite needs of real life.

"Ouija" criticizes the poet's previously safe reliance on those ossified, tarnished forms of sonnet, terza rima, and villanelle that Plath came to disrespect, just as she disparaged the subject matter those forms held: "Nature, I think: birds, bees, spring, fall, all those subjects which are absolute gifts to the person who doesn't have any interior experience to write about."[24]

Within the course of the poem, the conditions of the old god's poetic world are changed in mid-stanza. This formally signals the end of comfortable gentility and the introduction of new turbulence:

> Skies once wearing a blue, divine hauteur
> Ravel above us, mistily descend,
> Thickening with motes, to a marriage with the mire. (CW, 44)

The representative of the new poetry is the "rotten queen with saffron hair." She is courted by the doddering old god whose rules of courtship are as strictly formulaic—perhaps incongruous—as his forms of chronicling and poetasting. But the queen is compelling, seductive, and straightforward. Her manner is direct and brutal. Her stakes in the game called Love, Courtship, and Marriage are Sex and Death. And death, wormy couriers, and her "hot juices" are too quickly impatient with the old god's antiquated techniques of indirection. He smells of lavender, smacks of Shelley:

> He hymns the rotten queen with saffron hair
> Who has saltier aphrodisiacs
> Than virgins' tears. That bawdy queen of death,
> Her wormy couriers are at his bones.
> Still he hymns juice of her, hot nectarine. (CW, 45)

His effete style obstructs a truly productive union with the new queen.

"Ouija" is a cynical comment on the foppish limitations of Plath's academic style of poetry. That style ignored the compelling demands of a speaker's sensuous and immediate experience. The irony of the inverted (and failed) courtship-marriage metaphor is that the sentimental old god is not the aggressor: the power really belongs to the crassly practical, passionate, new queen. The task facing Plath in the development of a new art is to effect a real union between the skills of her early formal exercises and the newly discovered emotional awareness. Simply to court—to admire and isolate emblems of a uniformly ideal imaginative world—is to ignore the movements of the speaker's imagination, to fail to recover an emotional and dramatic register of a real voice in a real body. She seems to suggest that poetry should be a kind of birthing that, if it does not result in the creation of a definitive new self, at least explores a range of possible expressions for that self. Instead of clinging to barren and sedate professions of love, the new poetry should show ripeness, fullness, and the danger, risk, and turmoil of act; it should create, not stammer, in the face of death—art confronting experience.

That Plath thought this union of qualities important is evident from a BBC interview shortly before her death. While her poetry derived from the need to fix passionate life experiences, her life nevertheless remained the source of the poetry only as it was "controlled and manipulated" by the poetic imagination:

> I think my poems immediately come out of the sensuous and emotional experiences I have, but I must say I cannot sympathize with these cries from the heart that are informed by nothing except a needle or a knife, or whatever it is. I believe that one should be able to control and manipulate experiences, even the most terrifying, like madness, being tortured, this sort of experience . . . with an informed and an intelligent mind . . . personal experience is very important, but certainly it shouldn't be a kind of shut-box and mirror-looking, narcissistic experience. I believe it should be relevant . . . to the larger things, the bigger things. (PS, 169–70)

In "Stillborn," Plath describes the failure of her "juvenilia": "These poems do not live: it's a sad diagnosis," she says of her poetry before this volume. The traditional but spurious analogue for the creation of poetry—the act of childbirth—provides a crafty self-evaluation of her stylized, formal poetry. The tradition itself deserves some prefatory explanation.

The link between women's mind (voluntary creation) and woman's physiology (involuntary creation) has a lively and controversial history in literature. Such history exists quite apart from the positive use of the gestation metaphor by such modern male poets as Rainer Maria Rilke and Hart Crane. The Ovarian Theory of literature (in contrast to the Testicular Theory) claims that a woman writer's physiology determines the nature of her literary achievement. Female nature with its presumed psychology, emotional temper, endemic style, sensibility, and common preoccupations is posited on a basis of pure sexual function: "It assumed the writer's gender inherently circumscribed and defined and directed the writer's subject matter, perspective and aspiration."[25] The physiological vagueness of the blood flow and the brooding immobility of the ovum, for example, produce a supposedly recognizable sort of literature that distinguishes women's intellect and imagination from penile mental inventiveness.

A history of hostile convictions has been directed against the uterus-mind analogy, according to Mary Ellmann: "We assume it is necessary to escape from feminine influence if intellectual activity is to be free, inventive and original."[26] Virginia Woolf thought woman's most significant act was to kill the Angel in the House and finally rid herself of "unlady-like" critical thoughts.

Ellen Moers suggests that Mary Shelley in *Frankenstein* used the romantic birth myth with ironic awareness when she proposed the idea of a man's creating life:

> She brought birth to fiction not as realism but as Gothic fantasy, and thus contributed to Romanticism a myth of genuine originality. She invented the mad scientist who locks himself in his laboratory and secretly, guiltily, works at creating human life, only to find that he has made a monster. . . . He defies mortality not by living forever, but by giving birth.[27]

On the other hand, Anaïs Nin, in her *Diaries*, presents a Feminine Ideal, a model for constructive female art that reclaims and mirrors woman's role in biology: ". . . a woman's creation far from being like man's must be exactly like her creations of children, that is it must come out of her own blood, englobed by her womb, nourished with her own milk."[28] Cynthia Ozick has had the final word in puncturing the myth of women's creativity. That female nature espoused by Nin and the new feminists is misleading, according to Ozick:

> To call a child a poem may be a pretty metaphor, but . . . woman through her reproductive system alone is no more a creative artist than was Joyce by virtue of his kidneys alone, or James by virtue of his teeth (which, by the way, were troublesome). A poem emerges from a mind . . . an unknowable abstraction.[29]

With a wit as sharp as Ozick's, Plath uses the child-poem analogy in "Stillborn" to sever the reproduction-as-literature link. Emphatically, she dwells on the failure of literary reproduction, implying that she is aware of more than a few differences in poetic and embryonic art, creativity and procreation. The voice of the speaker charges the poems with lifelessness, with sitting "so nicely in the pickling fluid":

> These poems do not live: it's a sad diagnosis.
> They grew their toes and fingers well enough,
> Their little foreheads bulged with concentration.
> If they missed out on walking about like people
> It wasn't for any lack of mother love.
>
> O I cannot understand what happened to them!
> They are proper in shape and number and every part.
> They sit so nicely in the pickling fluid!
> They smile and smile and smile and smile at me.
> And still the lungs won't fill and the heart won't start.
>
> They are not pigs, they are not even fish,
> Though they have a piggy and a fishy air—
> It would be better if they were alive, and that's
>   what they were.
> But they are dead, and their mother near dead with
>   distraction,
> And they stupidly stare, and do not speak of her.
> (CW, 20)

Like stillborn children, her early poems promised vitality, but never delivered. Inexplicably, they "missed out on walking about like people," although they seemed to have all the drawing-board ingredients necessary for vitality: time, labor, and an enormous technical, if not emotional, investment. Plath indicts her earlier poetry: the Cambridge Manuscript poems for their philosophical edicts about imaginative temperance, and *The Colossus* poems for an admired but graphically one-dimensional world drawn from paintings, books, and myths. Early ideals were never put to the challenge of action, but merely intellectualized for their perfect union of opposite qualities. Armed with her thesaurus and thickly lined copy pages, Plath strove for formal and technical perfection in that adolescent work (poems "proper in shape and number and every part"). What she created, however, was only a single formulaic emotion (smiles pickled on faces; stupid stares). Now the question she raises in "Stillborn" is whether cultivating a poetic sensibility with a broader emotional range—"lungs that fill and a heart that starts"—is too grand an aspiration.

The end of the poem offers a moment of stark awareness for the mother-poet "near dead with distraction." She must explore new emotional possibilities for a protean self, then bring these discoveries to bear on a highly crafted but stillborn art.

Until the final stanza she has feigned naiveté about the reasons for the failure of her creation. She has assumed an innocent air about the difficulties that might accompany mental creativity. Her happy physiological vagueness suggests that the poem's germination is modeled on that of the embryo: an unconscious growth that needs only nurturance of love.

In the last stanza, however, she seems to recognize that the price of mental versus physical creativity is occasional failure. The poems do not live imaginatively, for the speaking voice plays no part in arriving at the calculatedly crafted perfection. The consequence of such a failure, she discovers, becomes the need for an even more stringent self-evaluation, one that is the subject or process of many *Crossing the Water* poems. In other words, it would be easier if one could follow the Ovarian Theory of creativity and produce simple, subhuman "piggy and fishy" things that unconsciously smile and are uncomplicatedly physical. But these poems exist apart from their nourishing source, the poet-mother self, who suffers "near death" and anxiety from her severance. She remains dislocated, distracted. Despite all their technical perfection and meticulous craft, the poems require a quickened "freedom of voice" and emotional vitality.

In short, Plath derides herself for previous mental inventiveness: her poems that were shaped as carefully as those separate blocks of her handwriting, checked according to a thickly lined thesaurus; measured in rhyme, meter, and part; and balanced in the total oeuvre. Now these diligent but dispassionate poems seem to be only a static simulacrum of the human.

Plath continues her poetic critique introduced by "Stillborn" in the neatly compact poem, "Metaphors." Within a perfect formal envelope (nine lines, nine syllables per line), she develops a wry linguistic mockery of that familiar link between the physical state of pregnancy and the poet's art of analogy:

> I'm a riddle in nine syllables,
> An elephant, a ponderous house,
> A melon strolling on two tendrils.
> O red fruit, ivory, fine timbers!
> This loaf's big with its yeasty rising.
> Money's new-minted in this fat purse.
> I'm a means, a stage, a cow in calf.
> I've eaten a bag of green apples,
> Boarded the train there's no getting off.
> (*CW*, 43)

The metaphors are numerous, quick-shifting, and disturbingly disparate. In themselves, they are riddles, not clarifications, and form a parodic comment on a poetic technique intended to enlarge the poet's sense of the world. The metaphors transfer little energy; instead, they are as flatly perfect as the "finger count" precision that is evident in all other formal aspects of the poem. They taunt us to discover a single transformation of meaning in their diverse particulars, but ultimately befuddle any attempt at analysis. Each comparison is stillborn in its isolated brevity, a wry comment on the state of embryonic growth that is supposed to eventually lead to production. The playfully familiar tone is in no way a preface to the final two sharp images of fear and entrapment. The final images are more dramatically poignant because they lack a preface to their force, preceded merely by a static anatomy of the poet's craft of comparison. Their tonal power, however, suggests a new authority of victimization that Plath will perfect in this and later volumes.

A New Tonal Authority: "I'm collecting my strength"

Taken together, "Stillborn" and "Ouija" make several important points within their combined poetic critique. In one poem, the rotten queen requires a new earthy sensuousness (a "marriage with the mire") to inform the old god's stilted pomposities. She wants the emotional and dramatic register of a real voice, not the old god's "talking whirlwind." Moreover, the mother-speaker in "Stillborn," as a last resort, would like to revert to cultivating a "piggy and fishy" air to her poems. This is a cure-all for the sad fact that they have been unnaturally arrested (the "pickling fluid" of domineering metrics and rhyme) before they fully matured. These child-poems are theoretically perfect but practically dead. Each poem offers a highly self-critical evaluation of Plath's transitional art within the context of the poem and the woman artist's biological and cultural heritage. By both re-creating the uterus-mind myth and tailoring romantic-love fictions to fit her individual aesthetic needs, Plath refuses to traffic in conventional women's mythology and stereotypes *uninformed* by her singular talents and imagination.

The restless, discursive voice with its startling dramatic authority becomes a trademark of Plath's *Crossing the Water* poems. She values a new freedom of choice in the emotional range available to that voice. It should come as no surprise that a woman whose work was in a perpetual state of flux with respect to titles and content (in both *The Colossus* and Cambridge Manuscript), and who modeled her early sensibility on the ebb and flow of the sea, should cultivate the same breathing, pulsating qualities—that lambent fluid movement—in the tonal range of her poems. Many of the poems display a "double-view." They seem to be quickened by a mercurial consciousness that moves easily between the mental and the physically concrete ("my mind runs with them," the poet says of the day's images), between the view of the self burrowed in marrowy tunnels at the "bowel of the root" and the metamorphic, grand self that swallows everything that "unwinds from the great umbilicus of the sun." Plath explores the whole gamut of possible emotional reactions in such poems, proclaiming an enlarged way of knowing by her power of metamorphosing from one state to another.

It has been pointed out that Plath frequently musters her creative energy toward becoming simple and inert. In doing so she lends paradoxical authority to her manipulating naiveté, an authority that recalls the adolescent ingenuity of a role willfully chosen, as her later bee sequence clarifies. But in these transitional poems the speaking self dwindles to a "cupboard of rubbish," to a simple but rich physicality that begs for a form elastic enough to catch the motion of the accompanying emotional awareness.

In "Last Words," she not only scales herself down to those "little particular lusters" of objects that remain permanent in their dumb endurance, but in the course of the poem actually allows the self to be bundled up for death:

> They will roll me up in bandages, they will store my heart
> Under my feet in a neat parcel.
> I shall hardly know myself. It will be dark,
> And the shine of these small things sweeter than the face
>   of Ishtar. (CW, 40)

The modest speaker adopts the voice of simple candor and confident unawareness ("I shall hardly know myself"), but not without a certain triumph of wit and prankishly imaginative humor:

> I do not want a plain box, I want a sarcophagus
> With tigery stripes, and a face on it
> Round as the moon, to stare up.
> I want to be looking at them when they come

Picking among the dumb minerals, the roots.
(*CW*, 40)

Such brief, colloquial declaratives only emphasize the hazard
the speaker must avoid: misleading dreams of the spirit, here
the promises of Ishtar, the Phoenician goddess of love and
fertility. Her preference—decidedly in favor of the "little things
that stay"—recalls the poet's reverence for the anti-illusionary
world in the Cambridge Manuscript poems, or the poet's expressed need for her "little Lares and Penates":

I do not trust the spirit. It escapes like steam
In dreams, through mouth-hole or eye-hole. I can't
   stop it.
One day it won't come back. Things aren't like that.
They stay, . . . (*CW*, 40)

Likewise in "Who," the energy with which the poet has
prepared herself for familiar inertia is itself a kind of resolution.
It ends in her reassigning value to the quality of passivity,
anticipating her single, strong statement of the bee sequence in
Ariel. Here she says:

I am at home here among the dead heads.

Let me sit in a flowerpot,
The spiders won't notice.
My heart is a stopped geranium.
. . . .
Cabbageheads: wormy purple, silver-glaze,
A dressing of mule ears, mothy pelts, but greenhearted,
Their veins white as porkfat. (*CW*, 48)

The important poem "Maenad" marks a slightly different
use of the poet's metamorphic powers in both social and poetic
realms. From an initial bold statement of separateness she hesi-
tates to adopt a more complex identity. She has outgrown the
"Good Ship Lollipop" world of her mother as well as the
father's legacy of protective fictions (those "fingers of wisdom"):

Once I was ordinary:
Sat by my father's bean tree
Eating the fingers of wisdom.
The birds made milk.
When it thundered I hid under a flat stone.

The mother of mouths didn't love me.
The old man shrank to a doll. (*CW*, 51)

Now she must accept the unconventional challenge of her testy muses. Within the simple narrative of the poem, a child's trust in an idyllic sensory world matures to an adult clarity about the factual world of change:

> O I am too big to go backward:
> Birdmilk is feathers,
> The bean leaves are dumb as hands. (CW, 51)

Step by step, the speaker reconstructs her personal history, showing her transformation from trust to disillusionment to a crass world of factual limitation. As if to prove this change, the speaker, midway through her reconstruction, suddenly shifts the fabular narrative couched in fairy tale imagery to a new stark linearity. She punctuates that paradoxical fall into fact by questions and direct imperatives. Tone, rhythm, and imagery trace her emotional rite of passage:

> A red tongue is among us.
> Mother, keep out of my barnyard,
> I am becoming another.
>
> Dog-head, devourer:
> Feed me the berries of dark.
> The lids won't shut. Time
> Unwinds from the great umbilicus of the sun
> Its endless glitter.
>
> I must swallow it all.
>
> Lady, who are these others in the moon's vat—
> Sleepdrunk, their limbs at odds?
> In this light the blood is black.
> Tell me my name. (CW, 51)

For the young speaker in "Maenad," the willful disingenuousness of the fairy-tale imagery and narrative are emotionally limited. They no longer suit her purpose. For now she is engaged in actively changing her poetics as well as her poetic identity. Aware that she lacks both precedent and directive for such metamorphosis, she momentarily begs for the security of an identity given by another: "Tell me my name," she pleads. By dramatic suggestion, not definition, she presents to us the overwhelming burdens of personal creativity that she alone must assume.

Plath's continual awareness of the actual process of change is recurrent in these poems. At the same time she recognizes the threat, yet the catalytic effect, of some impersonal force ("all

mouth," the "bullman," a "fat sort," "Mumblepaws," "Dogs-
body," or a "red tongue"). Plath has reached a critical juncture
in *Crossing the Water*. She must find the precise and nuanced
forms of expression (not the inherited repetitions of technique
displayed in earlier poems) to represent all the contours of the
poetic imagination: "the truth of the mental quirk of the moment, the individual feeling over the habitual one, the spon-
taneous over the rehearsed response, the fluctuations of consciousness rather than its rigidities" (Z, 17). Like her "Insomniac," she must live in a "lidless room," viewing full face the
"incessant heat-lightning flicker of situations," or catch in each
dramatic enactment the future's "dissolving series of promises."

All of Plath's personal fables, recast in idiosyncratic myths
(nodding bald-headed muses, beantree worlds, or tiger-striped
coffins), fail after a certain point to represent the pace and
rhythmic pitch of diction dictated by the poet's consciousness.
She often makes a plea to an ominous mother-figure or to an
unknown lady for an identity, a definition, or specific information. Perhaps she seeks some resolution to her willful self-
effacement: "I am a root, a stone, an owl pellet, / Without
dreams of any sort." In "Leaving Early," a final poignant question betrays the speaker's dislocation, her simple fear of going
ahead, and her need for some directive:

> Lady what am I doing
> With a lung full of dust and tongue of wood,
> Knee-deep in the cold and swamped by flowers? (CW, 19)

Occasionally, in the midst of changes or in the violent darkness
of a state of frenzy, she petitions the mother for assimilation,
absorption. She admires the "beauty of usage" in October's
rotting pumpkins ("mouldering heads"):

> Mother, you are the one mouth
> I would be a tongue to. Mother of otherness
> Eat me. Wastebasket gaper, shadow of doorways. (CW, 49)

But in *Crossing the Water* no petitioned mother performs a
dea ex machina rescue; nor is there a ready-made identity lurk-
ing in the catalysis by the "red tongues." Rather, emphasis is on
Plath's need to find new forms for her state of complication. She
must, in her paradoxical changes, construe the vagaries of
dramatic consciousness by means of her poems and image-
making. As George Stade says, Plath knows that something is

happening to her, but she simply does not have words for it yet. Her task is, above all, constructive and conscious, wholly her own: "I said: I must remember this, being small." Because the catalytic force in these poems remains undefined, the mother-figure mute or impersonal, the burden of describing and accounting for her changes rests totally with the poet: "Nobody can tell what I lack," she reluctantly admits.

The ideal situation is one where she is not precisely told an identity, or handed one "trapped in a laboratory jar," but where she can say: "Mother to myself, I wake swaddled in gauze / Pink and smooth as a baby." "Face Lift" seems to be a kind of tribute to assigned passivity. The clinic doctor changes the speaker's visage while she is unconscious:

> At the count of two
> Darkness wipes me out like chalk on a blackboard . . .
> I don't know a thing.
>
> For five days I lie in secret,
> Tapped like a cask, the years draining into my pillow. (CW, 5)

In its obvious metaphors, the poem compares two modes of anesthesia, pointing out the difficulty of the earlier unconscious state (ether) compared to the smooth facility with which one loses oneself nowadays (sodium pentothal):

> They've changed all that. Traveling
> Nude as Cleopatra in my well-boiled hospital shift,
> Fizzy with sedatives and unusually humorous,
> I roll to an anteroom where a kind man
> Fists my fingers for me. (CW, 5)

In fact, "Face Lift" celebrates the poet's power to poetically construe her lifetime of helplessness: the nine-year-old's world of bad dreams; "Jovian voices" and "lime-green" anesthetists feeding her "banana gas through a frog mask"; herself at twenty "broody and in long skirts." Her power to leap backward twenty years celebrates a kind of imaginative efficiency, even humor, in loss. Looking backward to "The Stones" and forward to the bee sequence, "Face Lift" establishes a wry authority for passivity. Ironically, for all the doctor's traditional power, the poet-speaker reclaims the new self by a metaphoric process of growing backward physically so as to grow forward imaginatively. It is she who finds words and images for change. And the process is wholly the poet's, one where she celebrates her paradoxical energy of passivity, not the doctor's overt authority:

> Now she's done for, the dewlapped lady
> I watched settle, line by line, in my mirror—
> Old sock face, sagged on a darning egg.
> They've trapped her in some laboratory jar.
> Let her die there. . . . (*CW*, 6)

It becomes obvious that for Sylvia Plath, in her transitional poems, truth is not a speaker's declarative authority or the presentation of a resolved identity. In contrast, Plath's process of shape-shifting becomes the dramatic focus of many memorable poems ("Maenad," "Witch Burning," "Love Letters," and "Face Lift"), just as truth becomes the poet's sincere effort to "play Pygmalion to her own Galatea," as Helen Vendler has shown.[30] Plath is concerned with the loss of the old familiar self, with what the process of changing feels like, and then with construing these ongoing changes poetically. As she claimed she loved to do, Plath tinkers with the process of making in all of its varying forms. She defines no single image of the self, although in the process of change she alternately recognizes states of greater complexity ("some things of this world are indigestible"), befuddlement ("Lady, who are these others at the moon's vat?"), simple exactitude ("staying put according to habit"), or willed passivity ("My mirror is clouding over / a few more breaths and it will reflect nothing at all"). Bursts of dramatic energy lend the power of continual metamorphosis to these individual images, yet allow no single definitive state to predominate.

"Witch Burning" is another poem that reexamines passivity, and in so doing reiterates the need for a new elastic poetic form. The poem establishes a new tonal authority of change. Everything that occurs in the poem is done to the speaker purposefully, with a kind of inevitability:

> I inhabit
> The wax image of myself, a doll's body.
> Sickness begins here: I am a dartboard for witches.
> . . . .
> . . . I climb to a bed of fire. (*CW*, 53)

She becomes little and insubstantial, a wax image of herself, a doll's body, a blown-out sparkler, a rice grain. She is pure victim, time after time choosing her passivity:

> If I am a little one, I can do no harm.
> If I don't move about, I'll knock nothing over. So I said.

Sitting under a potlid, tiny and inert as a rice grain.
They are turning the burners up, ring after ring.
We are full of starch, my small white fellows. We grow.
It hurts at first. The red tongues will teach the truth.
(*CW*, 53)

Even the metamorphic energy inherent in passivity seems to be countered by the tone of dutiful obedience.[31]

The speaking voice adopts the tone of moral trustfulness ("The red tongues will teach the truth"), as if to suggest that there is a properly lessoned certainty, a legacy of sisterhood available in witchcraft, but one that is nevertheless gullible. The act of growing larger or smaller, however, reveals no truth. Both the image of the inert grain of rice that puffs up and the speaker's tone of dependency that changes to imperative communicate the poet's need to reformulate what is happening and what has happened to her during the years she "coupled with dust" in the shadow of *The Colossus* poems:

Give me back my shape. I am ready to construe the days
I coupled with dust in the shadow of a stone.
My ankles brighten. Brightness ascends my thighs.
I am lost, I am lost, in the robes of all this light.
(*CW*, 53)

What she wants is her own narrative shape, words for the idiosyncrasies and rhythms of her own imaginative movements, not the false language or sense of power of borrowed truth. The poem's imagery makes this point: the "singeless moth" drawn to the candle flame or a rice grain exploding from heat only follow their own natures unexamined, unconstrued. By "construing her days," the poet becomes the real catalyst for her own growth as well as the manipulating authority in control of the final outcome.

What she has done within the poetic process of "Witch Burning" is turn pure victimage ("I climb to a bed of fire") into conscious metamorphosis. She has changed destructive fire into ritual purification that is visible in imagery of light, brightness, and airiness. Her initial nostalgia for victimage has become a testimony to her power of shape-shifting and reconstruction through art.

Self, however, is lost within the process of change. The poet gropes at the end of the poem for a form elastic enough to describe her expanded state: "I am lost, I am lost . . ." Yet she reserves for herself that ambivalent burden "to construe," to remember all poetically and imaginatively.

There is a lesson in Plath's "map-making" her way through the process of change by rehearsing the sheer constructive power of language. When the speaker in "The Beast" has been duped into accepting a diminished image of herself prescribed by the "beast-bullman" (a situation echoed in "Zoo Keeper's Wife"), she seizes her fate. With stark imperatives, shifts to narrative linearity, she spews forth a cacophonous disarray of metaphors and brief expletives. The energy of the poet's linguistic awareness celebrates the fact of her duping. Although her brilliant sounds cannot exorcise him or undo her own foolishness, the range and innovation of her clogged sounds of disgust (the phonemes that play on *ugh*) retrieves her from passive victimization. A new authority derives from the imaginative inventiveness of sheer name-calling:

> He won't be got rid of:
> Mumblepaws, teary and sorry,
> Fido Littlesoul, the bowel's familiar.
> A dustbin's enough for him.
> The dark's his bone.
> Call him any name, he'll come to it.
>
> Mud-sump, happy sty-face.
> I've married a cupboard of rubbish.
> I bed in a fish puddle.
> Down here the sky is always falling.
> Hogwallow's at the window.
> The star bugs won't save me this month.
> I housekeep in Time's gut-end
> Among emmets and mollusks,
> Duchess of Nothing,
> Hairtusk's bride. (CW, 52)

In quick retrospect, Plath's distinctive power in *Crossing the Water* is the vigorous and mobile self-consciousness of her achievement—or lack of it—in the areas of self-revelation and artistic form. Thematically and technically, the poems reiterate a tension between the urge to reveal the self in small physical images or dramatic bursts of energy, and the need to find an artistic form proper for expressing the imaginative rhythm of such new emotional forays. Plath is not sparing when it comes to self-evaluation. She reviews, and then reemploys, some traditional women's myths for her own artistic purposes. She explores a new tonal register for the speaking voice.

It is this dissociation of a faltering speaking voice from the lure of a timeless imaginative realm and the discovery of a new tonal authority for such a voice that best describes Plath's late work. However, the new power is also the source of her dilemma. As she outgrows the inflexible mold of her previous aesthetic and dramatically discovers its uselessness, she must reexamine every stage in the development of her consciousness for new language and forms. As one critic claims, "the expression of her vision in words unleashes reality, for her poems describe what is real—her own consciousness."[32]

"In Plaster" discusses this particular dilemma. The poem serves as a summary of Plath's developing poetic sensibility and style in *Crossing the Water*. While the narrative of the poem discusses the healing process, it is but a thin disguise for the real subject: an allegory about the art of writing poetry; specifically, the interdependence of style and voice. Plath's change in poetic modes is portrayed here in the dramatic conflict between a plaster of paris cast and the shrunken yellow flesh that it contains. "Old aureate poetry" is challenged by the new "foul declensions" of the yet unexercised voice that needs to assert itself in the poetic process. By means of a slow trial-and-error process the speaker dramatically comes to terms with the limitations of her art and with the peculiarities of self as artist. The voice is more vulnerable, more impassioned, and more ironic than in previous poems. It celebrates those very limitations, a paradox which Ted Hughes has pointed out: "The new thing in these poems is the freedom of the voice. And the more free it gets, the more musically exact it gets. . . . Every one of its casual free lines is like a sudden new melody—surprising and inevitable" (*R*, 170).

To date, critics have viewed "In Plaster" as an organizing principle for Plath's life, not her poetry: "The image of the poet that rises out of the poetry as we read it wears the aspect of her fate. Our knowledge of her suicide not only clarifies what she said and what she meant—it also certifies that she meant what she said" (*CLA*, 3). In the dialectic between the sulfurous, old, yellow self and the plaster saint, George Stade observes the key to Plath's life as she understood it—a constant struggle between the "imminent volcano" and the "prickly defense" (*CLA*, 5):

"The special horror and fascination derive from the fact that Sylvia Plath knew what was happening to her, knew where it would end, but could or would not do anything about it" (*CLA*, 7). As she claims in the poem: "I shall never get out of this! There are two of me now: / This new absolutely white person and the old yellow one" (*CW*, 16).

The autobiographical argument continues. For a while the poet's art, like the saintly white cast that replicates human form, acts as a force of containment, keeping disturbance at a distance. Later, in *Ariel*, the white saint is absorbed by these "ugly, hairy" forces, as "the repressed self exacts its revenge against the restraints that had held it both down and together." Stade hears the plaintive cry of a suicide in the final lines of the poem: "I'm collecting my strength; one day I shall manage without her, / And she'll perish with emptiness then, and begin to miss me" (*CW*, 17). Stade's analysis is echoed by another critic who views the poem as an ongoing death struggle between the superficial woman of appearances and the one inside.[33] Neither critic is able to keep one eye from wandering back over the shoulder to the demand for verification of suicide in the poetry.

Quite apart from suicide, "In Plaster" carefully delineates all the dramatic stages between disillusionment and awareness. The poem presents a sensitive seismograph of slowly awakening emotions. In a curiously searching monologue, the speaker gropes through degrees of developing awareness more to answer the difficult question, "What am I to make of these contradictions?" than simply "to anticipate the end" (*CLA*, 7). The ingenuous speaking voice (ugly yellow) inches away from its early, confident conformity toward a new, glaring disparity. After first admitting the superiority of the white cast, ugly yellow recounts a step-by-step acceptance of a necessarily vital separation:

> I used to think we might make a go of it together—
> After all, it was a kind of marriage, being so close.
> Now I see it must be one or the other of us. (*CW*, 17)

At first the speaker thinks of "superior white" with fear, admiration, and resentment:

> She doesn't need food, she is one of the real saints.
> At the beginning I hated her, she had no personality—
> She lay in bed with me like a dead body
> And I was scared, because she was shaped just the way
> I was. . . . (*CW*, 16)

Quickly she realizes that this white self is nonreactive. Next, she tries an emotional seduction:

> . . . I realized what she wanted was for me to love her:
> She began to warm up, and I saw her advantages. (CW, 16)

Finally, the poem's climax results from the dissociation of the two selves. The moment of truth comes when yellow cannot fit her voice to that "offish" perfection of mute, rigid white. The white cast, functioning like so many of Plath's metaphors in *Crossing the Water*, at one time offered a model for hairy yellow, but now destroys a vital symbiosis: it stops the transformation of energy. "Shrunken yellow" finds the plaster mold inhumanly, inflexibly perfect. Her early efforts to mold to the plaster form now only emphasize the worth of a much less dazzling but more vital self. This self sports all the imperfections of the speaking voice:

> Without me, she wouldn't exist, so of course she was
>   grateful.
> I gave her a soul, I bloomed out of her as a rose
> Blooms out of a vase of not very valuable porcelain,
> And it was I who attracted everybody's attention,
> Not her whiteness and beauty, as I had at first supposed.
> I patronized her a little, and she lapped it up—
> You could tell almost at once she had a slave mentality.
> (CW, 16)

As old yellow tries to exercise her fledgling powers, she discovers in a moment of psychological realism[34] that they are shrunken from dependency and withered from disuse:

> I wasn't in any position to get rid of her.
> She'd supported me for so long I was quite limp—
> I had even forgotten how to walk or sit,
> So I was careful not to upset her in any way
> Or brag ahead of time how I'd avenge myself. (CW, 17)

At first beneficial, all that white "tidiness, calmness and patience" now smothers, ossifies. Old white has failed to accommodate the new image of the healed yellow self, and by analogy provides a criterion for evaluating Plath's poetry. Her old mode of writing was a "fair chronicler of every foul declension," but ill-suited to the needs of a new elastic self-exploration. The exhausting struggle toward expression in "In Plaster" is the subject of many of the *Crossing the Water* poems.

What distinguishes Plath's speaking voice here and in other

poems is the classic reversal that occurs in self-disparaging irony; the device is as old as Chaucer pretending to be the humble bookworm for the Canterbury pilgrims, or Socrates fumbling with his questions at the feet of Plato.[35] The tone is willfully complaisant and deferent, but the reader must see through the initial deference in the character or personality of the speaker. When the disguise of the voice is penetrated, judgment is directed not against the naive speaker, but against the object of irony. Here the object is Plath's previous poetry, work that has eliminated by the primacy of its rigid forms all the tonal and emotional possibilities for the poetic speaking voice. The poet's voice engages us as co-investigators to discover, with old yellow, white plaster's inhuman criteria for existence: her impervious superiority, the lack of a protean sensibility, her ridiculous sense of immortality, her intolerance of risks, and, most importantly, her ignorance of the shortcomings of a struggling self that blooms out of "not very valuable porcelain." Such qualities belong to a world admired in *The Colossus*, but broken from in "Stones."

Charles Newman has said that, as her art develops, the poet's expression changes. She begins making a rhetorical, not psychological, analysis of that mysterious "other" that figures in a number of the transitional poems:

> It is the form of the expression, not the neurosis from which it may or may not issue, which concerns us, and which we can evaluate. . . . Her entire body of work can be seen as a dialogue with an "other," but it is not a dialectic in any academic sense, for her voice and her interlocutor metamorphose as the context of her private quarrel is enlarged.[36]

Formally, "In Plaster" heralds Plath's break with a strict imagistic mode and her discovery of a dissociated speaking voice. The wry irony of "In Plaster" looks backward to "Disquieting Muses" and "Stones," and forward to the self-performing spectacles that characterize the *Ariel* poems. In calculatedly naive tones, the speaking voice has slowly and self-consciously modified its original belief that old yellow and saintly white can coexist. This awareness has been gained serially through the investigative process. It is significant, too, that in her personal statements Plath has likened the process of making poems to the action of a child "forming itself finger by finger in the dark."[37] The speaker, not "saintly white," risks all the bumblings, gropings, and fitful stops and starts in an effort to puzzle out a truth. Saintly white is merely an abstraction that never changes, one that belongs, surely, to Plath's "juvenilia." The entire burden of self-disclosure is left to the painful metamorphosis of old yellow.

"In Plaster" ends on a carefully qualified note of hope, at once a childish boast (the poet *would* free herself from former rule-book exercises), yet a sound recognition of the transitional state of her art:

> She may be a saint, and I may be ugly and hairy,
> But she'll soon find out that that doesn't matter a
>   bit.
> I'm collecting my strength; one day I shall manage
>   without her,
> And she'll perish with emptiness then, and begin to
>   miss me. (CW, 17)

In *Crossing the Water*, Plath has abandoned narrative linearity for tonal nuance, villanelles for vernacular, impersonal ideals for personal ambivalence, external description for internal symbolism. She has suggested a new imaginative interdependence of theme, tone, and style: revised women's stereotypes borrowed from wider culture; new ranges of expression for the speaking voice; a guidebook of strengths and weaknesses for her task of poemmaking. Having gained confidence by investigating the state of her art and dramatically enacting a growing mobility of consciousness, she must find a way to represent this protean self in the poems of *Ariel* and *Winter Trees*.

IV.

Ariel and Winter Trees:
The Late Poems
"that theatrical comeback in broad day"

Introduction

> In a sense, these poems are deflections. I do not think they are an
> escape. For me, the real issues of our time are the issues of every
> time—the hurt and wonder of loving; making in all its forms.[1]

When Sylvia Plath taped a BBC broadcast shortly before her
death in 1963, she anticipated the central question that has
obsessed critics of her last poems. Is her poetry a murderous art,
one that reveals the poet "courting the experience that kills"; or
is it really a predicate of life, finding in its artistic control the
means to keep disturbances at a distance? Is death a foreclosed
theme or the source of renewed energy and imaginative performance for Sylvia Plath?

With the appearance of *Ariel* in 1965,[2] the critical tide
turned. Whereas formerly Plath's humor, her striking clarity,
and her precision with language skills had been praised, she
now seemed to brood over a broken landscape. Only by death
could she extricate herself from that "city of spare parts." As one
reviewer observed, "it's no good pretending that Sylvia Plath's
is not sick verse."[3] Such comment introduced the fashionable
cult of Sylvia, goddess of suicide, whose Pyrrhic victory defied a
societal taboo. Even more poignant was the fact that she prefaced the dramatic event with a written record that remained
unnoticed at the time of her death, but was exhumed by the
literary establishment during the next decade. Critics agreed
with Stephen Spender that "the guarantees of the authenticity
of the situation are insanity (or near-insanity) and death."[4] The
qualities of intensity, candor, and urgency were costly, thus all
the more valuable. In short, Sylvia Plath meant what she said.

As early as October 1965, George Steiner announced that
these last poems had "already passed into legend," readily
admitting that the spell didn't lie wholly in the poems themselves.[5] Reviews following the appearance of the British edition
of *Ariel* proved that the dramatic authority of the suicide had

indeed replaced critical discussion of the poems as linguistic acts. The rhetoric of the critics betrayed a frenzy equal to the sensational life described: Plath suffered a "sick room mutilation of the personality"; her work lingered like "the smell of morphia," while the persona in the poems was a "homonculus," the "all-mouth" from a "limbless fairy tale." Refusing to lie down on the page where "decency and good taste want them to stay," the poems belonged "to life rather than literature, nerve endings still squirming."[6]

The suicide fire was fanned by the appearance of *The Bell Jar*[7] on the best-seller list; *The Savage God*,[8] Alfred Alvarez's home companion to suicide; and the deaths of two other confessional poets, Anne Sexton and John Berryman. Feminists have tried to arraign Ted Hughes—that "one-man gynocidal movement"—for Plath's victimization and suicide.[9] This charge as well as psychovoyeuristic interest in self-laceration have made any attempts to quietly reread the poems for the merits of artistic control a challenge. Only a handful of critics—Barbara Hardy and Helen Vendler among the best—have been able to sufficiently counteract the risks of confessional platitudes, the fashionable cult of suicide, and the glib popularity of feminist and mythological subject matter to establish Sylvia Plath's protean talent for its imaginative forcefulness and control.

Winter Trees[10] received a considerably less dramatic response when the American edition appeared in 1972. Ted Hughes's preface to the volume promised that the poems were "all out of a batch from which the *Ariel* poems were more or less arbitrarily chosen . . . all composed in the last nine months of Sylvia Plath's life." Perhaps because *Ariel* had already been ransacked for every clinical symptom or verbal notation that might explain Plath's motivation for suicide, *Winter Trees* was treated to a more critical perspective. To read Plath's oeuvre as a protracted suicide note, a "melancholy long withdrawing roar," was to misread the work, critics of *Winter Trees* insisted. These poems were said to map out a territory that was "unique, harrowing, yet always controllable; and which [bred] its own distinctive landscapes: 'The wet dawn inks are doing their blue dissolve.' "[11] Praised for their detached control of language, variety of tones, and introduction of a principle of charity and tenderness, the poems of *Winter Trees* avoided a self-indulgent cashing in on misfortunes. As one critic rather wryly suggested about this new focus: "There can be no question but that Sylvia

Plath fulfilled the cruellest of the conditions that we, like petty gods, demand of our artistic martyrs: that they should convince us of their indifference to the regard we will subsequently fix upon them."[12]

Since the appearance of *Winter Trees* there have been two distinct trends in Plath criticism. After a brief lament for the legendary victimage and self-mutilation in the poetry, feminists have begun to explore Plath's muted but powerful views of maternal and domestic experiences. As Louise Bernikow points out, Plath legitimized "poems of the great female indoors," but she did so with terrible ambivalence. "Paradoxically, it is out of her domestic relationships and experiences, which she came to feel were stifling, even killing her, that the majority of her most powerful, most successful work was created."[13]

A second critical trend has avoided reductive suicidal or feminist categories and instead redirects Plath interest toward the mythologies behind her vision: "she demonstrates in her poetry how the mythic, in its immemorial pre-Christian, even pre-Graeco-Roman dress of birth and death, seasonal and vegetative changes, moon and sea phases, and archaic concept of beginnings and endings, is the only way to express the cosmos. . . ."[14] Karl Malkoff sets the stage for mythical interpretations of Plath by claiming that confessional poetry should not be read as a battery of "true facts" disclosing the poet's life:

> It is the myth of the self, which reaches inward to the archetypal patterns of the collective unconscious, and outward to the shared experiences of the poet's society, rather than the objective actions of the arbitrarily isolated individual, that forms the focus of Confessional poetry.[15]

Myths proliferate, whether they be the "paradoxical vision of her deathly paradise," the "generous humanity" she betrays in her death fixation,[16] or the "mythic drama of Greek necessity" acted out in a handful of late poems.[17] Even the social-sexual conflict in her short stories becomes a battle between the Apollonian and Dionysian principles, with Plath paying allegiance to the "repressed chthonic forces of darkness and death."[18]

But even goodwilled attempts to widen the scope for Plath interpretation can be insidious. Revisionist views often arrive at the same predetermined point as the old criticism: the focus on death. Malkoff ends his discussion of the poet's assertion of freedom by saying that "creation provides relief, but, for Sylvia

Plath in any case, only death provides final relief."[19] Ted Hughes suggests a foreclosed view of Plath when he discusses her problems in writing the short stories: "She had an instant special pass to the center, and no choice but to use it. She could no more make up an objective ingenious narrative than she could collect up all the letters in her handwriting, where nearly every symbol seems to sit perched over a gulf" (*JP*, 5).

While some critics are able to restate the problem of Plath's ambivalent feelings in "Daddy" with increased clarity, they discover a quality in her writing that still is expressed in only the most equivocal terminology. In such a way Ted Hughes described the nature of her talent: "This lightning pass through all the walls of the maze was her real genius. Instant confrontation with the most central, unacceptable things" (*JP*, 5). The new way to deal with Plath's poetic contradictions, it appears, is not to clinicize, but mythicize them, encouraging yet another form of deflection, transcendence. Death in the poems is sanctified as "the final relief," the "anti-Edenic vision," or viewed as a desirable "sweeping away of identity, a melding into the primal/impersonal."[20] Plath is even identified with the devouring Terrible Mother from whom she begs a transformation into a "purer existence, a terrible rebirth."[21]

A close review of *Ariel* and *Winter Trees* is the only antidote for contemporary criticism that continues to oversimplify her imaginative force while it avoids describing her poetic complexity. Both volumes dramatize the same tension, an emotional range expressed by two personifications in the poem "Death and Co.":

> Two, of course there are two.
> It seems perfectly natural now— (*A*, 28)

In this poem, rival aspects of death—energy and inertia—are actually rival aspects of life. They are accompanied by a competitive power that is celebrated throughout Plath's late poems. Both elements have grown familiar to the speaker in the poem. One figure—the "one who never looks up, whose eyes are lidded / And balled, like Blake's"—attempts to seduce the poet with the persuasion of simple, static perfection. He argues for the complete beauty of a "thing in itself":

> He tells me how badly I photograph,
> He tells me how sweet

The babies look in their hospital
Icebox, a simple

Frill at the neck,
Then the flutings of their Ionian
Death-gowns,
Then two little feet.
He does not smile or smoke. (*A*, 28)

His "beak claps sidewise," so the poet eludes his grasp. Vigor, dazzle, and seductive need are advertisements for the other image of death. Actively showy, autoerotic, this other character's self-spectacle begs for attention, not for necrophilia:

His hair long and plausive.
Bastard
Masturbating a glitter,
He wants to be loved. (*A*, 28)

The unresolved antagonism of these two figures suggests the larger tension of Plath's late poems: the pull between the "lithic impulse" toward homeostasis or diminishment, and the energy of dramatic performance.[22] The most startling poems enlarge upon the rivalry described in "Death and Co.," but do not attempt to resolve the tension between stasis and its counter impulse, a measured demonstration of energy. The poems either argue the wisdom of the first image—comfortable inertia and diminishment—or opt for the arrogant performing energy of the second. In *Ariel* and *Winter Trees*, Plath chooses to describe mobility, not choice, between the poles of passivity and theatrical display. Rhythmically, tonally, and imagistically, she cultivates a larger sensibility that she began to explore in the transitional poems of *Crossing the Water*. Now Plath's early insights into the poetic process and the dramatic possibilities for the self mature. She moves easily between the simple belief that "there is no great love, only tenderness," and a yearning for the "merciless churn of hooves," the drive of pistons, or the gala spectacle of diverse performances.

In sum, Plath creates a literary value out of poetic ambivalence, a state some biographical sleuths might call schizophrenia. The personae of these late poems actually dramatize the process of isolation, fragmentation, often disappearance, extending the earlier self-deprecating irony of "Disquieting Muses" or "I Am Vertical." Plath not only defines but sustains an authority of diminishment, particularly in her bee sequence. Inertia becomes no simple alternative to coercive authority but the dominant mode of power. Finally, an important group of poems addressed to her children completes the women's legacy introduced in *The Colossus* and continued in *Crossing the Water*. These poems also perfect, in technique and argument, the case for protection against total disillusionment.

Yet within the same group of late poems a counteraction renews Plath's interest in motion and energy: "Navel cords, blue-red and lucent, / Shriek from my belly like arrows, and these I ride." Both texture of language and construction of verse support the poet's attempt, through self-spectacle, to experience pure motion. Developments in rhythm, rhyme, and imagery all seem to reproduce this energy of process, of expanding in order to contract, and vice versa. Words themselves are "echoes travelling / Off from the center like horses." In "Lady Lazarus" and "Fever 103°," Plath's performing self at once searches contemporary culture for new experience, yet takes protective recourse from further personal vulnerability and confusion in poetic technique. Her final performances dissolve all the "old whore selves" described previously. They create a new shape and value for pure energy as it coexists with forms of inertia.

It is ironic that in her last poems—ones that gained her the reputation as pure, Pyrrhic victim—Plath's chief concern is to carve a space and develop a form of control for the largest possible range of expressive acts. She is bored by eternity and pays homage to a child's simplicity that is "right, like a well-done sum." She laments her inability to protect the child from indifference and disappointments. Then, as an embittered lover and wife, she hurls lively and ingenious expletives at her betrayer ("Hogwallow," "Mudsump," "Fido Littlesoul"). She flirts with the chilly perfection of death, adores "black statements" and the featureless "silences of another order." Yet she imagines death as a surprise birthday present one moment, suicide as a striptease act the next. She champions tenderness but considers marriage an institution hawked by advertising hype. She admits that myths are disillusioning, that the world is "blood hot and personal," yet she recommends eating its brutality "like Plato's afterbirth." Within this imaginatively elastic range of expression, Plath displays an uncanny mobility throughout *Ariel* and *Winter Trees*.

A Drama of Human Scale: "Is there no way out of the mind?"

The subjects of *Winter Trees* and *Ariel* are earmarked as Plath's own: beekeeping, domestic chores, bad marriage, family deaths, suicide attempts, childbearing and maternal love, even a threatened loss of identity. Despite a new congruity of language and content, the poems' provinces are turned curiously inward: "This is the light of the mind, cold and planetary. / The trees of the mind are black. The light is blue." (*A*, 41). Or:

> I am inhabited by a cry.
> Nightly it flaps out
> Looking, with its hooks, for something to love.
>
> I am terrified by this dark thing
> That sleeps in me;
> All day I feel its soft, feathery turnings, its malignity.
> (*A*, 16)

The poems dramatize the vague and undefined, but now in terms of a mental landscape that has no tangible equivalent like the house at Point Shirley, or the mussels of Rock Harbor:

> The womb
> Rattles its pod, the moon
> Discharges itself from the tree with nowhere to go.
>
> My landscape is a hand with no lines,
> The roads bunched to a knot,
> The knot myself, . . . (*WT*, 34)

As Alvarez has said of Plath's later poems, "the more vivid and imaginative the details, the more resolutely she turns them inwards. The more objective they seem, the more subjective they, in fact, become."[23] "I live here," the poet herself insists about the bleak mindscape.

The poem "Apprehensions" presents such a subjective, emotional geography. "This is what I am made of," the poet announces as she displays four graphic views of the mind. We progress from one to the other, from indifference through raw vulnerability back to a cold and final effacement, as if we were viewing four stage sets glimpsed through an antique stereopticon. In the first scene the poet describes her medium for creating, the great blank of imagination: a white wall or tabula rasa "above which the sky creates itself— / Infinite, green, utterly untouchable," and utterly removed from anything human. By the second glimpse, the wall is clawed and bloody:

> Is there no way out of the mind?
> Steps at my back spiral into a well.
> There are not trees or birds in this world,
> There is only a sourness. (*WT*, 3)

A restlessness, an undercurrent of vulnerability, informs the third view:

> A red fist, opening and closing,
> Two grey, papery bags—
> This is what I am made of, this, and a terror
> Of being wheeled off under crosses and a rain of pieties.
> (*WT*, 3)

It seems that the poetic imagination defies precise emotional equivalents: the red wall "winces continually," a "sourness" pervades. Each view of the mind is curiously static, graphically fixed. Each is an aftermath, a passive state that finally suggests total oblivion:

> On a black wall, unidentifiable birds
> Swivel their heads and cry.
> There is no talk of immortality among these!
> Cold blanks approach us:
> They move in a hurry. (*WT*, 3)

It is the emotional precision of an indelible mood, rather than description of an explicit event, that characterizes a number of late poems. "I lie / Whole / On a whole world I cannot touch," she says. Or the poet tries to answer her own question, "Is there no way out of the mind?" Location is simply "a place of force," somewhere "hung out over a dead drop," while hills "step off into whiteness." Mother and child meet in a "haloey radiance that seems to breathe" with the imperceptible energy felt in *The Colossus*, but now far less threatening. Pain itself is no more specific than the "small skulls, the smashed blue hills, the godawful hush." "Absence" grows beside a child without a father.

Throughout the last volumes, Plath poses—and repeats—questions, then leaves them unanswered: "The air is a mill of hooks / Questions without answers." "What am I to make of these contradictions?"; "Who has dismembered us?"; "What was she doing when it blew in?"; or "Who are these pietas?" she

asks. Even her rhetorical questions demand a profound understanding of despair: "O my God, what am I / That these late
mouths should cry open / In a forest of frost, in a dawn of
cornflowers" (*A*, 19). As if to suggest her indifference to a world
"out of the mind," she begins her poems in the middle of things,
leaves situations tantalizingly undefined. "Stopped Dead," for
example, begins:

> A squeal of brakes.
> Or is it a birth cry?
> And here we are, hung out over the dead drop
> Uncle, pants factory Fatso, millionaire! (*WT*, 17)

Most insistent are questions about her own dissolving and
forming identity: "It happens. Will it go on?— / My mind a rock,
/ No fingers to grip, no tongue . . ." (*A*, 77). "No use, no use,
now, begging Recognize!," she says in "Amnesiac." "There is
nothing to do with such a beautiful blank but smooth it."

Sometimes an ominous energy intrudes on the atmo-
spheric vagueness: the "shadow of ring-doves" chanting, the
"atrocity of sunsets," or the "sound of poisons." A "mind like a
ring" slides shut on "some quick thing / The constriction killing
me also" in "Rabbit Catcher." The skill of the poem is not the
metaphor of the hunt that describes a courtship (the tenor
reserved until the final stanza), but the mounting fear and
struggle that are dramatized in the poem's progression ("I felt
hands round a teamug, dull, blunt"). We participate in a nar-
rowing, a smothering ("there was only one place to get to"), and
finally entrapment:

> It was a place of force—
> The wind gagging my mouth with my own blown hair,
> Tearing off my voice, and the sea
> Blinding me with its lights, . . .
> . . . .
> The paths narrowed into the hollow.
> And the snares almost effaced themselves—
> Zeros, shutting on nothing,
>
> Set close, like birth pangs.
> The absence of shrieks
> Made a hole in the hot day, a vacancy. (*WT*, 35)

Spare images describe the frozen feelings of a couple in
"Event":

> How the elements solidify!—

The moonlight, that chalk cliff
In whose rift we lie

Back to back. (*WT*, 16)

Stars are "ineradicable, hard." "Apple bloom ices the night." A child in a crib is static as a woodcut, "his little face is carved in pained, red wood." The speaker walks in the same ring, a "groove of old faults, deep and bitter" in this landscape of estrangement. Yet, in the course of the poem, "elements solidify" as slowly and painfully as do the estranged emotions of the couple who only meet momentarily: "Love cannot come here. / A black gap discloses itself. / . . . The dark is melting. We touch like cripples" (*WT*, 16).

The collective atmosphere of many late poems suggests Plath's preoccupation with various forms of passivity. From early attempts to rhetorically accept the limitations of self to later emotional experiments with self-effacing speakers, Plath has been hinting at a new valuation for passivity. The authority she gives passivity does not uphold the old a priori qualifications about female nature, psychology, imagination, or intellect. Rather, her power of absence or inertia is distinct from its pejorative gender-assigned status.

"Birthday Present" is a good example of passivity reevaluated, for it describes the speaker's physical inactivity yet her imaginative forays. Although the subject of the poem is death as a surprise gift, this fact is never made clear to the speaker who imagines herself being reacted to, talked about, by a powerful anonymous force. The actual birthday present remains hidden and seems less important than the speaker's process of first discovering, then exploring, her range of feelings about the undeclared contents of the present. She gathers strength to move from polite silence to impolite declaration, becoming alternately impetuous, assertive, even cajoling. At first she merely asks for a description of the present: "Has it breasts, has it edges?" Then she wants specifics about its identity: "I would not mind if it was bones, or a pearl button." Still *it* remains only a vague motion (a "shimmering") or a brilliance (a "gleam" or "glaze" with "mirror variety").

Gradually she becomes recklessly impatient ("Can you not see I do not mind what it is"), guessing that it must be a "tusk" or a "ghost-column." In trying to adopt it as familiar domestic decor ("let us sit down to it . . . let us eat our last supper at it, like

a hospital plate"), she imagines being overtaken by lofty figures
from liturgical history, and mocked for her trivializing domestic-
ity:

> When I am quiet at my cooking I feel it looking, I
>   feel it thinking
>
> "Is this the one I am to appear for,
> Is this the elect one, the one with black eye-pits
>   and a scar?
>
> Measuring the flour, cutting off the surplus,
> Adhering to rules, to rules, to rules.
>
> Is this the one for the annunciation?
> My god, what a laugh!" (A, 42)

The more insistent she grows, the more the object remains a
mute and dazzling presence:

> There is this one thing I want today, and only you can give it
>   to me.
>
> It stands at my window, big as the sky.
> It breathes from my sheets, the cold dead centre
>
> Where spilt lives congeal and stiffen to history. (A, 44)

Now she becomes impertinent: she demands it whole, not
piecemeal, not by word of mouth, nor by mail. As the speaker
employs various emotional maneuvers, domestic images ac-
cumulate to create a dramatic terror. The ending is unresolved,
ambiguous, and deftly ironic understatement:

> If it were death
>
> I would admire the deep gravity of it, its timeless eyes.
> I would know you were serious.
>
> There would be a nobility then, there would be a birthday.
> And the knife not carve, but enter
>
> Pure and clean as the cry of a baby,
> And the universe slide from my side. (A, 44)

The hypothetical verb tense—the speaker's willful ignorance
that the nature of the present is death—dramatically exaggerates both the fear and the actual seriousness of the present.

Passivity as a power and a strategy for defining the self
(glimpsed in "Birthday Present") is used in a number of ways in
the late poems. Female figures dissolve, grow isolated in their
"wombs of marble," even disappear altogether. In another kind

of domestic chronicle, Plath praises the small constructiveness of motherhood. The mother-speaker pares away any hyperbolic hopes for her children. She knows at once her own separateness, knows that grand promises are but great disillusionments, that all one can hope for is to be "mirror safe" from abstractions and from the stain of dogmatic beliefs. Lastly, and perhaps most explicitly, the six poems of Plath's bee sequence, with their focus on the regal queen mother, offer the most unified statement of a new, authoritative valuation for passivity.

A Portrait of Woman: "the smell of years burning, here in the kitchen"

In the women figures of the last volumes, Plath gives conscious authority to an energy of limitation:

> Enigmatical,
>
> Shifting my clarities.
> . . . .
> My visibilities hide.
> I gleam like a mirror. ("Purdah," *WT*, 40)

No longer does she idealize mythical women ensconced like the Lorelei in their implausible perfections. Nor does she petition the stern directors and silent mothers with unsure voice. Now a conscious antagonism pervades the poems, resulting in ambiguous dramatic monologues or in slow dissolution of women's identity. As Harriet Rosenstein says, "She takes the standard deprecation of female 'subjectivity' and turns it into triumph."[24] Several images of women suggest that the poet is at once victim and victimizer of herself. Still it is Plath's elusive energy that triumphs over any single or collective portrait of woman in the late poems. Persistent passivity dominates any authoritative pose: "Each female figure is a facet of Plath, a momentary clarity, but none totally defines her, nor, for that matter, do all of them taken together. Thus, her women emerge with the authority of long familiarity but their limitations are necessarily her own."[25] The elusiveness she seeks provides her protection against further vulnerability, yet still allows her a measured control of energy.

One group of poems shows the variety of Plath's uses of passivity: the growing solitude of her personae ("The Rival," "The Other"); the dismemberment or fragmentation of the woman-figure into a series of rag-doll parts ("The Courage of

Shutting Up," "Purdah"); and finally the complete disappearance of the woman—"This is a case without a body. / The body does not come into it at all" (*WT*, 14).

A "growing isolation of the persona"[26] in several poems is an alienation more subtly felt than explicitly defined. Often it is described with no more detail than "my distractions, my pallors." "Cold glass, how you insert yourself / Between myself and myself," she says of that vague other whose "stolen horses, the fornications / Circle a womb of marble." In "Amnesiac" she warns: "O sister, mother, wife / Sweet Lethe is my life. / I am never, never, never coming home!" (*WT*, 20). The speaker in "Medusa" rages, "Off, off, eely tentacle! / There is nothing between us":

> Who do you think you are?
> A Communion wafer? Blubbery Mary?
> I shall take no bite of your body,
> Bottle in which I live,
>
> Ghastly Vatican. (*A*, 40)

It is sometimes true that for the poet "courage lies in living with the knowledge of outrage and not seeking the relief of utterance."[27] Occasionally her action is no verbal protest, no clean breast of dissatisfactions, but a silent performance of parts. The parts assume an authority of victimization over the weak protest of words, the bombast of rhetoric. In "The Detective" a woman's disappearance is no single act of murder, but a slow dissolution of various critical parts of the body—mouth, breasts, "then the dry wood, the gates, / The brown motherly furrows," and finally "the whole estate." When communication departs, sexuality and nurture follow, until at last the entire woman is gone:

> This is a case without a body.
> The body does not come into it at all.
>
> It is a case of vaporization. (*WT*, 14)

But her absence, her void, is turned into a cagey elusiveness. For years the woman has destroyed evidence of her disaffection. She has remained mute and passive, meticulously covering her tracks ("This is the smell of years burning, here in the kitchen / These are the deceits, tacked up like family photographs"). Her motives are too elusive for those professional fact finders, Holmes and Watson, who can only describe the obvious: the smell of polish in the house and the plush carpets. Lacking visible evidence, those sleuths are completely hamstrung, unable to speculate or discern psychological motives. Foiled by the woman's disappearance they can merely fumble about and mutter by way of excuse:

> We walk on air, Watson.
> There is only the moon, emblamed in phosphorous.
> There is only a crow in a tree. Make notes. (*WT*, 14)

The process of arrival at a state of willed and cultivated passivity is dramatized by "The Courage of Shutting Up." In this poem various vital parts of the self—the brain, eyes, tongue, even the "tits on mermaids and two-legged dream girls"—are now detached and, item by item, stashed away:

> Do not worry about the eyes—
>
> They may be white and shy, they are no stool pigeons,
> The death rays folded like flags
> Of a country no longer heard of,
> An obstinate independency
> Insolvent among the mountains. (*WT*, 9)

Animal imagery describes the various senses: the mouth is a "line pink and quiet, a worm, basking"; the tongue is an "antique billhook," a self-incriminating weapon:

> It has nine tails, it is dangerous.
> And the noise it flays from the air once it gets going!
> (*WT*, 8)

All the silenced senses defer to the revolving discs of the brain that are "asking to be heard." The mind, likened to a great surgeon now dwindled to a sleazy tattoo artist, engraves "over and over, the same blue grievances." Consciousness is at a premium. The brain's energy is the one continuous motion, the needle always "journeying in the groove," always in motion like the "muzzles of cannon." Passivity may be desirable, but it is nevertheless a very tenuous state of consciousness.

In "Purdah," the poet again superbly gathers her vulnerabilities into what she calls that "sheath of impossibles." Passive, gleaming like a mirror, she reflects the bridegroom. Rarefied and hidden like Indian women of higher castes, she is veiled to all but him:

> I am his.
> Even in his

Absence, I
Revolve in my
Sheath of impossibles,

Priceless and quiet
Among these parakeets, macaws! (*WT*, 41)

Once she has admitted her status as a "small, jeweled doll," she
recovers her senses and frees herself gradually by a measured,
dramatically timed release of energy:

Attendants of the eyelash!
I shall unloose
One feather, like the peacock.

Attendants of the lip!
I shall unloose
One note

. . . .
Attendants!
And at his next step
I shall unloose

I shall unloose—
From the small jeweled
Doll he guards like a heart—

The lioness,
The shriek in the bath,
The cloak of holes. (*WT*, 41–42)

The controlled calculation of the last three lines shifts the tone
significantly from sarcasm to the deadly serious, deadly because
the reference is to the murder of Agamemnon by Clytemnestra.
Gradually, the speaker has gathered up enough energy to turn
her limitations into strengths. Where once she might have been
the submissive doll, she is now the lioness. Where previously
there was docile silence, now there is a shriek. Where there was
the customary covering of the face (purdah), there is nothing
but a "cloak of holes."

Not content with the stereotype of the victim, the poet
energetically celebrates her dissolution in these poems. She
begins in stark terror, realizing how much of her identity has
been jeopardized: "If you only knew how the veils were killing
my days. / . . . the million / Probable motes that tick the years off
my life" (*A*, 43). A frequent defense or studied defiance exercises her full emotional mobility:

I have suffered the atrocity of sunsets.

Scorched to the root
My red filaments burn and stand, a hand of wires.

Now I break up in pieces that fly about like clubs.
A wind of such violence
Will tolerate no bystanding: I must shriek.
("Elm," *A*, 15)

Some protection against pain and vulnerability is gained by choosing to remain passive and unknown—the case without a body, a vacancy, a handful of burning red filaments, the bearer of a cloak of holes—but only if one can remove the taint of socially assigned passivity from these states and dramatically redefine the derogatory quality. Plath continues her reevaluation of passivity, perhaps more philosophically, in several of the poems about mothers and children.

A Small Constructiveness: "how I would like to believe in tenderness"

While *Ariel* has been likened to the last act of a revenge tragedy, *Winter Trees* is said to be "cut to a more human scale, a complete domestic drama."[28] Both volumes offer a cluster of subdued poems on a very human scale, ones in which Plath attempts to find not a grand transcendence from her own pain but a simple stay against total bleakness. "Mystic," "Brasilia," "You're," "Child," "For a Fatherless Son," "By Candlelight," "Nick and the Candlestick," and "Mary's Song" are some of her most directly despairing, yet candidly searching pieces, in *Winter Trees* and *Ariel*. They depart from the raging passions that have so stigmatized Plath and treat what Vendler calls the "small constructiveness of motherhood."[29] And they do so with a remarkable artistry, a matured sense of balance and timing. They portray a mother's feeling of powerful love for, yet vulnerable separateness from, her children's lives. With wistful despair, a speaker in "The Moon and the Yew Tree" says:

The moon is my mother. . . .
. . . .
How I would like to believe in tenderness—
The face of the effigy, gentled by candles,
Bending, on me in particular, its mild eyes.

I have fallen a long way. (*A*, 41)

The mother's hope for her children begs for the familiar "life no higher than the grasstops / Or the hearts of sheep." She wants for them a simple, factual existence where one is mirror-safe from the Grand Illusions (and consequent Great Letdown) of the Power and the Glory; from that "bastard masturbating a glitter"; from the "heavy notion of Evil." She wants for them an everyday life where "meaning leaks from the molecules." "Is there no great love, only tenderness?" she pleads. Plath wants no "pietas," no "stains" from the great cathedrals, no baggage of false hopes loaded onto those who have been redeemed by the "dove's annihilation."

She asks repeatedly for a remedy for seeing and feeling too much, for "having one too many dimensions to enter," as she said in *Crossing the Water*. In "Brasilia" the mother offers up an inverse prayer for her child to be spared the awesome Redemption—what she calls "that old story"—as well as her own complicated pain. For her children there must be respite from totally using ("wasting") oneself in ill-starred idealism:

> Not this troublous
> Wringing of hands, this dark
> Ceiling without a star. ("Child," WT, 18)

Comforting theories offer only a momentary distraction from inevitable despair, for the "sack of black" is "everywhere, tight, tight," according to the mother. She says to her child:

> But right now you are dumb.
> And I love your stupidity,
> The blind mirror of it. I look in
> And find no face but my own, and you think that's funny.
> It is good for me
>
> To have you grab my nose, a ladder rung.
> One day you may touch what's wrong—
> The small skulls, the smashed blue hills, the godawful hush.
> Till then your smiles are found money.
> ("For a Fatherless Son," WT, 33)

She feels "nearly extinct" with the weight of meaning imposed by the gray Magi who tote with them "the star, the old story," who gobble the "pill of the Communion tablet." For one moment, however, she is overheard asking:

> What glove
>
> What leatheriness
> Has protected
>
> Me from that shadow . . .
> ("Thalidomide, WT, 23)

"It is a terrible thing to be so open," the Wife in *Three Women* claims, asking: "How long can I be a wall keeping the wind off? / How long can I be gentling the sun with the shade of my hand, / Intercepting the blue bolts of a cold moon?"[30]

The mother cares not a whit for the rare or the exceptional throughout these poems. She admires the kind of life represented by the dark pheasant who paces oddly through the uncut grasses:

> I am not mystical: it isn't
> As if I thought it had a spirit.
> It is simply in its element. (*WT*, 28)

The pheasant's rarity is in its ease of movement, crossing and recrossing the hill, as kingly as a child in a mother's arm, wrapped in "rough, dumb country stuff." What is important to Plath's mother-speaker here is a simple brass paperweight (a rather tenuous distraction against the winter's night), the sun blooming like a geranium, the heart that "has not stopped," the "haloey glow" of a single candle's power, or "what green stars can make it to our gate." These are the tangible realities tendered to the child by the mother who knows the indifference of the world the child must enter ("a sky like a pig's backside, an utter lack of attention").

It should be clear that Plath is not preaching the old saw of women's limitations here, the cutting of the domestic cloth. Rather, her hopes for her children reclaim those derided "woman preferences" now as positive wishes for clarity and precision. She wants no contamination by the patrilineal world of male gods and "lamp-headed Platos" with their power-mongering legacy. After all, the father's world of the Magi is but a comically defunct backdrop ("People with torsos of steel / Winged elbows and eyeholes") against which the small and immediate constructiveness of the motherworld carries on: "In the lane I meet sheep and wagons, / Red earth, motherly blood."

Through a series of poignant questions, the poem "Mystic" makes a plea for the anticlimactic. The matter-of-fact lives of the "tame flower nibblers," humble and commonplace, are much to be desired over the glittering lives of the curious. Like the poet, the latter never seem to be granted answers. Visionaries, Plath would suggest, have no room for the everyday, no place for mere tenderness after the consuming fires of "Great Love":

> Once one has seen God, what is the remedy?

Once one has been seized up

Without a part left over,
Not a toe, not a finger, and used,
Used utterly, in the sun's conflagrations, the stains
That lengthen from ancient cathedrals
What is the remedy? (WT, 4)

Plath knows that a few, brief sensual moments—the "dead smell of sun on wood cabins," the feel of salt-stiffened sails—are more sobering realities than the misleading promise of miracles. Miracles only disappoint, for the grand finale of all great beliefs is unwarranted complexity, dashed illusions, and the misuse of simple human warmth. So in "Mystic" as well as "Pheasant," what Plath admires is the undramatic, scaled-down vision that is held by:

. . . the ones

Whose hopes are so low they are comfortable—
The humpback in her small, washed cottage
Under the spokes of the clematis.
Is there no great love, only tenderness? (WT, 4–5)

But admiration of the life of limited expectations is not enough. Barbara Hardy has already shown how one of these poems of maternal love, "Nick and the Candlestick," orchestrates humor and incongruous imagery with the mother's love and fear in order to enlarge a sense of personal terror.[31] The miner's cave and cold poison breath, the Nativity scene with mother and child, the rugs, roses, and the last of "Victoriana," the child, the "one / Solid spaces lean on" are brought together with a precision and timing that neither detracts from the mother and child, nor creates an unjustified hyperbole. Hardy quite movingly describes the internal coherence of the imagery, a tribute to Plath's control and skill with her medium:

The poet loves and praises, but in no innocent or ideal glorying.
. . . The expansion moves firmly into and out of a twentieth-century world, a medieval poetry, ritual, and painting, and the earliest Christ-story, and this holds for its pains and its loving. . . .
It uses—or, better, feels for—the myth of the Redemption not in order to idealize the particulars but rather to revise and qualify the myth to transplant it again cheerfully, to praise only after a long hard look at the worst. The love and faith and praise are there, wrung out and achieved against the grain, against the odds. (H, 169)

In the background of the poem "Morning Song" lurks the familiar universe of blank elements, blank windows that swallow "dull stars." This particular poem records a mother's loving surprise at the awesome separateness of her child:

> Our voices echo, magnifying your arrival. New statue.
> In a drafty museum, your nakedness
> Shadows our safety. We stand round blankly as walls.
> (*A*, 1)

It succeeds because it presents the child's existence as relatively uncontaminated by the mother's pain and gloomy foreknowledge about the world. Helpless in the face of the child's strange promise, she locates her own existence in those forming and dissolving elements of the universe:

> I'm no more your mother
> Than the cloud that distills a mirror to reflect
>   its own slow
> Effacement at the wind's hand.
> . . . .
> A far sea moves in my ear. (*A*, 1)

If the sexual love of the mother is responsible for the child's existence, so too is that solid slap to the footsoles delivered by the attending midwife. The "bald cry" of the child that takes its place among the "elements" (stanza one) foreshadows the mother's realm, a stanza later, of amorphous clouds, wind, and the "far sea." Counterpoint images—the rough horsehair simplicity of the child versus the Christian and classical references, or the Nativity "baby in the barn" versus the mother's child—demonstrate an intentional balancing. Such dialectic suggests the sure control of a poet who can move easily between the abstract and the concrete particulars with a tolerantly large consciousness (*H*, 171). In the end, as the mother's dull stars are swallowed into blankness, the child offers her a momentary respite from inevitable effacement:

> And now you try
> Your handful of notes;
> The clear vowels rise like balloons. (*A*, 1)

In her mother-child poems, Plath does not always find images as apt as "Morning Song" for describing the intermingling of the mother's pain and the child's promise. In the seven drafts of worksheets for "Thalidomide,"[32] the poet is unable to "carpenter / A space for the thing I am given." She finds no apt image for portraying her pain, but shows us instead a gradual process of discovering an absence bereft of expression. All exclamations and overtly dramatic references (bloodclots, abortion, sin, guilt) are pared away from the early drafts. More powerful is the sense of vagueness captured in "that shadow," "the thing," and "blood caul of absences." Gradually the child's existence is overwhelmed by the mother's own pain and hopelessness to become a "perilous thin dark fruit," or the "white spit / Of indifference." At first "smiles and perfections," the child soon borrows an undefined sense of dread belonging to the poet-mother and to the malforming drug of the title.

Curiously, the first half of the poem remains unchanged after the first of the seven worksheets. However, the following six drafts show, in the second half of each, the poet's increasing inability to discover an adequately descriptive image for the intermingling of the mother's promise and the child's pain. Although several dramatically violent expletives are omitted ("Nothingness. Black-ox!" "Unholy light," or "moon-smoke"), the wider dilemma that undercuts many later poems remains. Can fear of absence and void be staved off by the child's small physicality, "one candle's power worth of comfort," or a brass candelabra? Two final images of disintegration—revolving and falling fruits, and the cracking glass—seem to answer Plath's question negatively, at least in the poem "Thalidomide" which ends with a hint of disaster for the aspiring poet as well as the child: "the image / flees and aborts like dropped mercury."

The Bee Sequence: "but I have a self to recover"

In her six poems about the art of beekeeping,[33] Plath attempts to "recover a self" by exploring the various operations of power within the apiary. The highly organized, self-regulating hive becomes her model for conceptualizing human experience by reexamining power in its many shapes (seller, keeper, worker-drudge), or in its startling absence (queen). The poems suggest that there is a certain truth to psychologist David Holbrook's claim about Plath: "Be(e)ing seems a threat to one who doesn't know how to be."[34]

We have observed Plath's imaginative investigations of inertia, her growing sensitivity to a belief in factual limitation.

As early as her Cambridge Manuscript she realized that "though the mind like an oyster labors on and on, / a grain of sand is all we have." In *Crossing the Water* poems, the "Duchess of Nothing" announced boldly that "I housekeep in Time's gut-end / Among emmets and mollusks." Then she compared the task of mothering to the work of a cloud that distills a mirror in order to reflect its effacement by the wind. She attends to the moth-breath and horsehair simplicity of a small child. Too familiar with her own abstract truth and the "smashed blue hills" of her adult life, the mother "carpenters" a niche with her words for the child's "vowels like balloons." Her women personae are isolated, dismembered, even disappearing, but in each case, she resolves her investigation of passivity with a gesture of elusiveness that becomes her insurance against unwitting pain and vulnerability.

Now in the bee sequence Plath makes her most definitive and ambitious statement about passivity. She suggests that the absence of authoritative power is a form of strength and control, not merely a socially designated trait.[35] Her focus includes only a few relationships and facts: the beekeeper's inept control over the apiary, the deceived workers and virgins, and the royal captive, that bare old queen in hiding whose productive reign over her hive has drawn to a close, but who still remains the focal point both in and outside the colony. While Plath explores the concept of power central to the hive community, her focus is on the ambivalence of the queen. Through this paradoxical symbol of power, she questions the implausible status of heroine in the special category of queen bee, and hence the complexities of a woman artist. For the queen's existence represents a kind of feminocide, a double-edged tribute to uniqueness best described by the workings of apiculture.

Beekeepers know that the queen's world is one moment of terribly limited splendor circumscribed by sacrifice: she has given up daylight, a voice in major hive decisions, such as swarming, freedom of flight, gathering the nectar of flowers, even some power in the matter of her own life or death—all for her worshiped prison of procreation. Her status is deceptive, for the real mind power and occupational unity of the hive reside in the liaison of thousands of short-lived workers who cower in their disguise of mediocrity. The queen, a symbol of ambiguous achievement, becomes the central means by which Plath examines the contradictory workings of power and the dimensions of the poetic self that might be recovered in the aesthetic process.[36]

From the point of view of the speaker, the six bee poems describe a curve of maturation in their dramatic movement from youthful naiveté and disillusionment ("Beekeeper's Daughter") to vigorous exploration of contradictions inherent in power ("Arrival of the Bee Box," "The Bee Meeting," and "Stings"), and finally to a grasp of a new mode of power ("Wintering," "Swarm").[37]

To begin to puzzle out the complex intermingling of life and death in the bee poems, we must first take Plath at her word:

> . . . but I
> Have a self to recover, a queen.
> Is she dead, is she sleeping?
> Where has she been? (A, 62)

The narrative of the first poem in the series, "The Beekeeper's Daughter," is quite simple. The poet-child learns something about the pain and ecstasy of the "dark pa[i]rings" of sexuality within the bee kingdom. Her first glimpse of the apiarian world reveals the "maestro of bees" tending with ceremonial finesse the "many-breasted hives." She is fearful yet awed by the lush, androgynous sexuality in the miniature "garden of mouthings":

> The great corollas dilate, peeling back their silks.
> . . . .
> Trumpet-throats open to the beaks of birds.
> The Golden Rain Tree drips its powders down. (Col., 73)

As she looks within the hive and contemplates with childish delight the queen bee's immortal reign over such uncontained fertility, she makes a rather stark discovery:

> . . . The air is rich.
> Here is a queenship no mother can contest—
>
> A fruit that's death to taste: dark flesh, dark parings.
> . . . .
> I set my eye to a hole-mouth and meet an eye
> Round, green, disconsolate as a tear. (Col., 73, 74)

Looking for a reflection of herself—and the eye-I pun seems intentional—she finds only adult disillusionment and the unexpected complexity of a law that is central to the apiary. For the queen must suffer a uniquely regal motherhood. She neither directs nor participates in any of her subject's riches of cross-pollination. (The "uncontestable" queenship begins to sound slightly ironic.) For to one who never sees daylight, who has no bodily provisions for work, the virgin-workers' world of activity is really "death to taste." Literally, the fruit of flower (one meaning of "dark flesh, dark parings") is forbidden to this figurehead who remains ill-fated, hidden, and otherwise useless in her singular mission of motherhood.

Particularly significant about the queen's mission is its tragic nuptial flight, a blend of ecstasy and tragedy, life and death. It is in reference to this event that her first impressions are revised. She anticipates, first of all, the identification of father-maestro and the queen's mate, then the delusive power of sexual conquest and finally the union of death and sexuality in the remainder of the poem: "Father, bridegroom," she says, "the queen bee marries the winter of your year."

Apiarists know that the mate of the queen—chosen from thousands of suitors who pursue her high-spiraling nuptial flight—lives for a single moment of delight. But in this instant, the "dark pa[i]ring" is his undoing, the "winter of his year." For when he impregnates the queen, his abdomen splits open, loosing the entrails which the queen then totes behind her as a kind of triumphal banner. Dispensable, his death required for the propagation of the hive, the mate falls to the earth as a carcass; the queen, on the other hand, sports her murderous trophy, proof that she has guaranteed the future of the hive.

Within the poem, both maestro and bridegroom would seem to lose. The drone's taste of fruit in sexual union with the queen is costly. If we reexamine the poem with a purposeful child's-eye view, we see that the natural sexual world of the first half seems dark and funereal, forewarning the child's awakening. "Hieratical in his frock coat," the maestro suggests death as well as a wedding ceremony. Lush foliage smothers, asphyxiates, or is "nodding" or "dripping" as much with exhausted deadliness as with vitality:

Purple, scarlet-specked, black
The great corollas dilate, peeling back their silks.
Their musk encroaches, circle after circle
A well of scents almost too dense to breath in.
(*Col.*, 73)

As the child recognizes deathly, suffocating sexuality, her impression is echoed in the deadly nuptials of the queen bee and the father/bridegroom, the union of male and female principles. Neither the disconsolate queen nor her hapless male consort provides much encouragement to the young woman: the "wintry" drone dies, and the queen is but a tool of the hive's collective intent to ensure the future of the race. This is the rough adult lesson the maestro's daughter learns when her empathic "I" meets the "eye" of the old queen bee.

In sum, Plath's first bee poem anatomizes the process of discovery. The slow, calculated method by which the speaker arrives at awareness indirectly assumes importance over a smug, confident authority. The ambivalent imagery used to describe her growing awareness simulates a child's subliminal understanding that occurs gradually, well before the girl actually confronts the queen and grasps her paradoxical function.

The second poem in Plath's bee sequence, "The Bee Meeting," is a lengthy monologue that describes a mysterious rite of passage. The literal occasion, never made explicit, is a gathering of villagers who smoke out a beehive and get the honey. They move the virgin bees to another hive to prevent them from killing the old queen and, in this way, establish a new hive colony. A young girl is led by English country folk through various phases of an initiation ceremony where both the speaker's ignorance and the ambiguous imagery are calculated to suggest and sustain the life/death ambiguity of the event taking place.[38]

But more important than either the literal occasion or our gradual discovery of it is the poem's focus on the speaker's emotional range and her implied identification with the queen, both central to the poem's meaning. Real power lies in the speaker's powerless ignorance about place, time, direction, and event, all the physical and metaphysical realities of the ceremony. ("Who are these people at the bridge to meet me? . . . why did nobody tell me?") Her disingenuousness ("I am nude as a chicken neck, does nobody love me?") and her fear of uniformity ("A black veil moulds to my face, they are making me one of them") prompt repeated questions that form the dramatic center of the poem. Since she feels fixed and controlled by the village professionals, her defense is to diminish herself in an act of mental powerlessness, willing her own inertia in the ambiguous event: "I cannot run, I am rooted, and the gorse hurts me . . . If I stand very still, they will think I am cow parsley" (A, 57). Her choice for immobility is her only answer to those too-cheery voyeurs—the rector, sexton, and midwife—who merely witness the event, clapping one another in ritual gestures of approval.

Throughout the poem, the insistent questions of the naive young woman function in several ways. First, they signal that one is moving through and participating in an event. They shift the focus from the conclusion to the process of discovery. Finding the shape of the whole event undefined, the young woman feels increasing terror as the weight of every detail registers emotionally with her. "Is it some operation that is taking place," she asks, or are all these plateaus preparatory steps in bee etiquette? Is the progression—bridge to beanfield to the "shorn grove," the circle of hives, and finally to the empty chambers—a prescribed social ritual of conformity, or are we confronting the slow effacement of the dying process? Is this geography or mindscape?

The questions of the girl also sustain a powerful tension in imagery, keeping always before us the ambiguity between life and death, between scientific operation and transcendent ritual. Both the natural images (the beanfield and then the hawthorn grove) as well as the surgical imagery grow more ambiguous. They are comic yet deadly. Midwife, rector, and sexton are lumped together, "nodding square black heads." The rector, officiator at both deaths and entrances, chums with the midwife and the sexton during this formal ceremony, the three of them clad as sinister, depersonalized look-alikes. Vivid nature mingles with all that is antiseptically sterile:

> Strips of tinfoil winking like people,
> Feather dusters fanning their hands in a sea of bean flowers,
> Creamy bean flowers with black eyes and leaves like
>   bored hearts.
> (*A*, 56)

Gauzy white cheesecloth is set against black veils. The "milkweed silk" of a white garment hints at a hospital shift or a shroud slit ominously from neck to knee.

Even the technical details of beekeeping work paradoxically to sustain the life-death ambiguity. To avert death (the killing of the queen by her replacement), the virgins are moved by the villagers. To secure the future of the hive, a natural catastrophe ("smoking out") is simulated. Since smoke makes the bees emerge, believing their death to be imminent, it seems to the workers to be "the end of everything." Yet, for the queen, the smoking out is a new, if complex, freedom: "She is very clever. / She is old, old, old, she must live another year, and she knows it" (*A*, 57).

The traditional concept of power in the poem is paradoxical, relative, and, at best, suspect. The surgeon or mastermind of this mysterious operation is described as a science-fiction figure, a comic "apparition in a green helmet, / Shining gloves and white suit." Even the goodwilled villagers are wholly inept and clumsy. The speaker, ungloved and uncovered, is greeted by the high priests of conduct. Their garments scramble their identities and leave them looking like effete knights with no joust in sight: "Everybody is nodding a square black head, they are knights in visors, / Breastplates of cheesecloth knotted under the armpits" (*A*, 56). Physical power is undermined. Their confusing loss of identity is sad evidence of the need for collective disguise. Unanimous in their failure to make the most elementary distinctions between life and death, these folk conduct a witch-hunt through the hive's chambers and emerge with a misguided notion of their own success.

The controlling force of the poem is the shrewd queen bee, powerful in her very evasiveness. She proves her cleverness by refusing to show herself, whether to avoid a duel with the younger virgins or to escape some random fate from the villagers. To her, power is an attitude, a matter of perceiving life and death, the familiar and the terrible, simultaneously. She manipulates the visible from her vantage point of isolation. Physically, her fate is in others' hands. Mentally she remains untouched, undetected, her mind as well as her body "sealed in wax." Likewise, the inducted speaker—exhausted from the tedium of ignorance, fear, and unanswered questions—chooses immobility. Despite her outward conformity, she remains "a gullible head untouched by their [the bees'] animosity."

The poem's peculiar terror is that the link between the queen in her dotage and the young girl never becomes more overt than the final questions: "Whose is that long white box in the grove, what have they accomplished, why am I cold?" However, double-edged imagery and the speaker's helplessness intensify the identification. Both the queen and the speaker are mental rebels, yet physical pawns: the queen at the mercy of enterprising young virgins and villagers; the speaker besieged by workers on their "hysterical elastics," as well as by village elders. The queen eludes all forces of overt power. ("The old queen does not show herself, is she so ungrateful?") Likewise the speaker is physically passive, but conscious at every moment of the dramatic stakes of life and death:

> I am exhausted, I am exhausted—
> Pillar of white in a blackout of knives.
> I am the magician's girl who does not flinch. (*A*, 58)

In contrast to the naiveté of the first two poems, "Arrival of the Bee Box" is a prosaic study of rational control, of the brag of ownership, of the cheap physical coercion that can reject, kill, or merely unlock: "I ordered this, this clean wood box / Square as a chair and almost too heavy to lift." Assuming the power of the beekeeper-maestro, the speaker has ordered a box of undeveloped workers and finds herself faced with responsibility for their livelihood. "Tomorrow I will be sweet God, I will set them free," she asserts.

However, she deceives by her "unstable allegorical god-position,"[39] for the bulk of the poem reveals the obverse of the power that is authoritarian ownership. The bees control the speaker. As she becomes increasingly fascinated with their vitality and unintelligible noise, she abandons her declared pose of authority. She is lured to imagine various ways to dispose of the vital yet deadly threat:

> I have simply ordered a box of maniacs.
> They can be sent back.
> They can die, I need feed them nothing, I am the owner.
> (*A*, 59)

Again, a deathly vitality seems to overshadow any attempt to humorously diminish the contents of the dangerous bee box: the box is bursting with "maniacs," yet they are temporarily contained; they clamber vigorously with a "swarmy feeling," but still suggest decay ("African hands / Minute and shrunk for export"); reduced to a Roman mob chattering Latin, they are frighteningly alien. Whatever assertion of control has been cultivated in the tone, the imagery undercuts it. Her actual power becomes less convincing as her bravado grows. Fear, in fact, prompts her gradual stasis and effacement. She wildly scrambles the boundaries between herself and nature in a total defiance of the maestro's authority:

> I wonder if they would forget me
> If I just undid the locks and stood back and turned into a tree.

> There is the laburnum, its blond colonnades,
> And the petticoats of the cherry. (*A*, 60)

In the end, her grand resolve to play God is enfeebled by the boisterous liveliness of female drudges. Perhaps it is this sense of the bees' collective vitality that prompts the understated curious promise: "The box is only temporary."

After she recognizes the queen's isolation and the "dark pa[i]rings" of sexuality, a young girl dramatically experiences kinship with this paradoxical symbol of passivity. Miniature, invisible life ironically mocks the power of ownership. The speaker summarizes her progress in "Stings," a poem central to the developing drama of the bee sequence.

A scapegoat god whose presence was mere voyeurism has absconded from the poem.[40] He is even less effective than the "maestro" father, the "imaginary god" who is owner of the bee box, or the life/death professionals who conduct the "Bee Meeting" ritual. Here the speaker successively dons the roles of beekeeper, honey-drudge, and queen in a dramatic exploration of their functions. "It is almost over / I am in control," she says midway through the process of adopting and then rejecting various selves. The comment is crucial and links the aesthetic and scientific levels of awareness in the poem and in the sequence: the speaker conducts us from the literal level of "sweet" bargaining for honey, through the equally mechanical collection of it by drudges, and, finally, to the queen's controlling *in*activity, her last triumph.

"Stings" opens with the speaker engaged in that simple bargaining procedure of exchanging honey for clean combs. But suddenly she finds brood cells "grey as the fossils of shells." This brief confrontation with silence prompts her poignant question about the metaphysics of be(e)ing: "Is there any queen at all in it?" After this question, she shifts quickly to the imagined role of worker standing in a "column of unmiraculous women." Their "scurry," their cheerful mechanical existence, ignores a life of the mind. The speaker's link to these "industrious virgins" is her own honey-machine, the extractor:

> It will work without thinking,
> ....
> To scour creaming crests
> As the moon, for its ivory powders, scours the sea.
> (*A*, 62)

Unlike gathering honey from the "open cherry, the open clover," extracting honey from the cells is an arid, derivative process. The speaker's "strangeness" may be tenuous and likely to evaporate ("blue dew from dangerous skin"), but she is no drudge. Worker-drudges are easily deceived in their unconscious activity of searching for honey. Only too late do they discover their own deception, as happened with the poem's interloper:

> The bees found him out,
> Moulding onto his lips like lies,
> Complicating his features. (*A*, 62)

Although the bees obscure his identity with their stings, the cost to these workers is life itself, since honeybees die after they sting.

The speaker realizes—from the misleading third person now fled and from the impressionable workers—that no one, nothing, is worth sacrificing one's life for:

> They thought death was worth it, but I
> Have a self to recover, a queen.
> Is she dead, is she sleeping?
> Where has she been,
> With her lion-red body, her wings of glass? (*A*, 62)

The final image of the resurrected (recovered) queen is central to the bee sequence. The longtime elusive self, now visible, is a surprising triumph of contradictions. While most critics do recognize the importance of Plath's kinship with this bare, "plushless" queen, they nevertheless claim that it is "evidently only in death, if ever, that the queen, the persona (the identification seems complete), will recover her unique self."[41] But it is not death that is the "liberator of her unique personality." It is a peculiar meshing of those vital contradictions and the ritual, imagined deaths. Such contradictions have been at the very center of the life-death imagery throughout the sequence and culminate here in this recovery. Is hers a transcendence? A rebirth to death? A political exorcising of husband/father/domesticity, or a triumph over the male "to whom the false self has been servile?"[42] The movement through various roles central to the sequence, now enacted within the microcosm "Stings," has prepared the way for this self-styled queen of contradictions. The authoritative mode, seen in simple bartering and in the voyeur-god of "Stings," has been abandoned.

Like many of Plath's later high-energy poems ("Lady Lazarus," "Fever 103°"), "Stings" presents an ambivalence that makes the recovered queen image more realistic, more credible. The queen's feminocide is implicit in her action as well as in the persistent dualistic imagery. Queenship is a double-bind situation where the special category carries with it the threat of fossilization. The hive killed the queen by entombing her powers in its sealed waxen brood cells. She became a narrowly defined reproductive symbol and suffered a kind of death-in-life, the feminocidal hazard of "specialness." Now, however, the queen is:

> . . . flying
> More terrible than she ever was, red
> Scar in the sky, red comet
> Over the engine that killed her—
> The mausoleum, the wax house. (*A*, 63)

She is, to be sure, no antique replica emerging from "wormy mahogany." Imagery of transcendence commingles with hints of illness, vulnerability ("red scar," "her wings of glass") with ferocity ("lion-red body," "red comet"), to fashion a surprisingly resilient and vital queen. She both conquers and recognizes limitations.

After the queen's triumphal flight over "the mausoleum" in "Stings," "Wintering" praises the workers for their minimal survival. "It is they who own me," the keeper says of these workers who barely hang on, so slow that they are hardly recognizable. They possess the beekeeper by their sheer power of knowing how to survive ("neither cruel nor indifferent, / Only ignorant"), and how to scale subsistence down according to hibernal limitations. They endure the natural elements, the habits of the sponging drones, and even turn the deceptions of traditional authority (Tate and Lyle artificial sugar for honey) into life sustenance. The sugar ("refined snow") hints of the commingling of life and death: what nourishes the bees through the long winter appears to be like the white snow in which they bury their dead.

A deceptively profound efficiency governs this dark hibernaculum "at the heart of the house." The perfunctory labor of extracting honey has not prepared the beekeeper for the activities within the smothering room. After her initial boast ("This is the easy time, there is nothing doing. / I have whirled the midwife's extractor, / I have my honey"), the speaker faces a growing horror that her power is neither deep nor comprehensive enough to grasp so much sweetness with so much deathly decay. The beekeeper is no more a match for this inertia than she was for the puzzling, boxed vitality in "Arrival of the Bee Box":

> This is the room I have never been in.
> This is the room I could never breathe in.
> The black bunched in there like a bat,
> No light
> But the torch and its faint
>
> Chinese yellow on appalling objects—
> Black asininity. Decay.
> Possession. (*A*, 67)

Fearless, "rid of the men" now ("the blunt, clumsy stumblers, the boors"), these bees, all of whom are women, make a life for themselves "wintering in the dark without a window / At the heart of the house." Why? Because unlike the smug keeper whose efficiency is outwardly directed, these bees are self-determining. Their ability to perceive, accept, and project the reality of inner states is surely as purposeful as that "woman, still at her knitting, / At the cradle of Spanish walnut, / Her body a bulb in the cold and too dumb to think." Implicit in the poem's final seasonal renewal[43] is criticism of the beekeeper's defunct power that misunderstands inwardness. The beekeeper is possessed by neither cruelty nor indifference, but by those who collectively outlast death, fraudulence, cold, and grand expectations. These workers, in the end, "are flying." It is they who "taste the spring."

From praise for minimal activity in "Wintering," Plath moves to consider the historical plight of imaginative versus physical power in "The Swarm." "How instructive this is," she sarcastically remarks as she watches the antics of the man with a gun who attempts to shoot down a swarming hive. Two kinds of power—physical, self-defensive will (the smiling practical man with "grey hands"), and visionary, collective dreams (the "black intractable" mind of the swarm)—cancel each other out within the poem. By mutual deception and delusion, both are reduced to "the white busts of marshals, admirals, generals /

Worming themselves into niches" like white grubs germinating in hive cells.

It would appear that because the practical man with the gun and "asbestos receptacles" for hands can topple dreams to mere facts, or shoot fantasy hives into "cocked straw hats" ("Seventy feet high! / Russia, Poland and Germany . . . fields shrunk to a penny"), his power is triumphant: "Pom! Pom! They fall / Dismembered to a tod of ivy." Although he may have physical force and protective garb, his greed for honey, his contempt for bees, and his fear of stings ("It is you the knives are out for") prompt a feeble self-defense: "They would have killed *me*." In his misunderstanding of the bees' natural swarming patterns, he knows that "seventy feet up" is out of his control, and that he must exert corrective force:

> The dumb, banded bodies
> Walking the plank draped with Mother France's upholstery
> Into a new mausoleum,
> An ivory palace, a crotch pine. (*A*, 65)

The swarm is also deceived in several ways. Deserting to their "black pine tree," they mistake a gun for thunder ("the voice of God / Condoning the beak, the claw, the grin of the dog"). They are victims of self-delusion. The collective mind is prey to the aspirations of a Napoleon with his master plan for the "charioteers, the outriders, the Grand Army": "their dream, the hived station / Where trains, faithful to their steel arcs, / Leave and arrive, and there is no end to the country" (*A*, 65). Their absolute "notion of honor" causes them to sting the man with the gun who is a threat to their plans. Such action not only costs the bees their lives but exaggerates their failure to accept real limitations (the "tod of ivy," the "cocked straw hat," "stings big as drawing pins").

Central to the poem is the context of Napoleonic history that diminishes both the gunman's individual will-to-power and the swarm's collective delusions of grandeur. The bee itself, a public symbol of order in the sixteenth century and a private emblem for Napoleon, is ridiculed by this imagery. Either sort of power here is derivative; either is dependent upon some other person or force for definition. Of the so-called instructive aspects of the poem, it has been said that "from her own deep need to feel real, to be human, Plath can see the Napoleonic impulse to be Great through Hate with irony."[44] A psychic distance is gained by these cultural references. They puncture victories, dreams, jealousies that can "open the blood," greed, strengths, and even exiles, making them no more than a network of collective deceptions. Surely there is something mock-epic about Napoleon's conquests being reduced to arguing bees, "a flying hedgehog, all prickles," or to a "man with asbestos gloves" training his gun on bees in a tree. "Elba, Elba, bleb on the sea," the speaker chants in anagrammatic playfulness, pointing up the defeat of all grand aims "knocked into a cocked straw hat" of a hive. This mockery includes the practical gunman who believes he is more authentic than the bees:

> Shh! These are chess people you play with,
> Still figures of ivory.
> The mud squirms with throats,
> Stepping stones for French bootsoles.
> The gilt and pink domes of Russia melt and float off
>
> In the furnace of greed. Clouds, clouds. (*A*, 64)

Throughout her poetic investigation, Plath has formulated a new valuation for passivity based on the function of power within the hierarchy of the apiary, and most particularly on the interrelationship of the old queen, the beekeeper, and the workers, who are specialists in minimal survival. Plath has discovered that the power of inertia is, paradoxically, one of the greatest literary possibilities for contemporary women. Such "abandonment of authority as a rhetorical pose," is a point clarified by Patricia Spacks and Mary Ellmann:

> In our time, the "authoritative mode is no longer the mode of original, which is more than competent expression. At the same time, the exertion of sensibility is not marked in the most interesting writing by women now." The temper of the age is such that claims of authority are now likely to seem ludicrous.[45]

Passivity reevaluated as a form of power in the bee sequence is markedly different from the "Great Multiple Lie [about female nature] freshly got up in drag" that is described by Cynthia Ozick. According to Ozick, the new feminist strategy of isolating a female nature—a kind of "voluntary circumscription"—is really aimed toward the same authoritarian end as the old hostile, biologically based self-confinement:

> Thurber once wrote a story about a bear who leaned so far backward that he ended up by falling on his face. Now we are enduring

a feminism so far advanced into "new truths" that it has arrived at last at a set of notions undistinguishable from the most age-encrusted, unenlightened, and imprisoning antifeminist views.[46]

Again we see Plath rejecting the socially determined "new truth" of passivity (with its corollaries of evasiveness, indirection, deviousness, and apology) as a weakness. Instead, she assigns to passivity a positive value of choice, not of social situation, a function that Plath has already imaginatively dramatized in earlier poetry. The worst deception to Plath—seen repeatedly in her female images and culminating in the queen bee—is the act of merely subscribing to one's nature, unexamined. Rather, Plath is always in control of the kaleidoscopic selves that she explores in the process of trying to understand the limits of traditional power and the function of passivity. For her, passivity becomes an investigative resource, never so thoroughly yet succinctly stated as in her bee sequence.

"I have a self to recover," she asserts as she carves out a new value for contradiction. From a child's recognition of the paradoxical isolation and "dark pa[i]rings" of the queen bee, Plath's young speaker dramatically identifies with her in "Bee Meeting." The sheer vitality of those hidden but controlling female forces in "Arrival of the Bee Box" overpowers physical authority while the image of the angry red queen represents a new tolerance for contradictions in "Stings." In "Wintering," physical authority is possessed by the apparently passive and resigned worker bees and queen. Finally, in "Swarm," both physical and imaginative control are canceled out by Plath's mockery.

The commingling of life and death has strengthened the power of inertia in its many examples within the sequence: the "disconsolate" queen in her burrow; the double-edged survival of the workers in winter; the ambivalence of the red queen in "Stings." The many shifts in tone—naive wonderment, simple declaration, mock-epic allusiveness—show Plath exploring aesthetic possibilities as well as enlarging her tonal authority.

Her exploration within the apiary has developed originally, dramatically, in a crescendo that describes the "process of constructing meaning," not the correctness of a fixed body of critical facts about apiculture, power, or the "new feminism."[47] Within the microcosm of the bee world and this six-poem sequence, Plath's new space carved for contradictions suggests, once again, the rival energies at work in the late poems: the triumphal energy of performance coexists with a small constructiveness and counseled limitations. The late poems pose a challenge to the poet. As she realizes the benefits of being small, inert, and leading the scaled-down life, she also realizes that she is condemned to a state of complexity and continual change. Despite her knowledge that she had indeed "one too many dimensions to enter," Plath is still drawn to the difficult enlarged vision where neutrality and physical simplicity coexist with "some things of this world that are indigestible."

A Rival Energy: "there is no terminus"

The tension dramatized in "Death and Co." reminds us that Plath's passivity redefined has its rival aspect: energy or motion. That campy, public figure who posed as seductive death actually screamed vitality and need as he performed for the poet's attention. That showy figure protected himself by his elusive motion. In several late poems, Plath rejects structured states of being for such kinesis: "There is no terminus, only suitcases / Out of which the same self unfolds like a suit / Bald and shiny, with pockets of wishes . . ." (*A*, 76).

Plath worships energy for its own sake. Frequently she doesn't imagine a resolution or a final form to the gathering momentum. Instead, she admires the motion of the piston, the endless grinding of the "gigantic gorilla interior / Of the wheels" of a machine, the heart opening and closing its "bowl of red blooms," the flying arrow, the leaping horse, the shedding layers of the self in burlesque ("Lady Lazarus"), even the virginal immolation and mock Ascension ("Fever 103°") or the escape flight of the angry queen been with her "lion red body." "How far is it," becomes her constant refrain. The sense of progression, a going toward, replaces arrival at terminals, destinations, endpoints. "All the gods know is destinations," she says, for the stasis of religious beliefs, the "illusions of Greek necessity," are all identified with "the awful God bit," according to Plath. They belong to a world of hope, a "vacuous black / Stars stuck all over, bright stupid confetti," unlike this world of time and change:

> Eternity bores me,
> I never wanted it.
>
> What I love is

The piston in motion—
My soul dies before it.
And the hooves of the horses,
Their merciless churn. (*A*, 72)

In the poems "Gigolo," "An Appearance," and "The Munich Mannequins," Plath has a great deal of ambivalence toward mechanical motion. Total invulnerability—"perfection" Plath terms it—is to be automatic, mechanical, bloodless, and as voiceless as the dumb dolls, the "Munich Mannequins" who prop each other up. They are "intolerable" in all their "sulphur loveliness":

Perfection is terrible, it cannot have children.

. . . .

The tree of life and the tree of life

Unloosing their moons, month after month, to no purpose. (*A*, 73)

With his "tattle of gold joints," the gigolo is a timeless glorification of motion. It is precisely the character of his hedonism—the quantity not the quality of experience, his way of "turning / Bitches to ripples of silver," and his ever-replenishing prowess—that Plath presents as indefatigable momentum.

Unfortunately, many critics have labeled Plath's unresolved kinesis a death plunge. They require of her that confessional conformism which jots notations of neuroses and scrappy pathological facts. In their estimation, "the blood jet is poetry," but a murderous record, an apocalyptic vision, hysteria, suicidal madness, even the "autobiography of a fever" or a kind of Laingian "ontological insecurity":

The engine is killing the track, the track is silver,
It stretches into the distance. It will be eaten nevertheless.

Its running is useless. (*A*, 75)

Robert Lowell suggests that Plath is a kind of James Dean of modern poetry who "burns to be on the move, a walk, a ride, a journey, the flight of the queen bee":

Dangerous, more power than man, machinelike from hard training, she herself is a little like a racehorse, galloping relentlessly with risked, outstretched neck, death hurdle after death hurdle topped. She cries out for that rapid life of starting pistols, snapping tapes, and new world records broken. . . . Yet it is too much; her art's immortality is life's disintegration.[48]

In more recent years, Karl Malkoff has singled out the anxiety or restlessness in Plath's assertions of freedom that undermine strong meaning or permanency.[49] On the other hand, by noticing how often Plath uses spatial images that involve movement or distance, Barbara Howes has opened new critical doors to a view of Plath's enormous life energies: "Perhaps this emphasis on motion, on speed, was at first a search for experience rather than a result of the fever."[50] Energy for Plath becomes a freedom, a power, and an end in itself. It functions much like the quality of passivity which Plath reclaimed from the social arena in the bee poems and invested with an intransigent power. By her verbal contexts (rhyme, rhythm, and image patterns), as well as by her speaker's expressive dimensions, Plath creates a similar valuation for pure energy.

The fabric of the verse itself (from simple punctuation and rhyme to individual word choices and patterns) shows the extent that, as Ted Hughes has said, "crackling verbal energy" saturates Plath's poetry. The vigorous motion that infuses certain words and images answers Plath's own question negatively:

Is there no still place
Turning and turning in the middle air,
Untouched and untouchable. (*A*, 37)

Plath has developed her own codelike repertoire of words, what she calls her exhuberant "American" way of talking in these last poems that beg to be read aloud. A battery of aggressive nouns has become part of the Plath poetic idiolect: shrieks, discs, mills, filaments, hooks, glittering mirrors, and smiles.[51] An impressive litany of verbs is all in the form of verbals, demonstrating a physical gathering of freedom through motion: rising, grinding, crackling, flaking, bleeding, pumping, peeling, shimmering, flickering, dissolving, unloosing, opening and closing, sizzling, blooming, flashing, chanting, melting, tamping, dragging, shutting, and sliding. Such verbals lend unusual effect of ongoing movement to the surface of the poems. All the physical marks of direct, plain but extemporaneous, speech—dashes, exclamation marks, ellipses—dramatize a fluency and mobility that is formally represented by "quick-change" imagery. As Eileen Aird has said, "the stylistic simplicity is counterpointed by an agility and speed of association and reference which is also characteristic of the late work."[52] Plath leaves the calisthenic training ground of early syllabics and finely embroidered meter for new sound patterns that communicate the speaker's vital movement through or against the very substance of language. Even her compulsion to rhyme—both "rhyme at high noon" and ghost rhymes—always brings her back to a basic heart rhythm.[53]

In 1962 Plath said about her late poems: "I've got to say them, I speak them to myself, and I think that this in my own writing development is quite a new thing with me, and whatever lucidity they may have comes from the fact that I say them to myself, I say them aloud." A number of *Ariel* poems demonstrate this energy in utterance. As a first-degree religious relic, yet a sideshow striptease artist, the speaker in "Lady Lazarus" has returned from the grave for a repeat performance. Imagine the Boston-British bred accent pronouncing the following broad *a*s with a sarcasm that mocks both her own suicide attempt and the audience's voyeurism:

> There is a charge
>
> For the eyeing of my scars, there is a charge
> For the hearing of my heart—
> It really goes.
>
> And there is a charge, a very large charge,
> For a word or a touch
> Or a bit of blood . . . (*A*, 8)

The phonemes of the poem "Cut" spew out disgust with blood and pain, yet re-create the thump of the indefatigable heartbeat:

> How you jump—
> Trepanned veteran,
> Dirty girl,
> Thumb stump. (*A*, 14)

The mesmeric beginning and the incantatory nursery-rhyme meter in "Daddy" soon break the "heart rhythm." The timing of the break is significant, for it occurs when the poet expresses feelings of punishment for losing her father's love:

> You do not do, you do not do
> Any more, black shoe
> In which I have lived like a foot
> For thirty years, poor and white. . . . (*A*, 49)

David McKay describes the effect of such energetic poetry:

> Poetry which concentrates upon energy—its generation, control,

and unleashing—generally leaves readers with an exhilarating sense of kinesis, as skiing or flying does, but without a firm conception of content. It lives most fully in the act of reading, and recedes during the process of critical reflection when more tangible problems of "meaning" come naturally to the fore.[54]

Individual images—hooks, flakes, mouths, discs—as well as the dialectic between image patterns crackle with energy in poems such as "The Munich Mannequins," "Elm," "Poppies in October," "Tulips," "The Moon and the Yew Tree." Great kinetic force derives from the interplay in any given poem between the lofty and the homely, between "the poetic and the scientific (words like carbon monoxide, acetylene, ticker-tape, adding machine) . . . a constant and vivifying exchange between depth and surface."[55] The running together of the particular and the general, as Barbara Hardy has explained, lets Plath take the most outrageous or painful passions and imaginatively enlarge them. Like "Nick and the Candlestick," "Mary's Song" dissolves, by its syncretic image patterns, the ordinary limits of a mother's suffering. As the poem progresses through the various kinds of fire—historical, cultural, and religious—it enlarges the mother's narrow fears for her baby. She discovers that she lives in a world whose persecutions dishonor a mother's tender, protective wishes. Fire references begin with the fat browning on a Sunday leg of lamb. The mother's emotional center then shifts to include the fire of sun through stained glass windows, then those religious fires of sacrifice, "melting the tallow heretics," and finally the World War II gas ovens of Poland and Germany. Meanings intermingle subtly, gathering up and developing previous references. "Lamb" is at once the Sunday meal and the Old Testament sacrificial beast; hence, the joint in the oven "sacrifices its opacity." The idea of eating is at once a religious consummation, yet also an ordinary physical act. "Golden" suggests precious value, but also the singe that results from fire: "It is a heart, / This holocaust I walk in, / O golden child the world will kill and eat."

In sum, Plath's syncretic approach to her imagery, what has been termed her "transductive thinking," creates motion where one image bleeds into another as in the memories of the title poem in *Winter Trees*:

The wet dawn inks are doing their blue dissolve.
On their blotter of fog the trees
Seem a botanical drawing.

> Memories growing, ring on ring,
> A series of weddings.
>
> Knowing neither abortions nor bitchery,
> Truer than women,
> They seed so effortlessly! (*WT*, 43)

In another example nurse caps and the gulls run together in
"Tulips." Gulls introduce water, and water leads back to the
self, which is described as a slipping "thirty-year-old cargo boat
/ Stubbornly hanging on to [my] name and address." And when
the speaker is anesthetized, water flows: "I watched my tea set,
my bureaus of linen, my books / Sink out of sight, and the water
went over my head." In "Poppies in October" and "Cut," the
poet deals with other "weddings" of imagery. The bloodflow
from the cut fingertip becomes the occasion for references to
violent destruction: Indians by American pilgrims; the
brutalities of the Revolutionary War battles; the Second World
War ("Saboteur, / Kamikaze man"); and finally the persecution
of American blacks:

> The stain on your
> Gauze Ku Klux Klan
> Babushka
> Darkens and tarnishes and when
>
> The balled
> Pulp of your heart
> Confronts its small
> Mill of silence
>
> How you jump— (*A*, 14)

The quicksilver images in "Cut" create a violent momentum and
confusion of power ("whose side are they on?"), perhaps even a
sense of fluidity where the usual boundaries of the event continually merge with surrounding reality.[56] The metaphoric system of reference (recall "Metaphor") upholds pure speed. Certain images—poppies and tulips, in particular—evoke a center
of energy that is part of a wider dialectic between life or breath
(with its tangents of color, pulsing rhythm, heat, light, and
noise) and death or stasis (with reference to absence, silence,
darkness, and hardness).[57]

In her admiration for the energy of progress, Plath presents
a sketch of the human condition as a Sisyphean struggle, going
on endlessly in "Getting There." In all but four of sixty-eight
lines, the unknown speaker describes a painful attenuation of

life followed by a quick, brutal death. The central image is the revolving, devouring wheels of a death train whose journey is well underway as the poem opens ("black muzzles / Revolving, the sound / Punching out Absence!"). The insistent present tense, the terse elliptical phrases and rapid shifts in imagery, the pleading refrain and questions ("How far is it," "How far is it now," "Is there no still place"), dramatically mingle as they measure the agony of birth and death. As we will discover in the poem "Ariel," and as we have seen in the bee sequence, birth and death grow indistinguishable: "It is Adam's side, / This earth I rise from, and I in agony. / I cannot undo myself."

The textural sense of strain in the poem, the derangement of anything rational, and the widening sense of personal horror create a double movement: "a trope and a form for unbearable pain, and intolerable need for release."[58] So thoroughly interconnected are the poles of birth and death ("I step to you from the black car of Lethe, / Pure as a baby" or "the carriages rock, they are cradles") that either individual struggle or the cultural persecution becomes insignificant next to the simple energy of kinesis. The passion of process generated in the poem, with the endpoint undetermined, is primary. One has a physical sense of spent energy grating against accumulations of culture and history ("Why are there these obstacles"): Krupp, Russia, trains, nurses, men, "some war or other," charred bodies now garlanded in worship, even Hades's river of forgetfulness, sweet Lethe. To assign a temporal or spatial destination, or to call this a death-wish poem (Aird) or one that ends in a "purification that prepares for rebirth" (Kroll) is to shift focus from the velocity of journeying. A suffering portrayed en route is the matrix of the poem.[59] The only hint of "arrival" is to an undefined *you*, a throwback to the speaker's self-in-motion:

> The silver leash of the will—
> Inexorable. . . .
> . . . .
> I am a letter in this slot
> I fly to a name, two eyes. (*A*, 36)

With perfected structural, thematic, and technical unities, the title poem, "Ariel," is one of Plath's most comprehensive dramas of pure motion. The poem's literal event recounts an exhilarating instant on horseback when the rider and horse merge with each other and with the landscape. While this highly charged experience of blurring and merging has intense meaning for Plath, the logical explication of it can no more be captured by analyzing the poem's mechanical components than can the feeling of exhilaration be precisely defined. As M. L. Rosenthal has said, "the more intensely we pursue the exquisite essence, the more swiftly and surely we stare into the eye of mortality."[60]

"Ariel" enacts the coming together of object and movement, elements of life and death, sexuality and stasis, earthiness and spirituality.[61] "How one we grow," the poet says, as the rhythmic sound-weaving voice brings together the elation of sexuality ("And now I / Foam to wheat, a glitter of seas. / The child's cry / Melts in the wall") with the drive toward extinction ("Something else / Hauls me through air—"). The several levels of meaning in the title "Ariel" foreshadow the poem's unity of intermeshed emotions: "Ariel" is at once the poet's horse, a spirit in *The Tempest* who represents Prospero's control of the elements of air and fire, and the Hebrew lion of God, Jerusalem (Isaiah 29:7).

The craft of the poem welds stasis in cloddish earthly flesh to the sensation of speed. Spare, vivid language without surplus adjectival commentary moves rapidly through images that reenact (especially in the first six stanzas) the experience of riding. A swift, compressed use of rhythm and stanzaic form insists first on a sense of urgency by re-creating the rhythmic clatter of hoofbeats ("stasis in darkness"); then the long physical reaching motion of a galloping horse ("substanceless blue / Pour of tor and distances"); finally, the sense of land blurring as it passes by. Echoically, the meter falls, then rises. Verbs pull toward absolute kinesis, away from fleshly resistance (tor, heels, knees, brown neck, furrow). The poem moves toward impalpable energy and a purely vaporous state: pour, splits and passes, hauls, flakes, unpeels, foams, melts, then flies. Alliteration and assonance mime the motion of solid hoofbeat followed by airy suspension.

Throughout the poem, Plath has a curious way of knit-stitching or sustaining the same sounds—the same vowel sounds with different consonants, or different vowel sounds with the same final consonant. She inverts rhyme where the sound that ends one word begins the next, as in "wall . . . arrow," "catch . . . arc."[62] Stanzas six and seven interlock as do rider and horse ("How one we grow, / Pivot of heels and knees"), physical movement and metaphysical meaning ("heels" becomes "unpeel," "stringencies" moves into "seas"). After the break in the regularly established slant rhyme in the sixth stanza (the "unpeeling" of her own past and the adoption of the Godiva image), the sustained long *i* sound increases ("White / Godiva, *I* unpeel . . . and now *I* . . . the child's cry") until it finally insists not only on the unity of the horse ride with life, death, and sexuality, but the union of the persona's *I* with the "red eye" of the morning sun.

Colors in the poem tell the same story: black becomes blue, then white (a neutral moment), and finally red. If we are aware that Plath has developed certain color codes in her late poems, then this progression argues against the poem as a conventional death wish. The ambivalent vitality of tulips and poppies, not to mention the angry red resurgent queen bee ("Stings"), pushes toward energy and life, not pale death.[63] So too do the complex final images move in the direction of life, even if ambivalently.

A Performing Self: "the theatrical / comeback in broad day"

To discuss only Plath's self-sufficient system of poetic devices—even her imaginatively textured combinations that move organically toward energy—is to indulge narcissistically a kind of contextualism with some blatant indifferences. To demonstrate Plath's love of kinesis in only thematic or technical elements of verse is to ignore her audience, as well as the self-reflexive quality of her experiences. Rhyme, clearly ambiguous images, colloquialisms of the speaking voice, and bizarre juxtaposition of things public and private enlist our attention to those expressive dimensions of the poetry. In "Stillborn" and "Ouija" Plath directed her poetics away from "perfect" artifacts that exclude these expressive dimensions, away from the "florid, amorous nostalgias" of a world limned on paper. She has been moving toward a poetics where the poem functions not merely as language coming to terms with itself, but also as a dramatized verbal utterance that includes both expression and artifact, where the poet is both sayer and maker.[64] Poems such as "Birthday Present" and "The Bee Meeting" do not merely translate the theme of process, but formally re-create the velocity of the poet-speaker discovering in medias res, origin and end point obscured, the interrelationship of life and death. She weighs her role in the process of movement, watching herself act, react, and go through motions.

Now Plath's self-conscious spectacles mime the performance of the once showy figure in "Death and Co." The late public poems—monologue tours, interviews, journeys, investigations, sideshow acts for the "peanut crunching crowd," and cinematic flashes—invite our exploration of the nature and effect of her transforming energy. In these last, slowly unwinding dramas ("Lady Lazarus," "Daddy," "The Applicant," "The Tour," "Fever 103°"), Plath is engaged in a public watching, measuring, exploring, even parodying of both the personal and the cultural: images of Hiroshima, the *Divine Comedy*, and the Assumption combine with adulteries, fevers; suicide attempts and family deaths mingle with sideshow acts, biblical miracles, and Nazi murders. At best the performing poetic self puts on a theatrical show, puts the speaker in touch with moment-to-moment changes. The result is an immediate record of shifting sensibility, a close-up scrutiny of just how one is shaped by, and impelled to shape, her material. Richard Poirier describes such "performing energy" as a kind of stubborn vitality that "is its own shape." The self engaged in doing learns "how to keep from being smothered by the inherited structuring of things, how to keep within and yet in command of the accumulations of culture that have become a part of what he is."[65] Plath's speaker goes through the motions with the energy of ironic awareness. Perplexed, she questions the feasibility of ever constructing a final literary form for the self through the aesthetic process. In fact, Plath's peculiar self-conscious performances—those vitally rhythmical cadences of her last poems—become substitute assertions for a fixed identity. In their parody of the Assumption, the Nativity, the phoenix myth, and exorcism rituals, they form Plath's admission that any attempted literary shaping or definition of the self is inadequate and unfinished. Questions, theatrical acts, even disappearances become her boast. They provide her protective measure against ever having to define and locate a single, vulnerable self. They baffle critics on a snark hunt for precis or summary of the poems' complexity, finality, or perfection of the woman's image.

For we are told by Rosenthal (who coined the term *confessional poetry*) that the self, by "sheer energy of its insights into reality" and the sensuous excitement generated in the act of experiencing, brings the public-cultural and private-personal levels together in the poem as it dictates the aesthetic process.[66] The self placed at the center of the poem makes individual "vulnerability and shame" representative of a wider civilization. As private events are universalized through the speaking voice, private guilts are purged through universal events. But the real hazard of Rosenthal's definition of the "confessional self" is that shame and psychic fragility, in most instances, seem to be the *only* emotions communicated by the speaking voice. His explanation hints that if we were to plumb the imagery of a poem thoroughly enough, we would find unexpurgated "facts" from a kind of annotated notebook of the poet's personal neuroses.

Rosenthal does, however, mention one aspect of Plath's poetry that has been largely overlooked: her "marvelous buffoonery." While he admits that this tone exists in the poetry, he nevertheless fails to examine Plath's insistently manic and gay performances that promote it. Rosenthal—like Alvarez—cites only the suicidal urge and wildly realized madness as the focus for her passion and energy ("The Hanging Man," "Ariel," "Death and Co.," and "Tulips"). Like so many theorists who through personal need see Plath "sacrificed to her plot," he fails to examine the aesthetic risks she takes with her material. He ignores her comic hyperboles, her occasionally tasteless taunts, but particularly her dramatic performances in the face of accumulations of history, culture, and myth.[67]

Too many of the final poems ("Ariel," "Stings," "Fever 103°," "Lady Lazarus," and "Daddy") have been labeled "transcendent," poems of rebirth where Plath is said to achieve a purer self of a new order.[68] Actually, the poems are dramatically staged performances revealing a speaker's assertion, wit, ingenuity, and sheer life force. She performs even though she is faced with the suffering and pain of personal failure (suicide, adultery, death, self-hate) as well as inherited cultural myths. In the course of her poetic career, Plath rids herself of an impossibly idyllic vision of life (*The Colossus*). She rigorously scrutinizes her own talent and her woman's legacy (*Crossing the Water*), and then tailors the poles of behavior—passivity and motion—to her own aesthetic needs. All the while she narrowly avoids "confessional" or self-pitying overreactions (*Ariel* and *Winter Trees*).

The "performing self" in these late poems suggests the underlying feeling of comedy. Susanne Langer describes such feeling as "that pure sense of life" where one recovers the biological rhythm of sheer vitality or balance in a world of smothering coincidence.[69] What was previously mere name-calling based on a kind of savvy about sound ("Hogwallow," "Mudsump"), or the wheedling of an identity by an ironically naive voice ("Disquieting Muses," "Maenad"), now becomes an overstated sense of self-parody. Tonally and referentially, the speaker marshalls cultural and mythical imagery. She offers her own act as that very evidence of life, by performing against these patterns with all the vigor of the speaking voice. By her act, the poet within the course of the poem reminds herself of the exchange between the audience's reception and her own feelings. She imposes limits (rhyme, rhythm, code imagery, or pirated atrocities of culture) so as to measure changes within her personal situation. The sound-weaving, rhythmical energy of the speaking voice is a reminder of how sporting, playful, vengeful, or mocking she can be.[70]

A typical Plath performance is a slowly savored, dramatic peep show of loss, pain, and personal diminishment. Occasionally she uses lengthy monologues—eavesdropped, one-sided conversations—to show the emotionally charged process of discovery and reaction. Procedures such as the investigation ("The Detective"), or the interview ("The Applicant"), or even the tour ("The Tour"), demand through their pat formulas certain typical responses and assumptions. Plath's speaker defies these perfunctory, cliché reactions. Like her own "Detective" of exploited emotions, Plath assures us her motive is missing, the body had evaporated, and the killer is no more tangible than fingers "tamping a woman into the wall." She leaves us, her audience, the puzzled, boorish sleuths, "making notes."

In "The Tour," the speaker is surprised by a proper but nosey maiden aunt who demands to be shown about her "address." Like so many of the events in *Winter Trees*, this situation is a thinly camouflaged exposé of the psyche. In the course of the tour, increasingly bizarre and dangerous things are encountered in that psychological wreck of the self. The poet's damaged psyche is a conglomerate of dysfunctioning machines. On tour, they first come upon an icebox with its ominous "millions of needly glass cakes" that sometimes bite; then a furnace ("each coal a hot cross-stitch—a *lovely* light") that one night exploded, leaving the speaker bald and choking; then a "Morning Glory Pool":

It boils for forty hours at a stretch.
. . . .

O I shouldn't dip my hankie in, it *hurts*!
Last summer, my God, last summer
It ate seven maids and a plumber
And returned them steamed and pressed and stiff as shirts.
(*WT*, 38)

At last the speaker tells us that the aunt has tripped over a bald nurse on the floor who can "bring the dead to life."

Despite the psychological dangers, the most bizarre element of the poem is the persistent jauntiness in the voice of the speaker. With its unflagging colloquial vitality ("Not a patch on your place, I guess") her casual tone counters the contents of the damaged psyche. She speaks cordially with polite amenities: "But, Auntie, she's awfully nice," "Well, I hope you've enjoyed it, Auntie!" and the solicitous, "Here's a spot I thought you'd love—". She then resorts to a childlike naiveté ("wiggly fingers" and "creepy-creepy"). This is the controlled terror of a nursery rhyme world. The speaker's vitality (end-rhymed, patronizing) merely intensifies the slowly realized danger.

"The Applicant" satirizes the corporate interview where, in the course of the poem's canned questions, a decision is made about the person according to the talents or attributes possessed. But here "our sort of person" must have something missing, must be lacking some function in order to qualify:

First, are you our sort of a person?
Do you wear
A glass eye, false teeth or a crutch,
A brace or a hook,
Rubber breasts or a rubber crotch,

Stitches to show something's missing? No, no? Then
How can we give you a thing? (*A*, 4)

In typical wry fashion, the poem turns on a reversal of the use of power. Despite feigned bureaucratic politeness, the interviewer's hardsell hucksterism actually pushes the institution of marriage: "Will you marry it, marry it, marry it," insists the refrain throughout.

The marriage partner, the woman called "it" or "living doll," has an appreciating cash value by virtue of her tenure. She is advertised on the "program" as a conglomeration of service functions. She can fill teacups, roll away headaches, sew, talk, and cook. Thus, her ultimate value is her function or utility, not her substance:

It is guaranteed

To thumb shut your eyes at the end
And dissolve of sorrow.
We make new stock from the salt.
....
It works, there is nothing wrong with it. (*A*, 4, 5)

The promoted woman represents all the usefulness of a consumer product: she is emotionally biodegradable, recyclable!

The poem mocks other aspects of the stifling structure of
marriage: its reification of woman; woman's penchant for her
own victimization; function or utility as a priority over emotional satisfaction in marriage; and the old prescription of com-
plementarity in matchmaking:

Now your head, excuse me, is empty.
I have the ticket for that.
Come here, sweetie, out of the closet.
Well, what do you think of *that*?
Naked as paper to start

But in twenty-five years she'll be silver,
In fifty, gold.
A living doll, everywhere you look.
It can sew, it can cook,
It can talk, talk, talk. (*A*, 4–5)

Barbara Hardy accurately points out that the interview is
not merely a satire about marriage. Rather, the triumphant voice
that sustains a huckster's vitality broadens its scope to include
metaphysical issues from the larger world of life and death:

The enlargement works not just through the ill-assembled
fragments—hand, suit, and in the later stanzas, doll—but through
the satirized speech, which relates needs, deficiencies, depen-
dence and stupid panaceas to the larger world. Life (or love)
speaks in the cheap-jack voice, as well it may, considering what it
may seem to have to offer. This is an applicant not just for relationship, for marriage, for love, for healing, but for life and death.[71]

The poet's dramatically staged performances confirm more
abundant life and humor as they move through and against
personal pain in *Ariel* and *Winter Trees*. As the speaker in "Fever
103°" physically moves through earthbound images to the airy,
hell to paradise, she dramatically links the confusion attending a
high fever to adultery.[72] The first half of the poem defines
sensory limits—smell, taste, touch, those "yellow sullen

smokes" that cling to the earth, killing, choking, greasing, and "eating in" with their indelible smell. Long *o* and *u* sounds sustained by *m* and *n*, *r*, and *v* tonally underscore an earthly lack of purity:

> Love, love, the low smokes roll
> From me like Isadora's scarves, I'm in a fright
>
> One scarf will catch and anchor in the wheel.
> Such yellow sullen smokes
> Make their own element. They will not rise,
>
> But trundle round the globe
> Choking the aged and the meek,
> The weak
>
> Hothouse baby in its crib, . . . (*A*, 53)

Increasingly violent images drawn from personal, classical, cultural, even environmental realms mingle: adultery; Cerberus who guards the gates of Hades; Dante's "devilish leopard" of incontinence; Isadora Duncan's romantic death; radiation that kills people, pollutes the flora and fauna; finally, the fires of hell, "incapable of licking clean / The aguey tendon, the sin, the sin." As the poetic imagery grows vaporous, the poet's performing self moves away from sensual limitation toward a heavenly burning. The yellow, oily element in the opening of the poem becomes smoke, then a strobelike flickering, fire, light, and, finally, the "beads of hot metal" from a pure acetylene flare. This movement is also echoed in the repetitive abrasion and association of sounds that link developing images from line to line, "aural pivots that never achieve stasis," according to Stuart Davis:[73]

> Darling, all night
> I have been flickering, off, on, off, on.
> The sheets grow heavy as a lecher's kiss.
>
> . . . .
> I am too pure for you or anyone.
> Your body
> Hurts me as the world hurts God. I am a lantern—
>
> My head a moon
> Of Japanese paper, my gold beaten skin
> Infinitely delicate and infinitely expensive.
>
> Does not my heat astound you. And my light.
> All by myself I am a huge camellia
> Glowing and coming and going, flush on flush. (*A*, 54)

As the poet's image metamorphoses from Isadora to an outsized Japanese lantern, then to a neon camellia, and finally to a "pure, acetylene virgin," the boundaries between these identities disappear with the speed of the poet's shifting shape. She is absorbed into the perpetual process that dissolves her variable selves into pure gaseous motion. Energy creates its own shape and value here, albeit a comic one, for the final image is a parody. In a mock Assumption, the industrial virgin is hauled up by pulleys into heaven, dea ex machina, baffled by both event and props ("whatever these pink things mean"). The progression in tone and imagery ends in a wry comment on "mystical writing" or "transcendent" commentary that singles out the mythical archetypes of birth-rebirth:

> I think I am going up,
> I think I may rise—
> The beads of hot metal fly, and I, love, I
>
> Am a pure acetylene
> Virgin
> Attended by roses,
>
> By kisses, by cherubim,
> By whatever these pink things mean.
> Not you, nor him
>
> Not him, nor him
> (My selves dissolving, old whore petticoats)—
> To Paradise. (A, 54–55)

Among the other poems that display the performing self, "Daddy" and "Lady Lazarus" are two of the most often quoted, but most frequently misunderstood, poems in the Plath canon. The speaker in "Daddy" performs a mock poetic exorcism of an event that has already happened—the death of her father who she feels withdrew his love from her by dying prematurely: "Daddy, I have had to kill you. / You died before I had time—."

The speaker attempts to exorcise not just the memory of her father but her own *Mein Kampf* model of him as well as her inherited behavioral traits that lead her graveward under the Freudian banner of death instinct or Thanatos's libido. But her ritual reenactment simply does not take. The event comically backfires as pure self-parody: the metaphorical murder of the father dwindles into Hollywood spectacle, while the poet is lost in the clutter of the collective unconscious.

Early in the poem, the ritual gets off on the wrong foot both literally and figuratively. A sudden rhythmic break midway through the first stanza interrupts the insistent and mesmeric chant of the poet's own freedom:

> You do not do, you do not do
> Any more, black shoe
> In which I have lived like a foot
> For thirty years, poor and white,
> Barely daring to breathe or Achoo. (*A*, 49)

The break suggests, on the one hand, that the nursery-rhyme world of contained terror is here abandoned; on the other, that the poet-exorcist's mesmeric control is superficial, founded in a shaky faith and an unsure heart—the worst possible state for the strong, disciplined exorcist.

At first she kills her father succinctly with her own words, demythologizing him to a ludicrous piece of statuary that is hardly a Poseidon or the Colossus of Rhodes:

> Marble-heavy, a bag full of God,
> Ghastly statue with one grey toe
> Big as a Frisco seal
>
> And a head in the freakish Atlantic
> Where it pours bean green over blue
> In the waters off beautiful Nauset.
> I used to pray to recover you.
> Ach, du. (*A*, 49)

Then as she tries to patch together the narrative of him, his tribal myth (the "common" town, the "German tongue," the war-scraped culture), she begins to lose her own powers of description to a senseless Germanic prattle ("The tongue stuck in my jaw. / It stuck in a barb wire snare. / Ich, ich, ich, ich"). The individual man is absorbed by his inhuman archetype, the "panzer man," "an engine / Chuffing me off like a Jew." Losing the exorcist's power that binds the spirit and then casts out the demon, she is the classic helpless victim of the swastika man. As she culls up her own picture of him as a devil, he refuses to adopt this stereotype. Instead he jumbles his trademark:

> A cleft in your chin instead of your foot
> But no less a devil for that, no not
> Any less the black man who
>
> Bit my pretty red heart in two. (*A*, 50–51)

The overt Nazi-Jew allegory throughout the poem suggests

that, by a simple inversion of power, father and daughter grow more alike. But when she tries to imitate his action of dying, making all the appropriate grand gestures, she once again fails: "but they pulled me out of the sack, / And they stuck me together with glue." She retreats to a safe world of icons and replicas, but even the doll image she constructs turns out to be "the vampire who said he was you." At last, she abandons her father to the collective unconscious where it is *he* who is finally recognized ("they always *knew* it was you"). *She* is lost, impersonally absorbed by his irate persecutors, bereft of both her power and her conjuror's discipline, and possessed by the incensed villagers. The exorcist's ritual, one of purifying, cleansing, commanding silence and then ordering the evil spirit's departure, has dwindled to a comic picture from the heart of darkness. Mad villagers stamp on the devil-vampire creation.

In the course of performing the imaginative "killing," the speaker moves through a variety of emotions, from viciousness ("a stake in your fat black heart"), to vengefulness ("You bastard, I'm through"), finally to silence ("the black telephone's off at the root"). It would seem that the real victim is the poet-performer who, despite her straining toward identification with the public events of holocaust and destruction of World War II, becomes more murderously persecuting than the "panzer-man" who smothered her, and who abandoned her with a paradoxical love, guilt, and fear. Unlike him, she kills three times: the original subject, the model to whom she said "I do, I do," and herself, the imitating victim. But each of these killings is comically inverted. Each backfires. Instead of successfully binding the spirits, commanding them to remain silent and cease doing harm, and then ordering them to an appointed place, the speaker herself is stricken dumb.

The failure of the exorcism and the emotional ambivalence are echoed in the curious rhythm. The incantatory safety of the nursery-rhyme thump (seemingly one of controlled, familiar terrors) also suggests some sinister brooding by its repetition. The poem opens with a suspiciously emphatic protest, a kind of psychological whistling-in-the-dark. As it proceeds, "Daddy's" continuous life-rhythms—the assonance, consonance, and especially the sustained *oo* sounds—triumph over either the personal or the cultural-historical imagery. The sheer sense of organic life in the interwoven sounds carries the verse forward in boisterous spirit and communicates an underlying feeling of comedy that is also echoed in the repeated failure of the speaker to perform her exorcism.

Ultimately, "Daddy" is like an emotional, psychological, and historical autopsy, a final report. There is no real progress. The poet is in the same place in the beginning as in the end. She begins the poem as a hesitant but familiar fairy-tale daughter who parodies her attempt to reconstruct the myth of her father. Suffocating in her shoe house, she is unable to do much with that "bag full of God." She ends as a murderous member of a mythical community enacting the ritual or vampire killing, but only for a surrogate vampire, not the real thing ("the vampire who said he was you"). Although it seems that the speaker has moved from identification with the persecuted to identity as persecutor, Jew to vampire-killer, powerless to powerful, she has simply enacted a performance that allows her to live with what is unchangeable. She has used her art to stave off suffocation, and performs her self-contempt with a degree of bravado.[74]

Another performance, "Lady Lazarus," presents two unsuccessful suicide attempts as striptease acts while the third attempt is a genocidal dismemberment from which the speaker rises like a vengeful phoenix against her tormentors. Plath is energetically engaged in self-parody. She offers a triumph of vitality in the face of limiting biographical facts: her father's death when she was nine and her own suicide attempt at nineteen. The tonal conflicts and combinations of imagery demonstrate that energy itself has a consuming shape and value.

This view of the poem departs from the conventional canons of confessional criticism, which often ignore the poem's controlled aesthetic energy or treat it as a literal documentary of personal woes. A strict biographical reading demands of the poet a certain moral hush-hush that befits so weighty a subject as self-destruction. Irving Howe, for example, has viewed Plath's archness about suicide as "shocking in a way that she could not have intended."[75] Like Howe, the suicide mythologizers demand a certain clinical tone and demeanor of the poet, one that does not steal its personal grandeur from comparison with the Nazi holocaust.

In its wild concatenation of images and tones, "Lady Lazarus" defies simplistic confessional thinking. Here we see no naked ego wriggling on a couch, no private scrawls or disorientation. Instead, dying—at once the defeatist ritual of femininity

and the merit badge awarded to artists in extremis—is de-
bunked. The poet's peculiar strategic control—perfectly timed,
perfectly completed—suggests the smug finality of accomplishment:

> I have done it again.
> One year in every ten
> I manage it. . . . (A, 6)

The tone moves easily from bravado to sarcasm, from promise
to threat: "Do not think I underestimate your great concern," or
"Beware, beware."

But while the tone celebrates control, power, and mobility,
the imagery celebrates fragmentation, even dismemberment.
The transference of energy between the two is crucial to the
performer's final act:

> Peel off the napkin
> O my enemy.
> Do I terrify?—
>
> The nose, the eye pits, the full set of teeth?
> The sour breath
> Will vanish in a day. (A, 6)

The imagery is an audacious mixture of incongruities: the
Lazarus story from the Bible and the Nazi extermination. Recklessly, Plath mingles the miraculous with the cadaverous,
spiritual promise with witness of horror, a striptease act with
death, the myth of the phoenix with the parable of Lazarus, the
simple superstition of a cat's nine lives with the holocaust in the
Nazi ovens. She handles it all—the lampshades of skin and the
sideshow crowds—with reasoning, wit, and that pure bodily
gusto of the speaking voice. She dares, taunts, pities and shows
off, demythologizing dying to a habit or a skill one is conscious
of learning:

> Dying
> Is an art, like everything else.
> I do it exceptionally well.
>
> I do it so it feels like hell.
> I do it so it feels real.
> I guess you could say I've a call. (A, 7)

The keen, colloquial language ("what a trash," "I do it so it feels
like hell," and "that knocks me out") dares to speak of dismemberment by Nazis in a biting attack on those posturing artists
who write in extremis:

Ash, ash—
You poke and stir.
Flesh, bone, there is nothing there—

A cake of soap.
A wedding ring,
A gold filling. (*A*, 8)

With her art, and its pure energy of self-measuring process, Plath eludes her viewers as the inmates of Terezin used art to elude their persecutors. For her, energy in all its forms is that "pure gold baby," that "valuable," which is in, perhaps even beyond, the most painful facts of death.

Quite profoundly, the poet has isolated the quality of voyeurism that is common to both suicide and striptease. Her parody of self-enclosed dying is startling. Instead of presenting the performer as a cheesecake number who flaunts her sexual overtures with diaphanous scarves, the poet gives us a stark cadaver in quite a different display: "the nose, the eye pits, the full set of teeth," even the "sour breath." Instead of a titillating parade of flesh, there is only skin and bone, hands and knees, and worms to be picked off "like sticky pearls." The slangy voice that insists on physical vitality dares us to believe that despite visual differences she is substantially the same woman! By pitting her performing energy and tonal improvisations against the indefatigable energy of voyeurism, Plath redirects the attention of the "peanut crunching crowd" to the mundane, the everyday world of Lazarus arisen that is the antithesis of suicide spectacles. Here she lives, here she writes. This single fact holds more startling value for her than any suicide.

For the truly agonizing task, according to the poet, is not her highly acclaimed public spectacle, but the daily choice of continuing one's work despite the lure of high-profile stardom. Her emphasis, therefore, is not so much on the act, the grand event that is voyeurized ("ash, ash / you poke and stir / There is nothing there"), but on the aftermath, the anticlimactic, the everyday:

It's the theatrical

Comeback in broad day
To the same place, the same face, the same brute
Amused shout:

'A miracle!'
That knocks me out. (*A*, 7–8)

There's a skillful, comic ambiguity in the mention of "charge" to these folks, critics and voyeurs alike. Just as that call for dying is left intentionally vague, the "charge" has ambiguous sexual and religious connotations. Is it a monetary charge exacted by a sideshow barker for the peep show within? Or does it refer to religious awe and reverence—a mission—required of those believers prostrate before church relics? Perhaps the "charge" is simply the costly pain and anguish exacted from the cultists who observe Plath's performance only as pure victimization.

Read another way, "Lady Lazarus" is a peculiarly futuristic indictment of all those critics, editors, and collectors who promote the Plath legend, guest editor to ghastly suicide. As if predicting the lurid approach to her life, not her art, she mocks the glitter-seduced participants in the spectacle of her annihilation. This shoving crowd paws among the poetic ruins, reading and rereading for scraps of sensory details of her foreclosed end. Plath is their "opus" or "valuable," their classic archetypal victim reduced to a shriek. (Ironically, she "melts to a shriek"—her tonal escape-artistry as well as her status as hysterical goddess in women's canons—before they can carry off some scrap of the legend.) Hence, she eludes them and predicts her own marketability as a consumer product of the suicide enterprise. Plath is having her last laugh, a terribly sophisticated and ironic one, at the expense of those who are blind and deaf to her blatant self-exhibitionism in "Lady Lazarus." Oblivious to her poetic control and her sense of camp, they react only to the themes of negation and death and mythical rebirth. They do not perceive the rearranging, controlling, and freeing art.

"Lady Lazarus" is Plath's last act as pure performing energy by which she escapes a final identity imposed by critics and commentators, voyeurs and oppressors. Like a phoenix, with vital energy native to the comic spirit, she creates her own shape, that wild, protean admixture of passivity and spectacle. She utters her personalized warning:

Herr God, Herr Lucifer
Beware,
Beware.

Out of the ash
I rise with my red hair
And I eat men like air. (A, 9)

The warning of "Lady Lazarus" is one that applies to Plath's complete posthumous reputation. The poem is best read as her plea that the mundane be taken to heart. Proper critical attention should be redirected to the difficult, small constructiveness of her words, the everyday labor that continues despite the life-punctuating spectacles. From the ash of legends and myths, a self-styled phoenix of poetic art rises.

CONCLUSION

"Just to find a balance. . . ." For over thirteen years, Plath tinkered at reconciling the poles that determined both her life and her writing. As her art matured, the dilemma became less rhetorical, more personal, and more critical: the "fact of doubt" versus the "faith of dream"; engraved emblematic moments ("sign language of a lost otherworld") versus the menace of systematic degeneration; "wingy myths" of the imagination versus the slipping labor of verbal reconstruction; "stillborn" poetic metaphors versus the sensuously dramatic speaking voice; the love of stasis and passivity versus the flare for high-camp theatrics. What began as a description of social gesture quickly matured to a struggle with the creative process, a struggle that involved every fiber of her being.

Although Sylvia Plath grew practiced in spelling out her ideological options, she never seemed to resolve—or wanted to resolve—that "fatal equilibrium" by facile polemics or glib partisanship. "Suspense / On the quicksands of ambivalence" was less her "nemesis," as an early poem claimed, than a solid habit of mind and narrative, and eventually a positive individuating trait of her poetic. At first, Plath chided herself for that ambivalence, sparred with its presence, and postured in adolescent gesture about its conflicts. Gradually she learned to employ its challenge to create one of the most innovative emotional ranges of any modern poet. Plath transformed hollow philosophical argument and imitative technique into a linguistic portrait of her own complex consciousness.

More than a decade of readers and critics have been deceived in reading and reacting to Sylvia Plath. She has been neatly positioned under that confessional umbrella where life's irrefutable direction is deathward, where certain emotions have become clichés of madness. Her poems have been petrified into a handful of graven ur-myths ("preexisting options that constitute a state of being") that attempt to normalize Sivvy at the same time that they rob her poetry of its full range of wit and vitality. My work in the preceding chapters suggests that it is simply inaccurate to trace Plath's development to a final, glossy union of warring selves, woman and artist, or to place in a matrix the poet's sensibility in guilt over imagined incest with

"Dad." Such resolutions betray the same limitation: ultimately they dismiss Plath the poet, who seventeen years after her untimely death we are only beginning to appreciate for her emotional pioneering and remarkably skilled poetics.

From the early Cambridge and Smith poems, Plath was as capable of mocking herself for the practice of metaphorical overkill as for her naiveté about the perils of romantic love. And when her impossible imaginative world failed her, she faced the limits of her poetic sensibility with a "wry complaisance." She did not merely hide among female archetypes: she reinvented them. As she became more a "cold-vision" critic of her own poetry after *The Colossus*, she developed a highly personalized body of women's myths—an ogress's gallery of witches, maenads, muses, mannequins, and misplaced mothers. We have heard her startle with a colloquial voice that boasts or deprecates with equal ease. In *Ariel* and *Winter Trees* she worships pure energy. She dramatically and poetically cultivates an exhilarating velocity, yet frequently counsels a cowering stance to protect against disillusionment. Her tenderness toward children does not smother, but respects, otherness. She is wry, funny, capricious, theatrical, humble, humbling, dramatic, scholarly—all in quick succession. In sum, Plath the poet glories in her protean emotional range.

In these chapters I have discussed Sylvia Plath's poetry in terms that mattered a great deal to the poet herself. In her Cambridge diary (26 February 1956), Plath wrote:

> What I fear most, I think, is the death of the imagination. When the sky outside is merely pink, and the rooftops merely black: that photographic mind which paradoxically tells the truth, but the worthless truth, about the world. It is that synthesizing spirit, that shaping force, which prolifically sprouts and makes up its own worlds with more inventiveness than God which I desire. (*JP*, 260)

By charting the development of her "synthesizing spirit" from her early college poems to her posthumously published work, we have observed Plath reworking the sometimes marring, sometimes joyous details of real life with a startlingly fresh imagination. Yet she always measures the degree of synthesis in terms of human limitation. In her description of the metamorphosis of the poetic imagination from a dry-as-dust intellectual argument about scholarly abstractions to a movingly dramatic enactment of progress between contradictory poles, Plath struggles within the texture of the poems to find a theoretical balance.

Esther Greenwood's words in *The Bell Jar* ring only partially true of Plath's poetic career: "I'll be flying back and forth between one mutually exclusive thing and another for the rest of my days." Esther's forecast was accurate less for its reference to contradictory goals than for its hint at the significance of Plath's energy and movement. The act of moving—the worship of kinesis—becomes the focus for Plath's creative energies in her late volumes. While early in her career she may have postured intellectually that "the choice . . . has always to be made," as she matured poetically Plath realized that merely orchestrating the dualities of life's contradictions was task enough without requiring of herself resolution or choice. The dramatic portrayal of energy and movement was her form of protection against social and intellectual circumscription.

"Enigmatical, shifting [her] clarities," Plath struggled self-consciously into her own peculiar tonal and imagistic coherence. She developed a clever control of unconventional reactions, of unorthodox thematic and technical matters in her poetry. "What am I to make of these contradictions?" the poet asked in "An Appearance." Is the ingenue speaking? The diarist? The mother? The conjuror? The ironist? The striptease artist with "nine times to die"? The creations of over a decade—poems that forge a personal identity, span a wide range of emotions, and achieve a highly sophisticated form of artistic balance—give Plath's response to that question.

In Plath's early poems, words as well as philosophy are but echoes "traveling off from the center like horses," reverberating from modern poetry's hall of fame—Theodore Roethke, Dylan Thomas, Emily Dickinson, Wallace Stevens, Robert Frost, and Robert Lowell. The early poems jangle with overly athletic verbs, ornamental adjectives, and metaphors whose strained overstatement dissipates energy and makes the poem inelastic. The youthful exploration of contradictions in awkward allegories ("King Egg Head" versus "Barbarous Prince Ow") seem like deadlocked rehearsals for a high school debate. Thematically, this apprentice writing from the early fifties chronicles the poet's disillusionment with life and art, presenting Plath's philosophical despair in ever finding that elusive balance. She knows that her "casuist arguments" cannot suffice in a world that debunks the imagination and demands blunt facts. Three major groups of uncollected poems that predate *The Colossus* treat the cosmic sentiments of a neophyte who is yearning to write great poetry, to become one of the "philosophical heavies." But Plath is doomed to vagaries—and ironies—of romantic love and cursed with a handful of academic topics that reek with the musty scent of too many footnotes and too much homework in prosody.

In these Smith and Cambridge years, when she fitfully belabored argument and technique, Plath's burden was not so much an emotional weighing and balancing as it was the translation of her conflicts into borrowed verbiage and metrics. Like her own "Colossus," that run-down statue pilfered from mythology, she stands rakishly astride two worlds. Intellectually, she chides herself that a choice ought to be made between the "muck trap of skin and bone" and the "preposterous provinces of the madcap cloud cuckoo." In actuality, however, she remains content merely with stating the "ought." Plath never engages in niggardly false allegiances either to "lantern-jawed Reason" or to "squat Common Sense." Mere philosophical summary of the argument in borrowed terminology is a panacea for her malaise: discovery of analogues for her conflicts becomes an end in itself in the poems predating *The Colossus*.

What, then, is the value of this strained juvenilia in light of Plath's later achievement? First of all, Plath shows an early awareness of the value of ambivalence: "all absolutes that angels give / flounder in the relative." She discovers that even while frozen in a "cross of contradiction" she can engage in lively dialogue with the warring elements. Still, for the young poet this remains a purely rhetorical exercise where the bookish terms are not hers. Her philosophical tracts are less than convincing. Secondly, the public female figures of the early poems (queens, fortune-tellers, acrobats) prefigure her later personae. Engaged in flashy, debonair performances, each is confronted with a lesson in disillusionment: each is somehow humbled, tempered. Each emerges with some wry truth or perhaps an admonition about the ephemeral nature of romantic love or a caveat about the vanity of gluttonous wishes. These stubborn but comic women who populate the Cambridge Manuscript and the Smith poems are unwitting about the hazards of false ideals. However, the awareness they glean from the turn of events in the poems foreshadows the mother's tempered words of advice to her small child in the muted, late poems. These women also prefigure the self-deprecatory speaker in the *Crossing the Water* poems, and their comic plight anticipates Plath's new valuation of passivity in the bee sequence: they triumph mentally, if physically they are chastened.

Through her early exercises in intricate metrical and stanzaic forms Plath learned how to "leap through the hoop" of traditional structure. In several poems her variation, or at times clever defiance, of set forms undercuts thematic clichés. Though her early imagery remains jejeune and unsophisticated, her calculated, technical inversions of traditional forms suggest the later innovations found in *Crossing the Water*. There she uses her women's heritage, and not the universal twists of fate, as the optic through which to scrutinize her technical development. At times in the early poems she mocks her own technical literalism as prosody becomes her means of chiding those early, foolish illusions about love and the imagination: she makes her lexical and syntactic strategies, not a personal voice, bear the burden of self-criticism. Mechanical manipulation of set poetic forms (villanelle, sonnet, terza rima) anticipates the late dramatic performances that experiment with—and at times reinvent—domestic, cultural-historical, biblical, and holocaustal image patterns. These virtuoso performances become a last testament of skillful control and tonal audacity. Although thematic risks as well as formal defiances are minimal and cautious in this early stage of her career, Plath's undeveloped self-measuring spirit will mature in later volumes, as when she uses women's myths to evaluate her shifting poetics in *Crossing the Water* and sports her humor in high-energy performances in *Ariel* and *Winter Trees*.

Plath devises another approach to disillusionment in the poems predating *The Colossus*. One group of early poems recognizes the authority of practical facts and physical limits. These poems prefigure the mother's love of "two wet eyes and a screech," her humble retreat to dumb elements and the "pebbly, turnipy chambers" in *Ariel* and *Winter Trees*. By recommending the scaled-down life of tangible things as distinct from the confusing power and glory of mythmaking, Plath ends her poetic career as she began it. She discovers—in the Smith College poems in particular—that sole reliance on the imagination, with no recourse to a world of earthly facts, is doomed. One can either cultivate a tolerant irony or yield to a stark resignation—the "day of tarnish," or the "bent bow of thorns."

Of the two early stays against disillusionment, the most convincing is resignation to a simple, monochromatic life where "no glory descends." Understatement is Plath's protection, at least in theory. Throughout her poetic career, she never abandons her ethic of prescribed physical limits, an important option in the final poems. She dramatizes diminishment in the self-ironic postures of the speakers of the transitional poems ("I must remember this, being small"), while in the bee sequence she assigns passivity a new moral value.

In *The Colossus* we enter a world of fixed, changeless, perhaps even stillborn, energy—a world of poems promising to be as "dull as an old etching." Everything is safe, abstract, balanced, and framed in pictorial design. Here, however, the poet is a "literalist of the imagination" using the craft she has learned so well. She repeatedly describes perfect synchronic states of imagination that hold opposite qualities in a moment of simultaneity: "horses fluent in the wind / A place, a time gone out of mind"; the Lorelei in their "silver flux"—a song of passion, yet a seduction in stone; the timeless old man of the sea, half labyrinthine tangle, half "myth of origins / Unimaginable." Voiceless figures from the imagination beckon to the poet to join them in an emblematically perfect world of art, a world where there is not even the "scrape of a keel on the blank stones of a landing."

Always artistically self-conscious, Plath brings the aesthetic process into poetic focus, looking for the logic of imagination as it works on the raw material of life. She searches paintings and artifacts for imitative moments, lured by the safe past to recover a sense of personal history: "From the mercury-backed glass / Mother, grandmother, great-grandmother / Reach hag hands to haul me in." But most importantly, she explores the nature of the creative process in these artworks and artifacts, trying to understand the interaction between the moments of imaginative union that she has so repeatedly idealized and her own maturing poetic sensibility. Her focus is the watercolors of English landscape, the sculpture of Leonard Baskin, paintings of Rousseau, Gauguin, de Chirico, Brueghel, even Greek statuary. But these aesthetic objects remain external details; once again their emblematic perfection provides no directive for exercise of the poetic voice, no psychological mold for the poet's expanding consciousness. The longed-for world of aesthetics and metaphysics has obscured the blunt presence of that "one / Blue and improbable person" at the poem's center.

Clearly the ambivalence Plath courts at this stage in her career is an exercise in symmetry of verse and balance in poetic structure. She finds the comprehensive imaginative world she describes unavailable to her poetic sensibility. Her mode of perception is not as tidy, not as balanced as that ideal "reconciliation of opposites" so apparent in the compositional unity of the world she admires. She cannot translate its emblematically perfect moments into psychologically useful terms for the development of her sensibility: ". . . this thick air is murderous / I would breathe water." Instead, the "collusion of mulish elements" in the real things of this world menace her imaginative realm. A subtle threat of decay and ossification from nature reminds her of a practical, not a visionary, realm—the "dry-papped stones," the "blood-berried hawthorn," the indifferent iron hills.

Memories of a grandmother's fleeting love devour her as they eat at the spit of land, Point Shirley; and those monochrome ancestors "persevere in thinness" in her imagination as they do in physical pain. Elemental things threaten that "lost otherworld" of aesthetic perfection that she has mythologized. They loom over the poet's fragile self as nagging reminders of the mire of the factual world.

By her poetic explorations of mythology, antiquity, paintings, and sculpture ("Colossus" and "Burnt-out Spa"), Plath gradually relaxes and at the same time enlarges her too-pat theory of artistic integration to include the foibles and imperfections of the speaking self. For the poet who has failed to develop a perfectly balanced sensibility, "chagrin gives place / To a wry complaisance." A variety of mythical and godly models become her mentors in irony. Displaying boredom or a Machiavellian casualness, these figures are awkward creators: they discover their spheres of influence to be water, not traditional dust; they thumb out "a certain meaning green" about the nature of the world. Like her early women idealists, they are essentially comic: they foppishly form and then dissolve creation. Always the scholar of the aesthetic process, Plath learns from these figures a new self-consciousness and mobility in the role of creator. "Pared down to a pinch of flame," she recognizes human limitations in the face of sheer matter: "It is not I, it is not I," she insists of her vacant self-image throughout *The Colossus*. The final poem in the volume, "Stones," recounts not only a philosophical struggle with the integrative process, but, for the first time in her poetry, the struggle of the speaking voice to recover a whole range of reactions. This new, disingenuous speaking self becomes the focus of the poetic process in its dramatic metamorphosis from sickness to health. The self at the center of the metaphor—not an impersonal reconstruction modeled on a poetic theory—anticipates the central achievement of *Crossing the Water*.

Imaginative states are no longer described as perfect emblems of an inhuman order in *Crossing the Water*, Plath's third volume. Now the imagination is touched by the ragged, chewed edges of real life dilemmas—mother/daughter and husband/ wife rivalries, widowhood, stillbirth and abortion, aging, courtship, and everywhere the nostalgia of loss. A menacing world replete with disintegration, plus a speaker's restlessness and self-consciousness, characterize the poems of this transitional volume. Now an authority of tone prevails over any abstract, idealized states, over mere lip service to the illusion-free life. The poet is alternately slangy, casual, tender, tough, mocking, and sly as she rehearses the old imperfections of self ("fond masters") at the poem's center. Her manner of becoming—like a fitful and hesitant child "forming itself finger by finger in the dark"—is the focus of the poems. She explores and experiments, grows critical of fustian poetic forms that are ill-suited to her broader emotional range. No longer is the ostensible subject matter knowledge without experience, landscape unpeopled and cerebral, stones, breakwaters, paintings—that "morgue of old logs and images." The speaker now controls a personal world of maenads, witches, and cuddly mothers as well as mute, dumb elements: she moves among them to show her own maximum dramatic metamorphosis, anticipating the expansiveness, yet the self-depreciating limits, in the best late poems of *Ariel* and *Winter Trees*.

In *The Colossus* Plath failed to incorporate a perfect, unitive, imaginative vision into the functioning of her poetic sensibility. By using the most intimate subject matter available to her— women's blood and birth myths, voluntary and involuntary creation—she evaluates her old poetic, its failures and its promises in *Crossing the Water*. While Plath is exploring a new freedom in form, rhythm, and sound, she is also revising inherited stereotypes about women. These simultaneous functions form a more intimate commentary on—and guideline for—her future development than the distanced world of art provided her in *The Colossus*. Her poetic argument on the nature of the creative process has come to include new tonal possibilities for a speaking voice: "Once I was ordinary," she announces, "Sat by my father's bean tree / Eating the fingers of wisdom." She discovers new protean shapes for emotions, maunders over old nostalgias, enters the "contour of things," reveals the power in passivity, self-deprecation, and then boisterously exaggerates her energy: "I shone, mica-scaled, and unfolded / To pour myself out like a fluid." She minimizes and contracts her image ("I am silver and exact") so as to gain maximum emotional impact. In poem after poem, she flaunts her passage to awareness. She explores the new dramatic capacity for ironic detachment and newfound constructive powers of language (hermetic imagery, unusual rhythm combinations, colloquial voice). Sometimes her own dramatic register frightens the poet as she charts new areas for emotional and imaginative power: "Give me back my shape." Awestruck by so many options, uncertain about a single identity, the speaker sometimes begs in the midst of her repertoire of changes to be "told her name." The burden of consciousness, with its requisite self-scrutiny, is extraordinarily compelling.

What is Plath's aim in this highly self-critical transitional volume? That she wants a poetic form appropriate to her dramatic expansion is clear. By creating new emotional energies *within* the formal progress of the poem, and by doing this through a revision of women's heritage, Plath joins two significant processes of exploration and thus avoids the charges of narcissism and confessional self-indulgence. In this volume Plath arms the self with technique elastic enough to chart many protean changes and, by reexamining women's myth heritage as a means of measuring aesthetic progress, she forges a peculiarly succinct unity in her work. She gains confidence in her poetic inventiveness at the same time that she personalizes women's stereotypes. Both achievements complement her individual—heretofore critically unarticulated—poetic vocation.

From her struggles with the imagination, Plath knows that there is a life more grand than the mute existence of sheep or the "little particular lusters" of physical things. Yet the constructive urge of a mental life with its dreams of the spirit brings only pain and disillusionment. Self-protection as well as self-definition, she realizes, both rest in the ability to shift shape, to move swiftly, even surprisingly, from one state to another.

After "construing the days [she] coupled with / dust in the shadow of a stone" in *Crossing the Water*, Plath arrives at her technical and emotional center of gravity in her last two volumes of poems. Dramatically and emotionally, she now "comes of age," employing in the speaker's voice a full range of wit, imagination, and energy. As she moves between the poles of energy and inertia, she sheds a few "old whore selves" and puts on others. She glories in being able to isolate formally, and then to display, her transforming energy. She revels in the sheer life of it, asserting its vitality over stagnant images and conventional emotions. Just as she reversed and reexamined the legacy of women's myths in *Crossing the Water*, she takes similar technical and emotional risks with traditional imagery (religious, histori-cal, cultural, and psychological) in the last volumes. In her bee sequence and mother poems, she no longer merely implies a new authority in the fact of limitation but now creates complete symbolic microcosms that establish such authority: the apiary and the institution of motherhood. She reevaluates, even rede-fines, passivity, retrieving it from a socially pejorative status.

In *Winter Trees*, both external plot and character are dis-solved as if the poet cannot be bothered with anything but the pure consciousness of emotional states. The fact that these poems of mood and atmosphere coexist with Plath's final theat-rical spectacles ("Tour," "Fever 103°," "Lady Lazarus," and "Daddy") suggests to us, once again, that Plath was intent upon redefining the emotional gamut available to women. With star-tling comic vitality, she elasticizes conventional emotional reac-tions, thus forcing biography buffs to correct their sleuthing for suicidal motives in her poetry.

Thematically and technically, the last poems, defying both critical and psychological labels, argue for a positive, creative space for ambivalence. Plath demonstrates her mobility be-tween the contradictory extremes of self-effacement and the diminished life on the one hand, and theatrical energy on the other. The speaker reminds us that her enlarged sensibility is always at work weighing, balancing, and combining. Her ex-pansiveness is not a matter of diffused emotions out of control or schizophrenic inattention. Rather, it is a conscious love of motion.

The late poems of *Ariel* and *Winter Trees* prove how very ludicrous it is to "sacrifice Plath to her plot" or to the times that deem her a cultish victim. Nor can we summarize her achievement in a battery of themes now as weathered as old graveyard marble—lost youth, romantic love disappointment, marital discord, suicide, death, even an Electra complex. We do Plath a genuine disservice by ignoring her lively transformation of such preoccupations within the craft of each poem. Plath proves (by careful attention to her developing skills with sound, rhythm, and imagery) that control—not the dictates of illness or indecision—governs her wide-ranging emotional exploration. Her sheer vitality often takes no definitive shape, but parodies existing ones, suggesting that lables that subsume Plath in a psychological or mythical system of interpretation ignore an important element of her poetry. For the poems of the last volumes must be read as an ongoing, lively dialectic between inertia and energy in which the speaker continually takes different shapes, none final, all exploratory. Growth, motion, raucous humor, self-display, and sleight-of-hand reversals all suggest a negative answer to her earlier question, "Is there no way out of the mind?" As she dramatizes isolation, fragmentation, even disappearance, the poet does so with humor and aplomb, making a literary virtue and a personal moral strength out of passivity. She enlivens those still, perfect imaginative moments glimpsed in *The Colossus* with a newly mobile speaking voice developed in *Crossing the Water*.

Moreover, Sylvia Plath's wit and bodily gusto surely disprove any foreclosure of a "death track sensibility." She yearns for the "merciless churn of hooves," for the "piston in motion." She rides those blue-red navel cords that "shriek" from her belly, or she escapes a chilly marriage by a gaseous mock Assumption. Death to her is a surprise birthday present only very haltingly opened, suicide a striptease come-on that she turns to her own theatrical triumph. Marriage is hawked by a kind of hardsell hucksterism; an ostensible love song to "Daddy" becomes a backfired exorcism ritual. While Plath employs certain collectively significant images (the yew, the bee, the rose, and the moon) in her last poems, their meaning is eclipsed by a kind of worshipful life force, energy qua energy. She asserts this energy through self-parody, whimsy, ingenuous wit, jeering taunts, even respectful tenderness proffered to children.

Were these last poems a temporary stay against the rush of darkness? A culling oneself back to health (or to fiction) by verbal bravado? A brave litany in extremis? Why did Plath return again and again ("Point Shirley," "Mary's Song," "Stings") to a jarringly atypical relationship between life and death?

Once again we are humbled by how few facts, yet such a plethora of surmises, we have about the poet's life and art. The reckless critical assignment of motives and "complexes" has provided us with mere scrappy details. A generation of critics has cramped her full emotional range with their cavalier use of political, psychological, mythological, and now even anthropological labels. A few poetic Gradgrindians have become progressively myopic about her controlled craft.

The conclusions reached here are less dramatic than the claim for transcendence through art, less audacious than the designation of Plath as an initiate into a new ritual process. Quite simply, we have denied full existence to Plath's imaginative vision. By closely following the argument of the poems—the bickering between self-revelation and artistic form—we have observed Plath becoming her own best demythologist and offering criticisms and imaginative options for the female voice heretofore unheard. At each stage of her career, she evaluates the aesthetic process—specifically the development of her own poetic—from those handbook exercises in literary form to the blood-hot and personal canon of the late poems. Within the poetic fabric, Plath has developed her own masterful system of checks and balances.

Certain themes are present in slightly altered forms throughout her writings: she counsels physical limitations, warns against the hazards of an exclusive imaginative life, mocks romantic illusions and later marital-love delusions, recognizes the failure of a simple identity. Yet these themes seem less important, less defining, than Plath's consciousness of her changing poetic and her explorations of the startling gamut of emotional options for the speaking voice. By *Ariel* and *Winter Trees*, she has turned "fatal equilibrium" into creative ambivalence, giving a dual artistic authority to passivity and motion in her final poems.

A complete and fully nuanced evaluation of Plath's poetic talent remains an endeavor for the next generation of readers who will, we trust, return to the ever-growing Plath oeuvre with loving, renewed vision. The task will be less to structure Plath's psyche into yet another pattern than to remind us of the rich complexities and sophisticated poetics of a woman whose poetry is a field of landmines for the witting, a mere grave for the imperceptive.

Appendixes

Appendix I

The following poems were published in *The Smith Review* between 1952 and 1955:
Spring 1953: Mad Girl's Love Song, To Eva Descending the Stair, Doomsday.
Spring 1954: Admonition, Denouement, Never Try to Know More Than You Should, Verbal Calisthenics.
Fall 1954: Circus in Three Rings.
January 1955: Dialogue en Route.
Spring 1955: Danse Macabre.

Appendix II

The following eleven poems were awarded English Department prizes in 1954 and 1955 at Smith College, submitted under the pseudonym of Robin Hunter. The poems remain in the Sophia Smith Women's History Archive at Smith College: Insolent Storm Strikes at the Skull (Prize poem, 1955), Moonsong at Morning (Prize poem, 1955), Love Is a Parallax (Prize poem, 1955), Metamorphoses of the Moon (Prize poem, 1955), Lament (Prize poem, 1955), Second Winter (Ethel Olin Corbin Prize Poem, 1955), Winter Words (Prize poem, 1955), Prologue to Spring (Prize poem, 1955), Ice Age (Prize poem, 1955), Epitaph in Three Parts (Prize poem, 1955), Two Lovers and a Beachcomber by the Real Sea (Prize poem, 1955).

Appendix III

According to Eric Homberger, "this is the table of contents of the 'Cambridge Manuscript,' which was recently discovered at the English Faculty Library in Cambridge. It was submitted as an original composition by Sylvia Plath towards Part Two of the English Tripos in 1957" (*A Chronological Checklist of the Periodical Publications of Sylvia Plath*).

This checklist extends by one-third the periodical publications listed in the previous "Informal Checklist of Criticism" and "Bibliography" by Mary Kinzie, Daniel Lynn Conrad, and Suzanne D. Kurman included in Charles Newman's *The Art of Sylvia Plath*. I have discovered inaccuracies and omissions in Homberger's work, however: eleven poems from the Sophia

Smith Women's Archives at Smith College published under the pseudonym of "Robin Hunter"; two poems, "Never Try to Know More Than You Should," and "Verbal Calisthenics," from *The Smith Review*, 1954; two short stories and two poems from *Seventeen* ("Den of Lions," May 1951, and "Initiation," January 1953; "Ode to a Bitten Plum," November 1950, and "The Suitcases Are Packed Again," March 1953); and an important essay published two months after the poet's death ("Maids from School: 'America! America!' " *Punch*, pp. 482–84).

Section 1: Wreath for a Bridal, Monologue at 3 A.M., Street Song, Strumpet Song, Letter to a Purist, The Glutton, The Shrike, Two Sisters of Persephone, Spinster, Ella Mason and Her Eleven Cats, Miss Drake Proceeds to Supper, Vanity Fair, To Eva Descending the Stair, Tinker Jack and The Tidy Wives, The Snowman on the Moor, Apotheosis, Complaint of the Crazed Queen, Mad Girl's Love Song, Pursuit, Recantation, Mad Maudlin, Epitaph for Fire and Flower.

Section 2: Metamorphosis, Go Get the Goodly Squab, Sow, Touch and Go, On the Plethora of Dryads, Soliloquy of the Solipsist, on the Difficulty of Conjuring up a Dryad, Two Lovers and a Beachcomber by the Real Sea, Resolve, Natural History, Dream of the Hearse-Driver, Aerialist, Dream of Clam-Diggers, Pigeon Post, Black Rook in Rainy Weather, Lament, November Graveyard, Temper of Time, The Lady and the Earthenware Head, All the Dead Dears, Doomsday.

Appendix IV

This is the table of contents for *Lyonnesse*. A note accompanied this limited edition: "The poems in this volume are hitherto uncollected. A few of them will be included in *Winter Trees*, a collection of poems by Sylvia Plath to be published shortly by Faber and Faber, London and Harper and Row, New York." A further note with the table of contents claims that "the date after each poem indicates the year it was written; and the end-papers show two of Sylvia Plath's manuscripts slightly enlarged, in copies 1–100 only."

Contents: A Winter's Tale (1958), Mayflower (1955), Epitaph for Fire and Flower (1956), Old Ladies' Home (1958), Wreath for a Bridal (1956), Metamorphosis of the Moon (1953), Owl (1958), Child (1963), Electra on the Azalea Path (1958), In Midas' Country (1958), Tinker Jack and the Tidy Wives (1956), Two Campers in Cloud Country (1960), The Rabbit Catcher

(1961), The Detective (1962), On the Difficulty of Conjuring up a Dryad (1956), The Snowman on the Moor (1956), Widow (1961), The Other Two (1959), Gigolo (1963), Brasilia (1962), Lyonnesse (1963).

Appendix V

This is the table of contents for *Crystal Gazer and Other poems*. The title page includes an original drawing by Sylvia Plath. A note accompanying this limited edition explained that the date given after each poem indicated the year of composition. The note also explained that "the poems in this volume are previously uncollected in volume form and many of them appear here for the first time."

Contents: Ballade Banale (1951–1952), Alicante Lullaby (1956), Leaving Early (1961), Notes on Zarathustra's Prologue (1950–1951), Mad Girl's Love Song (1951), On the Plethora of Dryads (1956), The Dream of the Hearse-Driver (1950–1951), Go Get the Goodly Squab (1950–1951), The Beggars (1956), Circus in Three Rings (1951–1952), The Goring (1956), Admonitions (1950–1951), Recantation (1956), Crystal Gazer (1956), Stopped Dead (1962), Mirror (1961), Face Lift (1961), Zoo Keeper's Wife (1961), Heavy Women (1961), Last Words (1961), Fable of the Rhododendron Stealers (1958), Lament (1951–1952), Yadwigha, On a Red Couch, Among Lilies (1957).

Appendix VI

Uncollected Poems appeared in a limited edition of 150 copies and included the following comment:

> The poems in this booklet represent an intermediate stage in Sylvia Plath's development as a poet, and form the connecting link between the poems to be found in *The Colossus*, which was published in 1960, and those printed in her posthumous volume, *Ariel*, which appeared earlier this year. The booklet includes the poem, *Insomniac*, which was awarded the Cheltenham Festival Guinness Poetry Prize in 1961. The drawing on the cover is Sylvia Plath's own illustration to *Wuthering Heights*. One poem, *Half-Moon*, is presented in a facsimile of the manuscript to illustrate the author's working methods.

Contents: Blackberrying, Wuthering Heights, A Life, Crossing the Water, Private Ground, An Appearance, Half-Moon, Finisterre, Insomniac, I Am Vertical, Candles, Parliament Hill Fields.

Notes

Preface

1. Robert Conquest, ed., *New Lines I* and *New Lines II*.
2. Robert Lowell, *Life Studies/For the Union Dead*.
3. Conquest, *New Lines II*, p. xxviii.
4. Conquest, *New Lines I*, p. xiv.
5. Alfred Alvarez, *The New Poetry*, p. 27.
6. Sylvia Plath, "Context," pp. 45–46.
7. James Dickey, *The Suspect in Poetry*.
8. Robert Lowell, "Skunk Hour," *Life Studies*, p. 90.
9. M. L. Rosenthal, *The New Poets*, pp. 3–24.
10. Ibid., pp. 9–10.
11. A. R. Jones, in "Necessity and Freedom: The Poetry of Robert Lowell, Sylvia Plath, and Anne Sexton," *Critical Quarterly*, pp. 11–30, and Jones and C. B. Cox, in "After the Tranquilized Fifties," *Critical Quarterly*, pp. 107–22, were among the first to discuss the poets of the sixties in the context of the historical relationship between artistic creation and mental instability, the poet and neurotic. Their two excellent articles make a persuasive case for a new twentieth-century sense of personality: man as presented by clinical psychology.
12. Alvarez, *Beyond All This Fiddle*, pp. 12–13.
13. T. S. Eliot, *Selected Essays, 1917–1932*, p. 8.
14. Plath, "Context," pp. 45–46.
15. Alvarez, *Beyond All This Fiddle*, p. 15.
16. Plath, "Lady Lazarus," *Ariel*, p. 8.
17. David Holbrook, *Sylvia Plath: Poetry and Existence*, p. 2.
18. Lawrence Ries, *Wolf Masks: Violence in Contemporary Poetry*, p. 58.
19. Anne Sexton, "Wanting to Die," in "The Barfly Ought to Sing," *TriQuarterly*, p. 90.
20. Alvarez, *The Savage God*, pp. 267–84.
21. Marjorie Perloff, "Extremist Poetry: Some Versions of the Sylvia Plath Myth," *Journal of Modern Literature*, p. 585.
22. Ted Hughes, "Introduction," *Johnny Panic and the Bible of Dreams*, p. 1.
23. For references to these two articles on Plath's chronology, see bibliography. Judith Kroll (*Chapters in a Mythology*) carried on Hughes's mythical interpretation of the Plath canon, claiming that the late poems describe a static coded state of being, a foreclosed universe.
24. The bibliographic work of Mary Kinzie, Eric Homberger, Cameron Northouse, Thomas P. Walsh, Gary Lane, and Maria Stevens are listed in the bibliography.
25. Sylvia Plath, "Maenad," *Crossing the Water*, p. 51.

I: Early Fiction and Poetry

1. Aurelia Schober Plath, ed., *Letters Home by Sylvia Plath*, p. 59. Hereafter cited in the text as *LH* with page number.
2. Sylvia Plath, "Early Unpublished Poems by Sylvia Plath," *Times Literary Supplement*, p. 855. "Letter to a Purist" is also published in the Cambridge Manuscript, hereafter given as the source for individual early poems published in several different places and cited in the text as *CM*.
3. Sylvia Plath, *Johnny Panic and the Bible of Dreams: Short Stories, Prose, and Diary Excerpts*, p. 2. Hereafter cited in the text as *JP* with appropriate page number. This collection includes twenty stories (seventy are extant), three

journalistic pieces, and four brief notebook excerpts. Seven stories from the Lilly Library Plath archive (Indiana University) have been added to the original thirteen selected by Ted Hughes in a 1977 British edition of *Johnny Panic*.

4. While on the whole the problem of psychoanalytic legacies is disturbing in the Plath canon, certain conflicts in the parents' lives do provide a useful reference point for many dilemmas introduced in her early poetry.

5. See Appendix I for the titles of these ten poems, hereafter cited in the text as *SR*.

6. See Appendix II for the titles of these eleven poems, hereafter cited in the text as *RH*.

7. Circumstances surrounding the discovery of this manuscript are recorded by Alfred Alvarez, "Sylvia Plath: The Cambridge Collection," *Cambridge Review*, p. 246. See Appendix III for the contents of this manuscript.

8. Sylvia Plath, *The Bell Jar*, p. 98.

9. The early writing was published sporadically in various papers and magazines, ranging from popular journals such as *Seventeen* and *Mademoiselle* to the more staid *Christian Science Monitor* and *Smith Review*. The Homberger bibliography (see Appendix III) was one of the first to suggest the variety of that achievement: tourist descriptions, interviews, pen sketches, education essays, a guest editor's tribute, short fiction, and even a review of a book on Lord Byron's wife. Other bibliographies have followed: Thomas P. Walsh and Cameron Northouse, *Sylvia Plath and Anne Sexton: A Reference Guide*; Gary Lane and Maria Stevens, *Sylvia Plath: A Bibliography*; and the excellent bibliography of primary and secondary materials—particularly useful for the uncollected prose and poetry—that accompanies *Sylvia Plath: New Views on the Poetry* (Baltimore: Johns Hopkins, 1979) edited by Gary Lane. The Plath archive in the Lilly Library, Indiana University, houses a substantial number of stories, poems, and papers acquired from Sylvia in 1961 through a British bookdealer and from Mrs. Aurelia Plath in 1976. The arduous task of piecing together Plath's corpus continues.

10. There is no definitive edition of her writings to date, prose or poetry, though one has been promised for a number of years. Nor is there an apparent logistics of composition or publication. The Homberger checklist points out that most of the early poems were published individually in different places within the same year, making the body of early work even less cohesive, and the interpretation more problematic. Bibliographies proliferate in lieu of a volume of collected works. The chronology has been further complicated by the appearance since 1971 of a number of small editions of previously uncollected work. Two are mentioned here: *Lyonnesse* (see Appendix IV; citations are indicated as *L*), and *Crystal Gazer and Other Poems* (see Appendix V; citations are indicated as *CG*). These particular poems range over ten years and are too sparsely and randomly selected to give a real sense of Plath's development.

We learn only selectively about Plath's complete oeuvre from the current editorial practices. According to Ted Hughes's introduction in *Johnny Panic and the Bible of Dreams*, a substantial novel fragment, *Double Exposure*, "disappeared somewhere around 1970." Of Plath's seventy extant stories, only twenty have been collected. From over ten years of daily journals (three pages a day and more), we have four brief excerpts from the notebooks, complemented by three essays.

11. This poem, "On the Difficulty of Conjuring Up a Dryad," is a good example of the baffling publishing chronology that continues to surround Plath's early writing. Not only is this poem listed in the second section of the Cambridge Manuscript (Appendix III), but it is also included in *Lyonnesse* and in *Poetry* 90 (July 1957): 235–36.

Frequently, dates of composition included after each poem in the limited editions offer little directive to the chronology. At best these dates show intervals of four years between time of composition and that of publication, as is the case with two poems: "Admonition," *The Smith Review*, Spring 1954, and "Go Get the Goodly Squab," *Harper's Magazine* 209 (November 1954). Both are listed in *Crystal Gazer* as written in 1950–1951. "Lament," another poem composed at the same time, appeared later in *New Orleans Poetry Journal* 1 (October 1959). "Dream of the Hearse Driver" also dates from 1950–1951 (*Crystal Gazer*), and later appeared with "Lament" as part of the forty-three poems included in the Cambridge Manuscript.

At worst, the dates of composition in the limited editions provide information that conflicts with dates and circumstances previously cited about a poem's origin. We know, for example, that the composition date of "Dream of the Hearse Driver" given in *Crystal Gazer* is 1950–1951; yet an article, "Early Unpublished Poems by Sylvia Plath," *Times Literary Supplement*, dates the composition from 1954.

12. Lois Ames, "Notes Toward a Biography," *TriQuarterly*, p. 98.

13. Sylvia Plath, "And Summer Will Not Come Again," *Seventeen* (August 1950). Eric Homberger lists the date of publication as March 1950.

14. Alvarez, "The Cambridge Collection," p. 246.

15. Theodore Roethke, "How to Write Like Somebody Else," *On the Poet and His Craft: Selected Prose of Theodore Roethke*, ed. Ralph J. Mills, Jr., p. 62.

16. Sylvia Plath, "Million Dollar Month," *Million Dollar Month*.

17. According to Paul Fussell, the disproportion of the two parts has something farcical about it: "it invites images of balls and pins" (*Poetic Meter and Poetic Form*, p. 128).

18. See Appendix V for titles and contents.

19. Sylvia Plath, "Den of Lions," *Seventeen* (May 1951), p. 145.

20. Sylvia Plath, "Sunday at the Mintons," *The Smith Review* (Fall 1952), p. 3. The story is also included in *Johnny Panic and the Bible of Dreams*, pp. 295–305.

21. Sylvia Plath, "Sweetie Pie and the Gutter Men," *Johnny Panic and the Bible of Dreams*, pp. 131–42. This story was added to the 1979 American collection from the Plath archive in the Lilly Library, Indiana University.

22. Sylvia Plath, "Battle Scene from the Comic Operatic Fantasy, 'The Seafarer,' " *Times Literary Supplement*, no. 3518 (30 July 1969), p. 855.

23. Sylvia Plath, "Wishing Box," *Atlantic Monthly* (October 1964), pp. 86–89. The later date of publication is cited here although the story was originally published in *Granta*, 26 January 1957, pp. 3–5, and again reprinted in *Johnny Panic and the Bible of Dreams*, pp. 204–10. The most recent version is used in the text.

24. Margaret Shook, "Sylvia Plath: The Poet and the College," *Smith Alumnae Quarterly*, p. 8. This is an abridged version of a lecture delivered at Smith on 16 December 1971 as part 3 of a three-part Ziskind Lecture Series on "The Art of Sylvia Plath."

25. Alvarez, "The Cambridge Collection," p. 247.

26. Sylvia Plath, "Bitter Strawberries," *The Christian Science Monitor*, 11 August 1950, p. 17.

27. Sylvia Plath, "Superman and Paula Brown's New Snowsuit," *The Smith Review* (Spring 1955), pp. 19–21, and *Johnny Panic*, pp. 269–75.

28. Sylvia Plath, "The Shadow," *Johnny Panic*, pp. 143–51.

29. Alvarez, "The Cambridge Collection," p. 247.

II. *The Colossus*

1. Peter Dickinson, "Some Poets," *Punch*, p. 829.

2. John Wain, review of *The Colossus*, *The Spectator*, p. 50.

Notes

Notes 199

3. Judson Jerome, "A Poetry Chronicle, Part I," *The Antioch Review*, p. 11.

4. E. Lucas Myers, review of *The Colossus*, *The Sewanee Review*, p. 217. Another important critic who treats technique and formal elements is J. F. Nims, "The Poetry of Sylvia Plath: A Technical Analysis," *The Art of Sylvia Plath*, ed. Charles Newman, p. 136. Reviewers include: Dom Moraes, "Poems from Many Parts," *Time and Tide*, p. 1413; A. E. Dyson, "On Sylvia Plath," *The Art of Sylvia Plath*, p. 208; Thomas Blackburn, "Poetic Knowledge," *New Statesman*, p. 1016; Guy Owen, *Books Abroad*, p. 209.

5. Lynda B. Salamon, " 'Double, Double': Perception in the Poetry of Sylvia Plath," *Spirit*, p. 34. The most important of these critics are Richard Howard, "Five Poets," *Poetry*, pp. 412–13, and "Sylvia Plath: 'And I Have No Face, I Have Wanted to Efface Myself . . .' " *The Art of Sylvia Plath*, p. 77; Ted Hughes, "Notes on the Chronological Order of Sylvia Plath's Poems," *TriQuarterly*, p. 82, reprinted in *The Art of Sylvia Plath*. Other critics who are useful for this approach include: James Tulip, "Three Women Poets," *Poetry Australia*, p. 37; and Gary Kissick, "Plath: A Terrible Perfection," *The Nation*, p. 245.

6. Howard, "Five Poets," p. 412.

7. M. L. Rosenthal, "Metamorphosis of a Book," *The Spectator*, p. 456.

8. Alfred Alvarez, "Sylvia Plath," *The Art of Sylvia Plath*, p. 58.

9. Alvarez, "Sylvia Plath," p. 61. By the energy of their rereadings and by the highlighting of sensational details, critics as well as poets defined the nature of extremist art. In the words of poet Robert Lowell, "We are all old-timers, / each of us holds a locked razor" ("Waking in the Blue," *Life Studies/For the Union Dead*, p. 82). To poet Anne Sexton, the art of appreciation became the art of learning how to "crawl down alone into the death [I] wanted so badly and for so long":

. . . suicides have a special language.
Like carpenters, they want to know *which tools*.
They never ask *why* build ("Sylvia Plath's Death," *The Art of Sylvia Plath*, p. 179).

10. Sylvia Plath, "Verbal Calisthenics," *The Smith Review* (Spring 1954), p. 53.

11. T. S. Eliot speaks of the poet's "unified sensibility" that constantly amalgamates disparate experience, fusing emotional and intellectual aspects without distinction. John Ruskin, in defining both the imagination and fancy, speaks of the "dead earnestness" of the former. T. E. Hulme, despite his battle against the unbounded romantic imagination of Coleridge, pleads for new powers given to the intuitive faculty. In his article "The Creative Process: Science, Poetry and the Imagination," Murray Krieger (*The New Apologists for Poetry*, Bloomington: Indiana University Press, 1963) provides a more elaborate survey of theorists on poetic creativity.

12. Sylvia Plath, "The Net Menders," *New Yorker* 36 (20 August 1960), p. 36.

13. Sylvia Plath, "November Graveyard," *Mademoiselle* 1xii (November 1965), p. 134. The poem is also included in the Cambridge Manuscript.

14. Sylvia Plath, "The Colossus," *The Colossus and Other Poems*, p. 20. References to this edition of *The Colossus* will be indicated in the text by *Col.* and page number.

15. Dennis Welland in "The Dark Voice of the Sea: A Theme in American Poetry," *American Poetry*, ed. Irvin Ehrenpries, gives a comprehensive history of the use of sea imagery in American poetry.

16. Sylvia Plath, "Ocean 1212-W," *Writers on Themselves*, ed. Herbert Read, p. 110. References to this autobiographical essay will be cited within the text by *0* and page number. The essay has been reprinted in *Johnny Panic*, pp. 20–26.

17. Charles Newman, "Candor is the Only Wile," *TriQuarterly*, reprinted in *The Art of Sylvia Plath*, p. 22. Citations are from the later version.

18. George Stade, "Introduction," *A Closer Look at Ariel*, ed. Nancy Hunter Steiner, p. 12.

19. Alvarez, "Sylvia Plath," p. 59.

20. Sylvia Plath, *Johnny Panic and the Bible of Dreams* ("Introduction"), p. 5.

21. Alvarez, "Sylvia Plath," p. 59.

22. Howard, "Sylvia Plath: 'And I Have No Face,' " p. 81.

23. Other poems reinforce the ominous power of diminished things. In "Watercolor of Grantchester Meadows," menace is camouflaged in a small, silvered perfection; in "All the Dead Dears," the antique lady in that "mercury-backed glass" case has the power over an unwitting poet: she can "reach hag hands to haul her in"; quiet and discreet, those self-effacing "Mushrooms" suddenly become threatening despite the cautious syllabics of the poem:

> Soft fists insist on
> Heaving the needles,
> The leafy bedding,
>
> Even the paving.
> Our hammers, our rams,
> Earless and eyeless,
>
> Perfectly voiceless,
> Widen the crannies,
> Shoulder through holes. (*Col.*, 37–38)

24. "Snakecharmer" and "Yadwigha, on a Red Couch, Among Lilies" were inspired by two Rousseau paintings, *Le Douanier* and *La Reve*, respectively. "The Disquieting Muses" is based on de Chirico's *La Muse Inquietante*; "On the Decline of Oracles" was inspired in part by the same painter's *l'Enigme de l'Oracle*. "Two Views of a Cadaver Room" is based on Brueghel's *Triumph of Death*. *Letters Home* (pp. 336–37) reminds us that "Ghost's Leavetaking" is inspired by Paul Klee's *Departure of the Ghost*; "Battle Scene from the Comic Opera 'The Seafarer' " by another Klee painting on the opera; "Virgin in a Tree" and a ninety-line poem ("the biggest and best poem I've ever written," according to Plath), "Perseus, or the Triumph of Wit Over Suffering," are both modeled after early Klee etchings.

25. H. W. Janson, *History of Art*, pp. 527–28.

26. John Berryman, "Changes," *Poets on Poetry*, ed. Howard Nemerov, pp. 96–97. In this article, Berryman discusses the aestheticians' treatment of his poem, "Winter Landscape," which uses Brueghel's painting as a starting point for an "unusually negative war poem," not at all the subject of Brueghel's *Hunters in the Snow* (p. 96). The common interpretive mistake aestheticians make, he points out, is assuming Auden's "Musee des Beaux Arts" is a literal rendering of Brueghel's *Landscape with the Fall of Icarus*.

27. Most information about Brueghel here comes from the "Introduction" and "Plate Entries" in *Brueghel*, edited by Marguerite Kay.

28. W. H. Auden, "Musee des Beaux Arts," *The Norton Anthology of Poetry*, ed. Arthur M. Eastman, p. 1076.

29. Howard, "Sylvia Plath: 'And I Have No Face,' " p. 79.

30. Hughes, "Notes on the Chronological Order," p. 82.

31. Nan McCowan Sumner, "Sylvia Plath," *Research Studies*, p. 120.

32. Howard, "Sylvia Plath: 'And I Have No Face,' " p. 79.

33. The textual information is taken chiefly from Ingrid Melander, *The Poetry of Sylvia Plath: A Study of Themes*. The origin of "The Disquieting Muses" is pointed out in Melander's " 'The Disquieting Muses': A Note on a Poem by Sylvia Plath," *Research Studies*, p. 53. In the same article, she points to de Chirico's *l'Enigme de l'Oracle* as the inspiration for "On the Decline of Oracles."

34. Sylvia Plath, "Yadwigha, on a Red Couch, Among Lilies: A Sestina for

The Douanier," *Christian Science Monitor*, p. 8.

35. Melander, *Poetry of Sylvia Plath*, pp. 22–23. The poem's "strong final emphasis is . . . placed on the artist's privilege to follow his genius quite independently of established rules."

36. Ian Hamilton, "Poetry," *London Magazine*, p. 55.

37. Newman, "Candor," p. 29.

38. Donald Hall, "Knock, Knock," *The American Poetry Review*, p. 22.

39. Hughes, "Notes on the Chronological Order," p. 86.

III: Transitional Poems

1. Sylvia Plath, *Crossing the Water*. Hereafter cited in the text as *CW* with page number.

2. Douglas Dunn, "Damaged Instruments," *Encounter*, p. 70.

3. Helen Vendler, "The Poetry of Sylvia Plath," Ziskind Lecture Series, p. 23. This lecture is in the Sophia Smith Women's Archives, Smith College. Vendler's essay makes one of the most lucid and persuasive cases for reading Plath's quieter verses ("these poems come the closest to acknowledging the whole of life, its pull toward living, its pull toward death") and for tracing her changing concept of art over four volumes.

4. A few reviewers who filter *Crossing the Water* poems through *Ariel* are: Lee J. Richmond, "Books Covered and Uncovered," *Erasmus Review*, p. 162; Laurence Gonzales, "Sylvia Plath, Crossing Over," *Chicago Daily News*, 9–10 October 1971; Domenica Paterno, review of *Crossing the Water*, *Library Journal*, p. 3141. These transitional poems "kindle with a gleam that points forward to the eerie light of 'Lady Lazarus' and 'Daddy,' but for the most part they lag behind *Ariel* with its white heat temperament that sears deeply and ineradicably" (Victor Howes, "I Am Silver and Exact," *Christian Science Monitor*, p. 8). After *Ariel*'s "chilled simplicity of death," critics observed the Plath of *Crossing the Water* clinging to "death's apogean cold."

5. The contents of *Crystal Gazer* are listed in Appendix V, *Uncollected Poems* in Appendix VI. Two other limited editions appeared in England after 1971: *Fiesta Melons*, poems before 1958; *Pursuit*, containing a number of late poems combined with those from the Cambridge Manuscript. Several single poems exist: "Child," "A Winter Ship," and "Pursuit." In addition to "Million Dollar Month," Sceptre Press has also published "Wreath for a Bridal."

The following ten poems from *Crossing the Water* were first included in the British edition of *Colossus*: "Black Rook in Rainy Weather," "Metaphors," "Maudlin," "Ouija," "Two Sisters of Persephone," "Who," "Dark House," "Maenad," "The Beast," and "Witch Burning." Marjorie Perloff ("Extremist Poetry: Some Versions of the Sylvia Plath Myth," *Journal of Modern Literature*, p. 586) addresses the confusing chronology: "Of the thirty-eight poems in the volume, eleven were published before the end of 1960, and internal evidence suggests that an additional six were written in late 1959 or early 1960. Almost half of the poems in the volume belong to the period of *The Colossus*." Several other poems, she points out, are contemporaneous with *Ariel*.

6. Ted Hughes, "Notes on the Chronological Order of Sylvia Plath's Poems," *TriQuarterly*, p. 81. References will be cited in the text as *N*. Judith Kroll (*Chapters in a Mythology*) elaborates Hughes's tradition of interpreting Plath's poems: detached and impersonal, Plath's images and details grow increasingly "encoded," oblivious to any experience except rebirth or transcendence, according to Kroll (p. 6).

7. Ted Hughes, "Sylvia Plath's *Crossing the Water*: Some Reflections,"

Critical Quarterly, p. 165. When he speaks of "Insomniac," for example, he says, "an egg from *The Colossus* and *Ariel* is just cracking out of it" (p. 165). References to this essay will be included in the text and abbreviated as *R*.

8. Peter Porter, "Collecting Her Strength," *New Statesman*, p. 774. Plath's "zany, accurate and unexpected" imagery has prompted rather backhanded praise from Douglas Dunn ("Damaged Instruments," p. 69): "This demotic kind of simile-making is very feminine. She mocks the masculine world with flurries of domestic detail. The irritation and peevishness of this is profound, miles beyond the fashionable nonsense of Woman's Lib."

9. Paterno, review of *Crossing the Water*, p. 3141. It is amusing that Plath's growing sense of self-spectacle in this volume seems to infect the very methods of critics and reviewers who are wont to begin their commentaries in the manner of Lee J. Richmond: "To Hughes' wife, the late Sylvia Plath (she was a suicide in 1963), death's parcels were delivered for most of her thirty-one years . . . *Crossing the Water* . . . continues the poetic record of a fractured psyche beyond repair" (*Erasmus Review*, p. 160). And Helen Vendler vividly describes Plath's "exhilarating costumes" of literary influence, seeing Plath as a "rebellious adolescent dressed by her mother in unsuitable clothes"; ". . . the roaring ram disguise of Dylan Thomas; babbling exclamatory whispers-in-the-potting-shed after the manner of Theodore Roethke; duets between heaven and earth in Stevensian orchestration; and many plaintive familial brutalities learned from Lowell. What exhausting costumes these were" ("Crossing the Water," *New York Review of Books*, p. 4).

10. Suzanne Juhasz, *Naked and Fiery Forms: Modern American Poetry by Women—A New Tradition*, pp. 93, 101.

11. Barbara Hardy, "The Poetry of Sylvia Plath," *The Survival of Poetry*, ed. Martin Dodsworth, p. 171.

12. Adrienne Rich, "When We Dead Awaken: Writing as Re-Vision," *College English*, pp. 18–30.

13. Don Geiger, *The Dramatic Impulse in Modern Poetics*, p. 18.

14. Vendler, Ziskind Lecture, p. 21.

15. This poem was originally included in the British *Colossus* edition (William Heinemann, 1960). In her volume, *Naked and Fiery Forms*, Suzanne Juhasz sees the poet in this poem as "a Sleeping Beauty and contesting for her soul are her real mother and three evil fairies" (p. 98).

16. Vendler, Ziskind Lecture, p. 22. To distinguish this lecture from her published article, additional references will be abbreviated in the text as Z with page number.

17. Sylvia Plath, "Context," *London Magazine*, p. 46.

18. Paul Kameen, *Best Sellers*, p. 348.

19. Annette Lavers, "The World as Icon: On Sylvia Plath's Themes," *The Art of Sylvia Plath*, p. 111.

20. Mary Ellmann (*Thinking About Women*) says that "as we escape the exigency of sexual roles, we more fully indulge the avocation of sexual analogies" (p. 3). She offers a witty and pungent analysis of those overly simplified associations of female reproductive organs and female mind. All energetic enterprise is usually assigned to male thought, Ellmann claims. The supposed immobility of the ovum becomes the basis for analogy for the entire female constitution:

> In actuality, each month the ovum undertakes an extraordinary expedition from the ovary through the Fallopian tubes to the uterus, an unseen equivalent of going down the Mississippi on a raft or over Niagara Falls in a barrel. Ordinarily too, the ovum travels singly, like Lewis or Clark, in the kind of existential loneliness which Norman Mailer usually admires. One might say that the activity of ova involves a daring and independence

absent, in fact, from the activity of spermatozoa, which move in jostling masses swarming out on signal like a crowd of commuters from the 5:15. (p. 13)

21. Rich, "When We Dead Awaken," p. 18.

22. Ellmann, *Thinking About Women*, pp. 34–35.

23. George Stade, "Introduction," *A Closer Look at Ariel: A Memory of Sylvia Plath*, edited by Nancy Hunter Steiner, p. 3. References to this introduction will be included in the text and abbreviated as *CLA*.

24. Sylvia Plath, "Sylvia Plath," *The Poet Speaks*, ed. Peter Orr, p. 167. References to this interview will be abbreviated in the text as *PS*. Wary of too much gentility, Plath claimed that she preferred American to British poetry. "I feel that gentility has a stranglehold: the neatness, the wonderful tidiness which is so evident everywhere in England is perhaps more dangerous than it would appear on the surface" (p. 168).

25. Cynthia Ozick, "Does Genius Have a Gender?" *Ms.*, p. 81; Cynthia Ozick, "The Demise of the Dancing Dog," *The New Woman*, ed. Joanne Cooke, Charlotte Bunch-Weeks, and Robin Morgan.

26. Ellmann, *Thinking About Women*, p. 14. Most of the information in this section about women writers' approaches to motherhood is included in "Women Writers and the Element of Destruction," Ellen Peck Killoh, *College English*, pp. 31–38.

27. Ellen Moers, "Female Gothic: The Monster's Mother," *New York Review of Books*, pp. 25–26.

28. Anaïs Nin, *The Diary of Anaïs Nin II*, pp. 233–36.

29. Ozick, "The Demise of the Dancing Dog," p. 29.

30. Vendler, "Crossing the Water," p. 4.

31. Kroll sees the poem as the story of a firefly beetle on the verge of escaping the mother's clenched fist, "the self on the threshold of finding itself whole, the imminent emergence from the pupal phase" (*Chapters in a Mythology*, p. 101).

32. Juhasz, *Naked and Fiery Forms*, p. 102.

33. Ibid., pp. 99–101.

34. R. D. Laing in *The Divided Self* claims that the cherished inner self withers from disuse if one lives the outer mask for too long a time.

35. D. C. Muecke, *The Compass of Irony*, p. 87. Certainly the best examples and explanation of this ironic mode—Socratic irony and Chaucer's use of the persona—are offered in chapter 4, "The Four Modes."

36. Charles Newman, "Candor Is the Only Wile: The Art of Sylvia Plath," *TriQuarterly*, p. 42.

37. Sylvia Plath, "Context," p. 46.

IV. Late Poems

1. Sylvia Plath, "Context," *London Magazine*, p. 46.

2. Sylvia Plath, *Ariel*. Hereafter cited in the text as *A* with page number. The British edition, with slightly different contents, appeared in 1965, a year before the American edition.

3. P. N. Furbank, "New Poetry," *The Listener*, p. 379.

4. Stephen Spender, "Warnings from the Grave," *The New Republic*, p. 23.

5. George Steiner, "Dying Is an Art," *The Art of Sylvia Plath*, ed. Charles Newman, p. 211.

6. Alan Ross, review of *Ariel*, *The London Magazine*, p. 101.

7. Sylvia Plath, *The Bell Jar*.

8. Alfred Alvarez, *The Savage God: A Study of Suicide*.

9. Robin Morgan, "The Arraignment," *Monster: Poems by Robin Morgan*, p. 11.

10. Sylvia Plath, *Winter Trees*. Hereafter cited in the text as *WT* with page number. The British edition dates from 1971.

11. Review of *Crossing the Water* and *Winter Trees*, in *Times Literary Supplement*, p. 1602.

12. Dan Jacobson, "Mirrors Can Kill," *The Listener*, p. 482.

13. Jeannine Dobbs, " 'Viciousness in the Kitchen': Sylvia Plath's Domestic Poetry," *Modern Language Studies*, p. 11.

14. Constance Scheerer, "The Deathly Paradise of Sylvia Plath," *The Antioch Review*, p. 470.

15. Karl Malkoff, *Escape from the Self*, p. 126.

16. Lawrence R. Ries, *Wolf Masks: Violence in Contemporary Poetry*, p. 58. In speaking about Plath's humanity Ries has said: "Life, the poet has repeated over and over, is a greater violence than death. And in death is the last great human outcry against a world that will not permit humanity to be fulfilled" (p. 58).

17. Judith Kroll, *Chapters in a Mythology*, p. 6.

18. Josephine Donovan, "Sexual Politics in Sylvia Plath's Short Stories," *Minnesota Review*, p. 155.

19. Malkoff, *Escape from the Self*, p. 128.

20. Scheerer, "Deathly Paradise," p. 476.

21. Anthony Libby, "God's Lioness and the Priest of Sycorax: Plath and Hughes," *Contemporary Literature*, p. 399.

22. Richard Howard, "Sylvia Plath: 'And I Have No Face, I Have Wanted to Efface Myself . . .,' " *The Art of Sylvia Plath*, p. 79.

23. Alfred Alvarez, "Sylvia Plath," *The Art of Sylvia Plath*, p. 60.

24. Harriet Rosenstein, "Reconsidering Sylvia Plath," *Ms.*, p. 50.

25. Ibid.

26. Eileen Aird, *Sylvia Plath*, p. 69.

27. Ibid., p. 65.

28. Rosenstein, "Reconsidering," p. 98.

29. Helen Vendler, "The Poetry of Sylvia Plath," Ziskind Lecture Series, p. 11.

30. Sylvia Plath, *Three Women: A Poem for Three Voices*, reprinted in *Winter Trees: Late Poems*, p. 60.

31. Barbara Hardy, "The Poetry of Sylvia Plath: Enlargement or Derangement?" *Survival of Poetry*, ed. Martin Dodsworth, pp. 165–68. References to this essay are *H* with page number.

32. Seven plates of this poem, from the first boldly handwritten draft to the final typed version ("originals on quarto typewriting paper," we are told), are included in *The Art of Sylvia Plath*, pp. 273–79.

33. Four of the six poems ("The Bee Meeting," "The Arrival of The Bee Box," "Stings," "Wintering") are included in the British *Ariel*; "The Swarm" is published only in the American *Ariel* and so cited in the text. "Beekeeper's Daughter," dated much earlier than the other five poems, which were written in late autumn of 1962 in little more than a week, is included in *The Colossus and Other Poems* and so cited in the text.

34. David Holbrook, *Sylvia Plath: Poetry and Existence*, p. 212. Mary Ellmann (*Thinking About Women*) offers a brilliant and witty criticism of the Bruno Bettelheim-Erik Erikson school of thinkers that associate the female mind and female reproductive organs, isolating only the interiorizing, brooding, and enclosing qualities. "An immobility is attributed to the entire female constitution by analogy with the supposed immobility of the ovum [which is] like a pop art fried-egg-on-a-plate" (p. 13).

35. Patricia Meyer Spacks includes a chapter on "Power and Passivity" in *The Female Imagination* that explains the concepts as they were employed by Victorian women writers.

36. There are two particularly good sources of information on apiculture: Maurice Maeterlinck, *The Life of the Bee*, a particularly moving, poetic account of the workings of the hive; and *The Hive and the Honeybee*, ed. Roy A. Grout, a more detailed scientific collection of essays.

Sylvia Plath's father, an authority on bees, was author of the 1934 *Bumblebees and Their Ways*. Ingrid Melander (*The Poetry of Sylvia Plath: A Study of Themes*) points out that Plath's concern with honeybee imagery is significantly "independent of the father" whose scholarly work, unlike her own beekeeping, was on bumblebees, not honeybees (p. 91). Maeterlinck reminds us that beedom itself involves a curious inversion of sexual principles. The queen is parthenogenic, but this quality is another aspect of feminocide since she can only produce idle male drones ("the blunt, clumsy stumblers, the boors") who bring ruin to the hive. When she mates with a drone, however, he contributes the female principle in the coupling, thereby allowing the queen to produce female workers who will guarantee the future of the hive. David Holbrook mentions that the queenship with which the speaker identifies has "male-anther potency within itself" and is a kind of "male-femaleness" (*Poetry and Existence*, p. 26).

37. Hannah Arendt, in *On Violence*, makes fine distinctions among the phenomena *power, strength, force, authority*, and *violence*—terms she claims are mistakenly used synonymously in the world of public affairs. Power, for example, is never the property of an individual, but "corresponds to the human ability not just to act but to act in concert" (p. 44), a distinction particularly useful to an understanding of the apiary.

38. Barbara Hardy ("Enlargement or Derangement?") claims that the poem "moves between two poles of actuality and symbolic dimension right up to and including the ending" (p. 179). Kroll says that the speaker in this poem has evinced equally the attitude of a patient being led to surgery and that of an initiate to a sacred mystery. Although the speaker shares a moment of identification with the sacred queenship, "the event turned out to be an act of surgery; instead of exorcising her false self, it excised her principle of vitality" (*Chapters*, p. 142).

39. Hardy, "Enlargement or Derangement?" p. 180.

40. Ingrid Melander (*A Study of Themes*) claims that the interloper is a god manqué, perhaps Christ (p. 96), with his white linen shroud left behind in Gethsemane where he has suffered ("the sweat of his efforts a rain / tugging the world to fruit"). For a similar explanation, see Holbrook (*Poetry and Existence*, p. 225), or Kroll, who deals with this puzzling and magical scapegoat figure as one "appropriate, finally, to carry off her [the speaker's] sins" (*Chapters*, p. 149).

41. Melander, *Themes*, p. 95.

42. Kroll, *Chapters*, pp. 149–50.

43. Holbrook claims that the imagery "of seasonal renewal, of Christ's rebirth (Christmas roses, sugar roses at Easter), of sweetness, honey, effort and love, give these Bee poems a creative impulse and an 'intentionality' widely lacking in Sylvia Plath's work" (*Poetry and Existence*, p. 231).

44. Ibid., p. 237. Holbrook claims that the poet treats "problems of collective, psychic infection" (p. 234) or offers Plath's profound vision of the "consequences of schizoid hate in the world at large" (p. 234).

45. Patricia Meyer Spacks (*The Female Imagination*, p. 31) here quotes Mary Ellmann.

46. Cynthia Ozick, "Does Genius Have a Gender?" *Ms.*, pp. 80–81.

47. Dorin Schumacher, "Subjectivities: A Theory of the Critical Process, *Feminist Literary Criticism: Explorations in Theory*, ed. Josephine Donovan, p. 36. In

this article, which defines the best modes of feminist criticism, Dorin Schumacher sets up a model that values correctness and completeness of process, over "truths" lifted from a body of knowledge.

48. Robert Lowell, "Introduction," *Ariel*, p. vii.

49. Malkoff, *Escape*, p. 128.

50. Barbara Howes, "A Note on *Ariel*," *Massachusetts Review*, p. 226.

51. Annette Lavers, "World as Icon: On Sylvia Plath's Themes," *The Art of Sylvia Plath*, p. 101.

52. Aird, *Plath*, p. 66.

53. John Frederick Nims, "The Poetry of Sylvia Plath: A Technical Analysis," *The Art of Sylvia Plath*, p. 147.

54. D. F. McKay, "Aspects of Energy in the Poetry of Dylan Thomas and Sylvia Plath," *Critical Quarterly*, p. 53.

55. Lavers, "World as Icon," p. 103.

56. Malkoff, *Escape*, p. 131.

57. Charles Newman, "Candor Is the Only Wile: The Art of Sylvia Plath," *TriQuarterly*, p. 61.

58. Hardy, "Enlargement or Derangement?" p. 184.

59. See Aird, *Plath*, p. 85; Kroll, *Chapters*, pp. 158–59 and 161.

60. M. L. Rosenthal, *The New Poets: American and British Poetry Since World War II*, p. 86.

61. Ernest Fenollosa, in his essay "The Chinese Written Character as a Medium for Poetry" (Ezra Pound's *Instigations*, Freeport, 1967), discusses this sort of unity through the nature of representation of nouns and verbs in the Chinese character. His chief idea is that in Chinese perception the eye sees both the noun and verb united as one ("things in motion, motion in things"), and the Chinese character preserves this relationship. D. W. McKay treats Plath's desire to regain the "simultaneity of experience by the strategic manipulation of language, to bring together dancer, the act of dancing and the dance" ("Aspects of Energy," p. 54), with Fenollosa's description of the Chinese ideogram as starting point. For the best analyses of "Ariel" see McKay and William V. Davis, "Sylvia Plath's 'Ariel,' " *Modern Poetry Studies*, pp. 176–84.

62. Stuart A. Davis, "The Documentary Sublime: The Posthumous Poetry of Sylvia Plath," *The Harvard Advocate*, p. 12.

63. For a recent analysis, see Kroll, *Chapters*, pp. 180–85.

64. Don Geiger (*The Dramatic Impulse in Modern Poetics*) gives a superb explanation of poem as dramatic verbal utterance, especially in his chapter "Toward a Poetics for Making, Seeing, and Saying."

65. Richard Poirier, *The Performing Self: Compositions and Decompositions in the Languages of Contemporary Life*, pp. xiii. Poirier's introduction to literature, his discussion of the "performing self," seems to apply to the interpretation of much contemporary poetry. Perhaps the closest approximation of a self shaped in the process of performance is simply the energy of awareness, the wonder of irony, that a self can never emerge from the literary waste heap. At best we can have performance that "creates life in literature in the sense that it is itself the act and evidence of life. It is a way of being present, in every sense of that word" (p. 44).

66. Rosenthal, *New Poets*, p. 13.

67. Ibid., p. 14.

68. Kroll, *Chapters*, p. 172. According to Kroll, "this kind of rebirth, egoless transcendence, is an identification not with individual forms of self, but with the larger, impersonal "Self" of the universe. Not only the false self, but the mythic true self as well (insofar as its selfhood is a limitation or barrier) are transcended" (p. 172).

69. Susanne Langer, "Great Dramatic Forms: The Comic Rhythm," *Feeling and Form*, pp. 351–66.

70. Poirier, *Performing Self*, p. 36.

71. Hardy, "Enlargement or Derangement?" p. 183.

72. According to Ted Hughes ("Notes on the Chronological Order of Sylvia Plath's Poems," *TriQuarterly*, pp. 81–88), Plath has said that "Fever" is about "two kinds of fire—the fires of hell, which merely agonize and the fires of heaven, which purify. During the poem, the first sort of fire suffers itself into the second" (p. 86). Malkoff (*Escape*) has an interesting analysis of the imagery of this poem, pp. 130–31.

73. Davis, "Documentary Sublime," p. 10.

74. What remains the most thorough and enlightening account of the poem is A. R. Jones, "On 'Daddy,' " *The Art of Sylvia Plath*, pp. 230–36.

75. Irving Howe, "Sylvia Plath: A Partial Disagreement," *Harper's Magazine*, pp. 89–90.

Bibliography

Aird, Eileen. *Sylvia Plath: Her Life and Work*. Edinburgh: Oliver and Boyd, 1973; New York: Harper and Row, 1975.

————. "Variants in a Tape Recording of Fifteen Poems by Sylvia Plath." *Notes and Queries* 19 (February 1972):59–61.

Aldrich, Elizabeth. "Sylvia Plath's 'The Eye-mote': An Analysis." *Harvard Advocate* 101 (May 1967):4–7.

Allen, Mary. "Sylvia Plath's Defiance: *The Bell Jar*." In *The Necessary Blankness: Women in Major American Fiction of the Sixties*, edited by Mary Allen, pp. 160–78. Urbana: University of Illinois Press, 1976.

Alvarez, Alfred. "The Art of Suicide." *Partisan Review* 37 (1970):339–58.

————. "Beyond All This Fiddle." *Times Literary Supplement* (23 March 1967):229–32.

————. "Epilogue: American and Extremist Art." In *Under Pressure: The Writer in Society: Eastern Europe and the U.S.A.*, pp. 183–89. Baltimore: Penguin Books, 1965.

————. "The New Poetry or Beyond the Gentility Principle." In *The New Poetry*, pp. 21–31. London: Penguin, 1962.

————. "The Poet and the Poetess." *The Observer* (18 December 1960):21.

————. "Poetry in Extremis." *The Observer* (14 March 1965):26.

————. "The Problems of the Artist." In *Under Pressure: The Writer in Society: Eastern Europe and the U.S.A.*, pp. 154–80. Baltimore: Penguin Books, 1965.

————. "Sylvia Plath." In *The Art of Sylvia Plath*, edited by Charles Newman, pp. 56–68. Bloomington: Indiana University Press, 1970; London: Faber and Faber, 1970.

————. "Sylvia Plath: The Cambridge Collection." *Cambridge Review* 90 (7 February 1969):246–47.

————. "Sylvia Plath: A Memoir." In *New American Review #12*, pp. 9–40. New York: Simon and Schuster, 1971.

————. "Sylvia Plath: A Memoir." In *The Savage God: A Study of Suicide*, pp. 3–42. London: Wiedenfeld and Nicolson, 1971; New York: Random House, 1972.

Ames, Lois. "Notes Toward a Biography." In *The Art of Sylvia Plath*, edited by Charles Newman, pp. 155–73. Bloomington: Indiana University Press, 1970; London: Faber and Faber, 1970.

————. "Notes Toward a Biography." *TriQuarterly* 7 (Fall 1966):95–107.

Arb, Siv. "Dikter nar forvanensvärt langt." *Ord och Bild* 83 (1974): 459–60.

Arendt, Hannah. *On Violence*. New York: Harcourt, Brace and World, 1969.

Ashford, Deborah. "Sylvia Plath's Poetry: A Complex of Irreconcilable Antagonisms." *Concerning Poetry*, vol. 7, no. 1:62–69.

Bagg, Robert. "The Rise of Lady Lazarus." *Mosaic* 2 (Summer 1969): 9–36.

Balitas, Vincent D. "On Becoming a Witch: A Reading of Sylvia Plath's 'Witch Burning.' " *Studies in the Humanities* 4 (February 1975):27–30.

Ballif, Gene. "Facing the Worst: A View from Minerva's Buckler." *Parnassus: Poetry in Review* (Fall/Winter 1976):231–59.

Barnard, Caroline King. *Sylvia Plath*. Boston: Twayne Publishers, 1978.

Baro, Gene. Review of *Ariel. New York Times Book Review* (26 June 1966):10–11.

Bere, Carol. Review of *Letters Home. Ariel* 8:4 (1977):99–103.

Berman, Jeffrey. "Sylvia Plath and the Art of Dying: Sylvia Plath (1932–1963)." *University of Hartford Studies in Literature* 10 (1978):137–55.

Berryman, John. "Changes." In *Poets on Poetry*, edited by Howard Nemerov, pp. 94–103. New York: Basic Books, 1966.

Bewley, Marius. "Poetry Chronicle." *Hudson Review* 19 (Autumn 1966):479–93.

Birje-Patil, J. "The Autobiography of a Fever: The Poetry of Sylvia Plath." *Indian Journal of American Studies* 5:1–2 (1976):10–20.

Blackburn, Thomas. "Poetic Knowledge." *The New Statesman* 60 (24 December 1960):1016.

Blodgett, E. D. "Sylvia Plath: Another View." *Modern Poetry Studies* 2 (1971):97–106.

Boyers, Robert. "Sylvia Plath: The Trepanned Veteran." *Centennial Review* 13 (Spring 1969):138–53.

Brink, Andrew. "Sylvia Plath and the Art of Redemption." *Alphabet* 15 (December 1968):48–69.

Broe, Mary Lynn. "Demythologizing Sivvy: that 'theatrical comeback in broad day.' " *Poet and Critic* 10:1 (1977):30–39.

———. "Recovering the Complex Self: Sylvia Plath's Beeline." *Centennial Review* 24 (Winter 1980).

———. " 'Oh Dad, Poor Dad': Sylvia Plath's Comic Exorcism." *Notes on Contemporary Literature* 9:4 (1979):2–4.

———. Review of *Letters Home. Journal of Modern Literature* 5:4(1976):787–89.

———. "A Subtle Psychic Bond: Sylvia and Aurelia Schober Plath in *Letters Home*." In *The Lost Tradition: A History of Mothers and Daughters in Literature*, edited by Esther Broner and Cathy Davidson, pp. 217–30. New York: Frederick Ungar, 1980.

Brownjohn, Alan. "Awesome Fragments." *The New Statesman* 82 (1 October 1971):446–47.

Buell, Frederick. "Sylvia Plath's Traditionalism." *Boundary* 2 (Fall 1976):195–211.

Burke, Herbert C. Review of *The Colossus. Library Journal* 87 (15 June 1962):2385.

Burnham, Richard E. "Sylvia Plath's 'Lady Lazarus.' " *Contemporary Poetry* 1:2 (1973):42–46.

Butscher, Edward. "In Search of Sylvia: An Introduction." In *Sylvia Plath: The Woman and the Work*, edited by Edward Butscher, pp. 3–29. New York: Dodd, Mead, 1977.

———. *Sylvia Plath: Method and Madness*. New York: Seabury Press, 1976.

———, ed. *Sylvia Plath: The Woman and the Work*. New York: Dodd, Mead, 1977.

Campbell, Wendy. "Remembering Sylvia." In *The Art of Sylvia Plath*, edited by Charles Newman, pp. 182–86. Bloomington: Indiana University Press, 1970; London: Faber and Faber, 1970.

Caraher, Brian. "The Problematic of Body and Language in Sylvia Plath's 'Tulips.' " *Paunch* 42–43 (December 1975):76–89.

Claire, William F. "That Rare, Random Descent: The Poetry and Pathos of Sylvia Plath." *Antioch Review* 26 (Winter 1966):552–60.

Cleverdon, Douglas. "On 'Three Women.' " In *The Art of Sylvia Plath*, edited by Charles Newman, pp. 227–29. Bloomington: Indiana University Press, 1970; London: Faber and Faber, 1970.

———. "Preface" to *Three Women: A Monologue for Three Voices* by Sylvia Plath. London: Turret, 1968.

Cloud, Jeraldine Neifev. "Robert Lowell, Sylvia Plath, and the Confessional Mode in Contemporary Poetry." Master's thesis, Emory University, 1976.

Cluysenaar, Anne. "Post-culture: Pre-culture?" In *British Poetry Since 1960*, edited by M. Schmidt and G. Lindop, pp. 215–32. Oxford: Carcanet Press, 1972.

Conquest, Robert. *New Lines I*. London: Macmillan, 1957.

———. *New Lines II*. London: Macmillan, 1963.

Cooley, Peter. "Autism, Autoeroticism, Auto-da-fe: The Tragic Poetry of Sylvia Plath." *Hollins Critic* 10 (February 1973):1–15.

Corrigan, Sylvia Robinson. "Sylvia Plath: A New Feminist Approach." *Aphra* 1 (Spring 1970):16–23.

Cunningham, Stuart. "Bibliography: Sylvia Plath." *Hecate* 1 (July 1975):95–112.

Dale, Peter. " 'O Honey Bees Come Build.' " *Agenda* 4 (Summer 1966):49–55.

Davis, Robin Reed. "The Honey Machine: Imagery Patterns in *Ariel*." *New Laurel Review* 1 (Spring 1972):23–31.

———. "Now I have Lost Myself: A Reading of Sylvia Plath's 'Tulips.' " *Paunch* 42–43 (December 1975):97–104.

Davis, Stuart A. "The Documentary Sublime: The Posthumous Poetry of Sylvia Plath." *Harvard Advocate* 101 (May 1967):8–12.

Davis, William V. "Sylvia Plath's 'Ariel.' " *Modern Poetry Studies* 3 (1972):176–84.

Davison, Peter. "Inhabited by a Cry: The Last Poetry of Sylvia Plath."

Atlantic (August 1966):76–77.

———. "Three Visionary Poets." *Atlantic* 229 (February 1972):104–7.

Dettmering, Peter. "Personal Goal and Self-Destruction." *Praxis der Psychotherapie* 21 (1976):131–38.

Dickey, James. *Spinning the Crystal Ball: Some Guesses at the Future of American Poetry*. Washington, D.C.: Library of Congress, 1967.

———. *The Suspect in Poetry*. Madison, Minnesota: The Sixties Press, 1964.

Dickey, William. "Responsibilities." *Kenyon Review* 24 (August 1962):756–64.

Dickinson, Peter. "Some Poets." *Punch* 239 (7 December 1960):829.

Dobbs, Jeannine. " 'Viciousness in the Kitchen': Sylvia Plath's Domestic Poetry." *Modern Language Studies* 7:2 (Fall 1977):11–25.

Dodsworth, Martin, ed. *The Survival of Poetry: A Contemporary Survey*. London: Faber and Faber, 1970.

———, ed. *Feminist Literary Criticism: Explorations in Theories*. Lexington: University Press of Kentucky, 1975.

Donovan, Josephine. "Sexual Politics in Sylvia Plath's Short Stories." *Minnesota Review* 4 (Spring/Summer 1973):150–57.

———, ed. *Feminist Literary Criticisms: Explorations in Theories*. Lexington: University Press of Kentucky, 1975.

Doran, Rachel S. "Female—or Feminist: The Tension of Duality in Sylvia Plath." *Transition* 1:2 (1977–1978):14–20.

Dunn, Douglas. "Damaged Instruments." *Encounter* 37 (August 1971):68–74.

———. "King Offa Alive and Dead: Ten Poets." *Encounter* 38 (January 1972):67–74.

Dyroff, Jan M. "Sylvia Plath: Perceptions in *Crossing the Water*." *Art and Literature Review* 1:49–50.

Dyson, A. E. "On Sylvia Plath." In *The Art of Sylvia Plath*, edited by Charles Newman, pp. 204–10. Bloomington: Indiana University Press, 1970; London: Faber and Faber, 1970.

Efron, Arthur. "Sylvia Plath's 'Tulips' and Literary Criticism." *Paunch* 42–43 (December 1975):69–75.

———. " 'Tulips': Text and Assumptions." *Paunch* 42–43 (December 1975):110–22.

Ehrenpreis, Irvin. "The Age of Lowell." In *Robert Lowell: A Portrait of the Artist in his Time*, edited by Michael London and Robert Boyers, pp. 155–86. New York: David Lewis, 1970.

Eliot, T. S. *Selected Essays*. New York: Harcourt Brace Jovanovich, 1950.

Ellmann, Mary. "The Bell Jar: An American Girlhood." In *The Art of Sylvia Plath*, edited by Charles Newman, pp. 221–26. Bloomington: Indiana University Press, 1970; London: Faber and Faber, 1970.

———. *Thinking about Women*. New York: Harcourt Brace Jovanovich, 1968.

Eriksson, Pamela Dale. "Some Thoughts on Sylvia Plath." *Unisa English Studies* 10 (1972):45–52.

Feldman, Irving. "The Religion of One." *Book Week* (19 June 1966):3.

Ferrier, Carole. "The Beekeeper and the Queen Bee." *Refractory Girl* (Spring 1973):31–36.

Fraser, G. S. "A Hard Nut to Crack from Sylvia Plath." *Contemporary Poetry* 1 (Spring 1973):1–12.

Frye, Northrup. "Towards Defining an Age of Sensibility." In *Fables of Identity: Studies in Poetic Mythology*, pp. 130–37. New York: Harcourt, Brace and World, 1963.

Furbank, P. N. "New Poetry." *The Listener* 73 (11 March 1965):379.

Fussell, Paul. *Poetic Meter and Poetic Form*. New York: Random House, 1965.

Geiger, Don. *The Dramatic Impulse in Modern Poetics*. Baton Rouge: Louisiana State University Press, 1967.

Gilbert, Sandra M. " 'A Fine White Flying Myth': Confessions of a Plath Addict." *Massachusetts Review* 19 (1978):585–603.

Gonzales, Laurence. "Sylvia Plath, Crossing Over." *Chicago Daily News* (9–10 October 1971):12.

Gordon, Jan B. " 'Who Is Sylvia?': The Art of Sylvia Plath." *Modern Poetry Studies* 1 (1970):6–34.

Goto, Akio. "Sylvia Plath no Sekai." *Eigo Seinen* 122 (1977):584–87.

Gross, Harvey. *Sound and Form in Modern Poetry*. Ann Arbor: University of Michigan Press, 1968.

Grout, Roy, ed. *The Hive and the Honeybee*. Hamilton, Illinois: Dadant and Sons, 1970.

Guttenberg, Barrett. "Sylvia Plath, Myth, and 'The Hanging Man.' " *Contemporary Poetry* 3 (1977):17–23.

Hakeem, A. "Sylvia Plath's 'Elm' and Munch's 'The Scream.' " *English Studies* 55 (December 1974):531–37.

Hall, Donald. "Knock, Knock." *The American Poetry Review* (May/June 1974):22.

Hamilton, Ian. "Poetry." *The London Magazine* 3 (July 1963):54–56.

Hardwick, Elizabeth. Review of *Crossing the Water* and *The Bell Jar*. *The New York Review of Books* 17 (12 August 1971):3, 5–6.

———. "Sylvia Plath." In *Seduction and Betrayal: Women and Literature*, pp. 104–24. New York: Random House, 1970.

Hardy, Barbara. "The Poetry of Sylvia Plath: Enlargement or Derangement?" In *The Survival of Poetry: A Contemporary Survey*, edited by Martin Dodsworth, pp. 164–92. London: Faber and Faber, 1970.

Hawkes, Terence. *Metaphor*. London: Methuen, 1972.

Herman, Judith B. "Plath's 'Daddy' and the Myth of Tereus and Philomela." *Notes on Contemporary Literature* 7:1 (1977):9–10.

———. "Reflections on a Kitchen Table: A Note on Sylvia Plath's 'Black Rook in Rainy Weather.' " *Notes on Contemporary Literature* 7:5 (1977):5.

Higgins, Judith. "Sylvia Plath's Growing Popularity with College Students." *University: A Princeton Quarterly* 58 (Fall 1973):4–8; 28–33.

Himelick, Raymond. "Notes on the Care and Feeding of Nightmares: Burton, Erasmus, and Sylvia Plath." *Western Humanities Review* 28 (Autumn 1974):313–26.

Holbrook, David. "Out of the Ash: Different Views of the 'Death Camp'—Sylvia Plath, Al Alvarez, and Viktor Frankl." *The Human World* 5 (November 1971):22–39.

———. "R. D. Laing and the Death Circuit." *Encounter* 31 (August 1968):35–45.

———. "Sylvia Plath and the Problem of Violence in Art." *Cambridge Review* 70 (7 February 1969):249–50.

———. *Sylvia Plath: Poetry and Existence*. London: Athlone Press, 1976.

———. "The 200-Inch Distorting Mirror." *New Society* 12 (11 July 1968):57–58.

Homberger, Eric. *A Chronological Checklist of the Periodical Publications of Sylvia Plath*. Exeter: Exeter University Press, 1970.

———. "I am I." *Cambridge Review* 90 (7 February 1969):251–53.

Hope, Francis. Review of *Ariel*. *The New Statesman* 69 (30 April 1965):687–88.

Hosbaum, Philip. "The Temptations of Giant Despair." *Hudson Review* 25 (Winter 1972–1973):597–612.

Howard, Richard. "Five Poets." *Poetry* 101 (March 1963):412–13.

———. "Sylvia Plath: 'And I Have No Face. I Have Wanted to Efface Myself . . . .' " In *The Art of Sylvia Plath*, edited by Charles Newman, pp. 77–88. Bloomington: Indiana University Press, 1970; London: Faber and Faber, 1970.

Howe, Irving. "The Plath Celebration: A Partial Dissent." In *Sylvia Plath: Method and Madness*, edited by Edward Butscher, pp. 225–35. New York: Seabury Press, 1976.

———. "Sylvia Plath: A Partial Disagreement." *Harper's Magazine* (January 1972):88–91.

Howes, Barbara. "A Note on *Ariel*." *Massachusetts Review* 8 (Winter 1967):225–26.

Howes, Victor. " 'I am silver and exact.' " *Christian Science Monitor* (30 September 1971):8.

———. "Sometimes, A Walker of Air." *Christian Science Monitor* (4 October 1972):11.

Hoyle, James F. "Sylvia Plath: A Poetry of Suicidal Mania." *Literature and Psychology* 18 (1968):187–203.

Hughes, Ted. "Notes on the Chronological Order of Sylvia Plath's Poems." In *The Art of Sylvia Plath*, edited by Charles Newman, pp. 187–95. Bloomington: Indiana University Press, 1970; London: Faber and Faber, 1970.

———. "Notes on the Chronological Order of Sylvia Plath's Poems." *TriQuarterly* 7 (Fall 1966):81–88.

————. "Sylvia Plath's *Crossing the Water*: Some Reflections." *Critical Quarterly* 13 (Summer 1971):165–72.

————. "Winter Trees." *Poetry Book Society Bulletin* 70 (Autumn 1971).

Isaacs, J. "The Coming of the Image." In *The Background of Modern Poetry*, pp. 34–51. New York: E. P. Dutton, 1952.

Jacobson, Dan. "Mirrors Can Kill." *The Listener* 86 (7 October 1971):482.

Jaffe, Dan. "An All-American Muse." *Saturday Review* 49 (15 October 1966):29–30.

Jerome, Judson. "A Poetry Chronicle, Part I." *Antioch Review* 23 (Spring 1963):110–11.

Jones, A. R. "Necessity and Freedom: The Poetry of Robert Lowell, Sylvia Plath, and Anne Sexton." *Critical Quarterly* 7 (Spring 1965):11–30.

————. "On 'Daddy.' " In *The Art of Sylvia Plath*, edited by Charles Newman, pp. 230–36. Bloomington: Indiana University Press, 1970; London: Faber and Faber, 1970.

Jones, A. R., and Cox, C. B. "After the Tranquilized Fifties." *Critical Quarterly* 6 (Summer 64):107–22.

Juhasz, Suzanne. *Naked and Fiery Forms: Modern American Poetry by Women–A New Tradition*. New York: Harper and Row, 1976.

Kamel, Rose. " 'A Self to Recover': Sylvia Plath's Bee Cycle Poems." *Modern Poetry Studies* 4 (1973):304–18.

Kameen, Paul. Review of *Crossing the Water*. *Best Sellers* (1 November 1971):347–48.

Kay, Marguerite. *Brueghel*. New York: Hamlyn House, 1970.

Kenner, Hugh. " 'Ariel'—Pop Sincerity." *Triumph* 1 (September 1966):33–34.

Killoh, Ellen Peck. "The Woman Writer and the Element of Destruction." *College English* 34 (October 1972):31–38.

King, Nicholas. "Poetry: A Late Summer Roundup." *New York Herald Tribune* (26 August 1962):4.

Kinzie, Mary. "An Informal Check List of Criticism." In *The Art of Sylvia Plath*, edited by Charles Newman, pp. 283–304. Bloomington: Indiana University Press, 1970; London: Faber and Faber, 1970.

Kissick, Gary. "Plath: A Terrible Perfection." *The Nation* 207 (16 September 1968):245–47.

Kopp, Jane. " 'Gone, Very Gone Youth': Sylvia Plath at Cambridge." In *Sylvia Plath: Method and Madness*, edited by Edward Butscher, pp. 61–80. New York: Seabury Press, 1976.

Kostelanetz, Richard. "Reactions and Alternatives: Post World War II American Poetry." *Chelsea* 26 (1969):7–34.

Kroll, Judith. *Chapters in a Mythology: The Poetry of Sylvia Plath*. New York: Harper and Row, 1976.

Krook, Dorothea. "Recollections of Sylvia Plath." In *Sylvia Plath: Method and Madness*, edited by Edward Butscher, pp. 49–60. New York: Seabury Press, 1976.

Laing, R. D. *The Divided Self*. New York: Penguin, 1965.

Lameyer, Gordon. "The Double in Sylvia Plath's *The Bell Jar*." In *Sylvia Plath: Method and Madness*, edited by Edward Butscher, pp. 143–65. New York: Seabury Press, 1976.

———. "Sylvia at Smith." In *Sylvia Plath: The Woman and the Work*, edited by Edward Butscher, pp. 32–41. New York: Dodd, Mead, 1977.

Lane, Gary, ed. *Sylvia Plath: New Views on the Poetry*. Baltimore: Johns Hopkins University Press, 1979.

———. "Sylvia Plath's 'The Hanging Man': A Further Note." *Contemporary Poetry* 2 (Spring 1975):40–43.

Lane, Gary, and Maria Stevens. *Sylvia Plath: A Bibliography*. Metuchen, N.J.: Scarecrow Press, 1978.

Langer, Susanne. *Feeling and Form*. New York: Charles Scribner's Sons, 1953.

Lanser, Susan Sniader. "Beyond *The Bell Jar*: Women Students of the 1970s." *Radical Teacher* 6 (1977):41–44.

Lask, Thomas. "A Kind of Heroism." *The New York Times* (8 June 1966):45.

Lavers, Annette. "The World as Icon: On Sylvia Plath's Themes." In *The Art of Sylvia Plath*, edited by Charles Newman, pp. 100–135. Bloomington: Indiana University Press, 1970; London: Faber and Faber, 1970.

Levertov, Denise. *The Poet in the World*. New York: New Directions, 1973.

Levy, Laurie. "Outside the Bell Jar." In *Sylvia Plath: The Woman and the Work*, edited by Edward Butscher, pp. 42–48. New York: Dodd, Mead, 1977.

Libby, Anthony. "God's Lioness and the Priest of Sycorax: Plath and Hughes." *Contemporary Literature* 15 (Summer 1974):386–405.

Lindberg-Seyersted, Brita. "Notes on Three Poems by Sylvia Plath." *Edda* 74 (1974):47–54.

———. "On Sylvia Plath's Poetry." *Edda* 72 (1972):54–59.

Lindop, G., and Schmidt, M., eds. *British Poetry Since 1960*. Oxford: Carcanet Press, 1972.

Lowell, Robert. "Introduction to *Ariel*." New York: Harper and Row, 1966.

———. "Waking in the Blue." In *Life Studies / For the Union Dead*, pp. 81–82. New York: Farrar, Straus and Giroux, 1967.

Lucie-Smith, Edward. "A Murderous Art." *Critical Quarterly* 6 (1964):355–63.

———. "Sea-Imagery in the Work of Sylvia Plath." In *The Art of Sylvia Plath*, edited by Charles Newman, pp. 91–99. Bloomington: Indiana University Press, 1970; London: Faber and Faber, 1970.

McCann, Janet. "Sylvia Plath's Bee Poems." *South and West* 14:4 (1978):28–36.

McClatchy, J. D. "Staring from Her Hood of Bone: Adjusting to Sylvia Plath." In *American Poetry Since 1960*, edited by R. B. Shaw, pp. 155–66. Oxford: Carcanet Press, 1973.

McKay, D. F. "Aspects of Energy in the Poetry of Dylan Thomas and Sylvia Plath." *Critical Quarterly* 16 (Spring 1974):53–67.

Maeterlinck, Maurice. *The Life of the Bee*. New York: Dodd, Mead and Co., 1905.

Malkoff, Karl. *Escape from the Self*. New York: Columbia University Press, 1977.

Marcus, Jane. "Nostalgia Is Not Enough: Why Elizabeth Hardwick Misreads Ibsen, Plath, and Woolf." *Bucknell Review* 24:1 (1978):157–77.

Martin, Wendy. "God's Lioness—Sylvia Plath, Her Prose and Poetry." *Women's Studies* 1 (1973):191–98.

Meissner, William. "The Opening of the Flower: The Revelation of Suffering in Sylvia Plath's 'Tulips.' " *Contemporary Poetry* 1 (Spring 1973):13–17.

———. "The Rise of the Angel: Life Through Death in the Poetry of Sylvia Plath." *Massachusetts Studies in English* 3 (Fall 1971):34–39.

Melander, Ingrid. " 'The Disquieting Muses': A Note on a Poem by Sylvia Plath." *Research Studies* 31 (March 1971):53–54.

———. *The Poetry of Sylvia Plath: A Study of Themes*. Stockholm: Almquist and Wiksell, 1972.

———. " 'Watercolour of Grantchester Meadows': An Early Poem by Sylvia Plath." *Moderna Sprak* 65 (1971):1–5.

Miles, Josephine. "American Poetry in 1965." *Massachusetts Review* 7 (1966):321–35.

Mills, Ralph J. *Creation's Very Self: On the Personal Element in Recent American Poetry*. Fort Worth: Texas Christian University Press, 1969.

Moers, Ellen. "Female Gothic: The Monster's Mother." *New York Review of Books* 21 (21 March 1974):24–27.

Mollinger, Robert N. "Sylvia Plath's 'Private Ground.' " *Notes on Contemporary Literature* 5:2 (1975):14–15.

———. "A Symbolic Complex: Images of Death and Daddy in the Poetry of Sylvia Plath." *Descant* 19:2 (Winter 1975):44–52.

Moraes, Dom. "Poems from Many Parts." *Time and Tide* 41 (19 November 1960):1413.

Muecke, D. C. *The Compass of Irony*. London: Methuen, 1969.

Murphy, Francis. "Going It Alone: Estrangement in American Poetry." *Yale Review* 56 (1966):17–24.

Myers, E. Lucas. Review of *The Colossus*. *The Sewanee Review* 70 (Spring 1962):216–17.

Nance, Guinevara, and Jones, Judith P., "Doing Away with Daddy: Exorcism and Sympathetic Magic in Plath's Poetry." *Concerning Poetry* 11:1 (1978):75–81.

Nemerov, Howard, et al., eds. *Poets on Poetry*. New York: Basic Books, 1966.

Newman, Charles, ed. *The Art of Sylvia Plath: A Symposium*. Bloomington: Indiana University Press, 1970; London: Faber and Faber, 1970.

———. "Candor Is the Only Wile: The Art of Sylvia Plath." *Tri Quarterly* 7 (Fall 1966): 39–64.

Nguyen, Thanh-Binh. "A Stylistic Analysis of Sylvia Plath's Semantics." *Language and Style* 11 (1978):69–81.

Nims, John Frederick. "The Poetry of Sylvia Plath: A Technical Analysis." In *The Art of Sylvia Plath*, edited by Charles Newman, pp. 136–52. Bloomington: Indiana University Press, 1970; London: Faber and Faber, 1970.

Oates, Joyce Carol. "The Death Throes of Romanticism: The Poems of Sylvia Plath." *Southern Review* 9 (July 1973): 501–22.

———. Review of *Winter Trees*. *Library Journal* 97 (1 November 1972):3595.

Oberg, Arthur. "The Modern British and American Lyric: What Will Suffice?" *Language and Literature* 7 (Winter 1972):70–88.

———. "Sylvia Plath and the New Decadence." *Chicago Review* 20 (1968): 66–73.

———. "Sylvia Plath: 'Love, love, my season.' " In *The Modern American Lyric: Lowell, Berryman, Creely, and Plath*, pp. 127–73. New Brunswick, N.J.: Rutgers University Press, 1978.

Oettle, Pamela. "Sylvia Plath's Last Poems." *Balcony* 3 (Spring 1965):47–50.

O'Hara, J. D. "An American Dream Girl." *Washington Post Book World* (11 April 1971):3.

Oliva, Renato. "La Poesia d: Sylvia Plath." *Studi American* 15 (1969): 341–81.

Orr, Peter. "Sylvia Plath." In *The Poet Speaks*, pp. 167–72. New York: Barnes and Noble, 1966.

Oshio, Toshiko. "The Romantic Agony? Sylvia Plath no Jojo no Shitsu." *Eigo Seinen* 123 (1977):166–67.

———. "Sylvia Plath no Shi." *Oberon* 14 (1973):45–59.

Ostriker, Alicia. " 'Fact' As Style: The Americanization of Sylvia." *Language and Style* 1 (Summer 1968):201–12.

Owen, Guy. Review of *The Colossus*. *Books Abroad* 37 (Spring 1963):209.

Ozick, Cynthia. "Does Genius Have a Gender?" *Ms.* 6 (December 1977):56, 79–81.

———. "The Demise of the Dancing Dog." In *The New Woman*, edited by Joanne Cooke, Charlotte Bunch-Weeks, and Robin Morgan, pp. 23–42. New York: Fawcett, 1971.

Paterno, Domenica. Review of *Crossing the Water*. *Library Journal* 96 (1 October 1971):3141.

Pearson, Sheryl Sherman. "The Confessional Mode and Two Recent Poets." *Rockham Literary Studies* 2 (1972):1–10.

Perloff, Marjorie. "Angst and Animism in the Poetry of Sylvia Plath." *Journal of Modern Literature* 1 (1970):57–74.

———. "Extremist Poetry: Some Versions of the Sylvia Plath Myth." *Journal of Modern Literature* 2 (November 1972):581–88.

———. "On Sylvia Plath's 'Tulips.' " *Paunch* 42–43 (December 1975): 105–9.

———. "On the Road to Ariel: The 'Transitional' Poetry of Sylvia Plath." In *Sylvia Plath: The Woman and the Work*, edited by Edward Butscher, pp. 125–42. New York: Dodd, Mead, 1977.

———." 'A Ritual for Being Born Twice': Sylvia Plath's *The Bell Jar*." *Contemporary Literature* 13 (Autumn 1972):507–22.

Phillips, Robert. "The Dark Funnel: A Reading of Sylvia Plath." *Modern Poetry Studies* 3 (1972):49–74.

Plath, Sylvia. *Ariel*. New York: Harper and Row, 1966.

———. *The Bed Book*. New York: Harper and Row, 1976.

———. *The Bell Jar*. London: Faber and Faber, 1966.

———. *Child*. Exeter: Rougemont Press, 1971.

———. *The Colossus and Other Poems*. New York: Alfred A. Knopf, 1962.

———. "Context." *London Magazine* 1 (February 1962): 45–46.

———. *Crossing the Water*. New York: Harper and Row, 1971.

———. *Crystal Gazer*. London: Rainbow Press, 1971.

———. *Johnny Panic and the Bible of Dreams, and Other Prose Writings*. New York: Harper and Row, 1979.

———. *Letters Home: Correspondence 1950–1963*. Selected and edited with commentary by Aurelia Schober Plath. New York: Harper and Row, 1975.

———. *Lyonnesse*. London: Rainbow Press, 1972.

———. "The Magic Mirror: A Study of Doubles in Two of Dostoevsky's Novels." Senior thesis, Smith College. Sophia Smith Women's Archives.

———. "Maids from School: 'America! America!.' " *Punch* (3 April 1963):482–84.

———. *Million Dollar Month*. Frensham: Sceptre Press, 1971.

———. "The Net Menders." *The New Yorker* 20 (August 1960):36.

———. "Ocean 1212–W." In *Writers on Themselves*, edited by Herbert Read, pp. 102–10. London: Cox and Wyman, 1964.

———. *Pursuit*. London:Rainbow Press, 1973.

———. "Sunday at the Mintons." *The Smith Review* (Fall 1952):3–9.

———. "Superman and Paula Brown's New Snowsuit." *The Smith Review* (Spring 1955): 19–21.

———. "Sylvia Plath." In *The Poet Speaks*, edited by Peter Orr. New York: Barnes and Noble, 1966.

———. *Sylvia Plath: A Dramatic Portrait*. Assembled by Barry Kyle. New

York: Harper and Row, 1977.

―――. *Three Women: A Monologue for Three Voices*. London: Turret Books, 1968.

―――. *Uncollected Poems*. London: Turret Books, 1965.

―――. *A Winter Ship*. Edinburgh: Tragara Press, 1960.

―――. *Winter Trees*. New York: Harper and Row, 1972.

―――. "Wishing Box." *Atlantic Monthly* 214 (October 1964):86–89.

―――. *Wreath for a Bridal*. Frensham: Sceptre Press, 1970.

―――. "Yadwigha, on a Red Couch, Among Lilies: A Sestina for the Douanier." *Christian Science Minotor* (26 March 1959):8.

Poirier, Richard. *The Performing Self: Compositions and Decompositions in the Languages of Contemporary Life*. New York: Oxford University Press, 1971.

Porter, Peter. "Collecting Her Strength." *New Statesman* 81 (4 June 1971):774–75.

Pratt, Linda Ray. " 'The Spirit of Blackness Is In Us . . . .' " *Prairie Schooner* 47 (Spring 1973):87–90.

Pratt, William. *The Imagist Poem: Modern Poetry in Miniature*. New York: E. P. Dutton, 1963.

Rapone, Anita. "The Body is the Role: Sylvia Plath." In *Radical Feminism*, edited by Anne Koedt, Ellen Levine, and Anita Rapone, pp. 407–12. New York: Quadrangle Press, 1973.

Rich, Adrienne. "When We Dead Awaken: Writing As Re-Vision." *College English* 34 (October 1972):18–30.

Richmond, Lee J. "Books Covered and Uncovered." *Erasmus Review* (September 1971):157–62.

Ries, Lawrence R. *Wolf Masks: Violence in Contemporary Poetry*. Port Washington, New York: Kennikat Press, 1977.

Roche, Clarissa. "Sylvia Plath: Vignettes from England." In *Sylvia Plath: The Woman and the Work*, edited by Edward Butscher, pp. 81–96. New York: Dodd, Mead, 1977.

Roethke, Theodore. "How to Write Like Somebody Else." In *On The Poet and His Craft: Selected Prose of Theodore Roethke*, edited by Ralph J. Mills, Jr., pp. 61–70. Seattle: University of Washington Press, 1966.

―――. "On Identity." In *On The Poet and His Craft: Selected Prose of Theodore Roethke*, edited by Ralph J. Mills, Jr., pp. 18–27. Seattle: University of Washington Press, 1966.

―――. "Open Letter." In *On The Poet and His Craft: Selected Prose of Theodore Roethke*, edited by Ralph J. Mills, Jr., pp. 36–43. Seattle: University of Washington Press, 1966.

―――. "Some Remarks on Rhythm." In *On The Poet and His Craft: Selected Prose of Theodore Roethke*, edited by Ralph J. Mills, Jr., pp. 71–84. Seattle: University of Washington Press, 1966.

Roland, Laurin K. "Sylvia Plath's 'Lesbos': A Self Divided." *Concerning Poetry* 9 (1976):61–65.

Romano, John. "Sylvia Plath Reconsidered." *Commentary* 57 (April 1974):47–52.

Rosenblatt, Jon. " 'The Couriers.' " *Explicator* 34 (December 1975):no. 28.

———. *Sylvia Plath: The Poetry of Initiation*. Chapel Hill: University of North Carolina Press, 1979.

Rosenstein, Harriet. "Reconsidering Sylvia Plath." *Ms.* 1 (September 1972): 44–51, 96–99.

Rosenthal, M. L. "Alienation of Sensibility and 'Modernity.' " *Arts and Sciences* (Spring 1964):19–24.

———. "Metamorphosis of a Book." *The Spectator* 218 (21 April 1967): 456–57.

———. "Other Confessional Poets." In *The New Poets: American and British Poetry Since World War II*, pp. 79–89. New York: Oxford University Press, 1967.

———. "Poetic Theory of Some Contemporary Poets or Notes from the Front." *Salmagundi* 1 (1967):69–77.

———. *Poetry and the Common Life*. New York: Oxford University Press, 1974.

———. "Sylvia Plath and Confessional Poetry." In *The Art of Sylvia Plath*, edited by Charles Newman, pp. 69–76. Bloomington: Indiana University Press, 1970; London: Faber and Faber, 1970.

———. "Uncertain Odysseus: The Critic of Current Poetry." *Shenandoah* 19 (1968):59–66.

Ross, Alan. Review of *Ariel*. *The London Magazine* 5 (May 1965): 99–101.

Rukeyser, Muriel. *The Life of Poetry*. New York: William Morrow, 1974.

Salamon, Lynda B. " 'Double, Double': Perception in the Poetry of Sylvia Plath." *Spirit* 37 (1970):34–39.

Salop, Lynne. *Suisong*. New York: Vantage Press, 1978.

Scheerer, Constance. "The Deathly Paradise of Sylvia Plath." In *Sylvia Plath: The Woman and the Work*, edited by Edward Butscher, pp. 166–76. New York: Dodd, Mead, 1977.

Schrickx, W. "De Dichtkunst van Sylvia Plath." *Dietsch Warande er Belfort* 116 (1971):191–210.

Schvey, Henry I. "Sylvia Plath's *The Bell Jar*: Bildungsroman or Case History." *Dutch Quarterly Review of Anglo-American Letters* 8 (1978):18–37.

Schwartz, Murray M., and Bollas, Christopher. "The Absence at the Center: Sylvia Plath and Suicide." *Criticism* 18 (1976):147–72.

Sexton, Anne. "The Barfly Ought to Sing." In *The Art of Sylvia Plath*, edited by Charles Newman, pp. 174–81. Bloomington: Indiana University Press, 1970; London: Faber and Faber, 1970.

Shapiro, Karl. *Prose Keys to Modern Poetry*. New York: Harper and Row, 1962.

Shook, Margaret. "Sylvia Plath: The Poet and the College." *Smith Alumnae Quarterly* (April 1972):4–9.

Sigmund, Elisabeth. "Sylvia in Devon: 1962." In *Sylvia Plath: The Woman and the Work*, edited by Edward Butscher, pp. 100–107. New York: Dodd, Mead, 1977.

Simon, John. "More Brass than Enduring." *Hudson Review* 15 (Autumn 1962):455–68.

Simpson, Louis. "Black Banded With Yellow." In *A Revolution in Taste: Studies of Dylan Thomas, Allen Ginsberg, Sylvia Plath, and Robert Lowell*. New York: MacMillan, 1978.

Skelton, Robin. "Britannica's Muse Revisited." *Massachusetts Review* 7 (Autumn 1965):834–35.

Smith, Pamela. "Architectonics: Sylvia Plath's *Colossus*." In *Sylvia Plath: The Woman and the Work*, edited by Edward Butscher, pp. 111–24. New York: Dodd, Mead, 1977.

———. "The Unitive Urge in the Poetry of Sylvia Plath." *New England Quarterly* 45 (September 1972):323–39.

Smith, Stan. "Attitudes Counterfeiting Life: The Irony of Artifice in Sylvia Plath's *The Bell Jar*." *Critical Quarterly* 17 (Autumn 1975):247–60.

Spacks, Patricia Meyer. *The Female Imagination*. New York: Avon, 1975.

Spendal, R. J. "Sylvia Plath's 'Cut.' " *Modern Poetry Studies* 6 (Autumn 1975): 128–34.

Spender, Stephen. "Warnings from the Grave." In *The Art of Sylvia Plath*, edited by Charles Newman, pp. 199–203. Bloomington: Indiana University Press, 1970; London: Faber and Faber, 1970.

Stade, George. "Introduction" to *A Closer Look at Ariel: A Memory of Sylvia Plath*, edited by Nancy Hunter Steiner. New York: Harper's Magazine Press, 1973.

Stainton, Rita T. "Vision and Voice in Three Poems by Sylvia Plath." *Windless Orchard* 17 (Spring 1974):31–36.

Steiner, George. "Dying Is an Art." In *The Art of Sylvia Plath*, edited by Charles Newman, pp. 211–18. Bloomington: Indiana University Press, 1970; London: Faber and Faber, 1970.

———. "In Extremis." *Cambridge Review* 90 (7 February 1969):247–49.

Steiner, Nancy Hunter. *A Closer Look at Ariel: A Memory of Sylvia Plath*. New York: Harper's Magazine Press, 1973.

Stevens, Wallace. "Effects of Analogy." In *The Necessary Angel: Essays on Reality and the Imagination*, pp. 107–30. New York: Vintage, 1951.

———. "Imagination as Value." In *The Necessary Angel: Essays on Reality and the Imagination*, pp. 133–56. New York: Vintage, 1951.

Stilwell, Robert L. "The Multiplying Entities: D. H. Lawrence and Five Other Poets." *Sewanee Review* 76 (July-September 1968):520–35.

Sumner, Nan McCowan. "Sylvia Plath." *Research Studies* 38 (June 1970):112–21.

Talbot, Norman. "Sisterhood Is Powerful: The Man in Sylvia Plath's Poetry." *New Poetry* 21 (June 1973):23–36.

Taylor, Andrew. "Sylvia Plath's Mirror and Beehive." *Meanjin* 33 (September 1974):256–65.

Taylor, Eleanor Ross. "Sylvia Plath's Last Poems." *Poetry* 89 (January 1967): 260–62.

Times Literary Supplement. "Early Unpublished Poems by Sylvia Plath." (31 July 1969):855.

———. Review of *Crossing the Water* and *Winter Trees* (24 December 1971):1602.

Tulip, James. "Three Women Poets." *Poetry Australia* 19 (December 1967):35–40.

Uroff, Margaret D. *Sylvia Plath and Ted Hughes*. Urbana: University of Illinois Press, 1979.

———. "Sylvia Plath on Motherhood." *Midwest Quarterly* 15 (October 1973):70–90.

———. "Sylvia Plath's 'Tulips.' " *Paunch* 42–43 (December 1975):90–96.

———. "Sylvia Plath's Women." *Concerning Poetry* 7:1 (1974):45–56.

Vendler, Helen. "Crossing the Water." *The New York Review of Books* (10 October 1971):4, 48.

———. "La Poésia de Sylvia Plath." *Plural* 33 (1974):6–14.

———. "The Poetry of Sylvia Plath." Ziskind Lecture Series, Part I, 13 December 1971. Smith College: Sophia Smith Women's Archives.

———. "Recent American Poetry." *Massachusetts Review* 8 (1967):541–60.

Wagner, Linda. "Plath's 'Ariel': 'Auspicious Gales.' " *Concerning Poetry* 10:2(1977):5–7.

Wain, John. "Farewell to the World." *The Spectator*(13 January 1961):50.

Walsh, Thomas P., and Northouse, Cameron. *Sylvia Plath and Anne Sexton: A Reference Guide*. Boston: G. K. Hall, 1974.

Welland, Dennis. "The Dark Voice of the Sea: A Theme in Modern Poetry." In *American Poetry*, edited by Irvin Ehrenpreis, pp. 197–219. New York: St. Martin's Press, 1965.

Wheelwright, Philip. *Metaphor and Reality*. Bloomington: Indiana University Press, 1967.

Whittier, Gayle M. "The Divided Woman and Generic Doubleness in *The Bell Jar*." *Women's Studies* 3:127–46.

Williamson, Alan. "I Am That I Am: The Ethics and Aesthetics of Self-Revelation." *American Poetry Review* (January/February 1974):37–39.

Yoshida, Sachiko. "Incense of Death: Sylvia Plath no Sonzai no Kaku." *Eigo Seinen* 120:488–89.

Zollman, Sol. "Sylvia Plath and Imperialist Culture." *Literature and Ideology* 1 (1969):11–22.

Index

223